EYEWITNESS COMPANIONS

Trees

COLIN RIDSDALE
JOHN WHITE
CAROL USHER

Foreword by
DAVID MABBERLEY

LONDON, NEW YORK,
MUNICH, MELBOURNE, DELHI

Senior Art Editor Ina Stradins
Senior Editor Angeles Gavira Guerrero
Art Editor Vanessa Marr
Project Editor Cathy Meeus
Designers Kavita Dutta, Shefali Upadhyay, Romi Chakraborty, Arunesh Talapatra, Enosh Francis
Editors Dipali Singh, Glenda Fernandes, Rohan Sinha, Aekta Jerath, Mary Lindsay
Managing Art Editor Phil Ormerod
Managing Editor Liz Wheeler
Art Director Bryn Walls
Reference Publisher Jonathan Metcalf
DTP Co-ordinator Pankaj Sharma
DTP Designers John Goldsmid, Balwant Singh, Sunil Sharma
Production Controller Kevin Ward
Illustrators Gill Tomblin, Ann Winterbotham

First published in 2005 by
Dorling Kindersley Limited
80 Strand, London WC2R ORL

A Penguin Company

2 4 6 8 10 9 7 5 3 1

Colour reproduction by Colourscan, Singapore
Printed and bound in Hong Kong,
China by L. Rex

See our complete catalogue at
www.dk.com

Foreword 10

WHAT IS A TREE?
12

Tree Classification *14*

Tree Evolution *16*

Tree Structure *18*

How Trees Work *20*

Tree Reproduction *22*

Forests of the World *24*

Coniferous Forests *26*

Temperate Broadleaf Forests *28*

Tropical Broadleaf Forests *30*

Tropical Rainforests *32*

Barren Lands *34*

Identifying Trees *36*

CONTENTS

LIVING WITH TREES
38

Early People
and Trees 40

Tree Myths and
Spirits 42

Trees for Sustenance 44

Trees for Wood
and Building 46

Trees for Paper
and Pulp 48

Other Products
from Trees 50

Trees for Amenity
and Ornament 52

Planting and Caring
for Trees 54

Forest Practice 56

Trees and the
Environment 58

Tree Conservation 60

TREES OF
THE WORLD
62

Spore Trees 64
Seed Trees 66
Cycads 68

Ginkgo 70

Conifers 74

Flowering Trees 110

Primitive Angiosperms 112

Monocotyledons 122

Dicotyledons 141

Glossary 344

Tree Families 349

Index 350

Acknowledgments 359

"THE FOREST IS A PECULIAR ORGANISM OF
UNLIMITED KINDNESS AND BENEVOLENCE THAT
MAKES NO DEMAND FOR ITS SUSTENANCE AND
EXTENDS GENEROUSLY THE PRODUCTS OF ITS LIFE
ACTIVITY: IT AFFORDS PROTECTION TO ALL BEINGS,
OFFERING SHADE EVEN TO THE AXEMAN WHO
DESTROYS IT." *The Buddha*

FOREWORD

In every society, trees provide food in terms of fruits and nuts, flavourings, and even edible flowers and leaves. Trees are the source of pharmaceuticals, as well as building timber and firewood. Their protective bark provides not only medicines but also resins, barkcloth, and cork. Their heartwood and water-transport systems produce long-lasting wood that is used to make furniture and the pulp for all modern books and newspapers. Trees provide the bases for the perfume industry.

As a whole, forests harbour 75 per cent of the world's biodiversity. Trees intercept rainfall and gently release it in watersheds; they absorb carbon dioxide and replenish the air with oxygen. Trees are planted to restore degraded landscapes and provide forage for hungry animals. They protect coastlines and river-banks. Some act as important shade trees and wind-breaks; many others are grown as ornamentals.

The original vegetation of much of the world was dominated by trees, and our ancestors were tree-living primates. Trees were the sources of food and medicine long before there was human consciousness. They still feature strongly in our human psyche: the forbidding forests of fairy tales, sacred groves, the Tree of Knowledge,

and the Tree of Life – in Christianity, Jesus's cross is often called "the Tree". We have a great fascination with the tallest and oldest trees, which span generations of human lives. Their majestic gigantism is as attractive as that of the dinosaurs.

Perhaps even more importantly, trees have provided the building materials and fuel for most civilizations, either as wood or fossilized as coal. More trees are used for fuel than construction – indeed the North American tribes thought that the first European settlers could only have left their country because they had run out of firewood.

Brought up in the English countryside before it was so mercilessly pressed into intensive agriculture, I was privileged, as a boy, to wander through woodlands and along hedgerows, learning for myself about the trees and the animals that they sheltered. Standing in a tropical rainforest, amongst the redwoods of California, the giant eucalyptus of southwestern Australia, or even the relic pine forests of Scotland, inspires an awe that few other experiences can.

Not merely for economic reasons, then, should we do all we can to conserve these bases of civilization, trees, but because we rely on them so much for our spiritual welfare too.

SWAMP CYPRESS
The buttresses of this deciduous conifer rise from the freshwater swamps of the southeastern, USA. The Swamp Cypress (*Taxodium distichum*) displays rich, orange-brown colours in autumn.

DAVID MABBERLEY
University of Washington, Seattle;
Universiteit Leiden, The Netherlands;
University of Western Sydney & Royal
Botanic Gardens Sydney, Australia

WHAT IS
A TREE?

Tree Classification

The definition of a tree accepted by science and the forestry industry is "A woody plant (arboreal perennial) usually with a single columnar stem capable of reaching six metres in height". Less than six metres (21ft) of potential height is regarded as a shrub.

This definition is not absolute; gardeners contest the height threshold, some preferring five metres (17ft) and others choosing a threshold of three metres (13ft). It is likely that bonsai enthusiasts would entirely dismiss any figures suggested. Horticultural selections of dwarf conifers also fall into a grey area usually called "dwarf trees".

BOTANICAL CLASSIFICATION

Classification is the process of arranging plant groups into an order. This helps with the identification of individual species and indicates natural relationships between groups. Attempts to classify plants were made by the Ancient Greeks and Romans, including Theophrastus in the 3rd century BCE. and Pliny the Elder before 79CE. Their methods relied on sometimes very long descriptions instead of succinct names.

Over the centuries several other systems were proposed. The two-part scientific naming system still in use today (see right) was devised by Carl von Linné (known as Linnaeus) a Swedish botanist who published his Species Plantarum in 1753. Linnaeus used a classification system known as artificial classification,

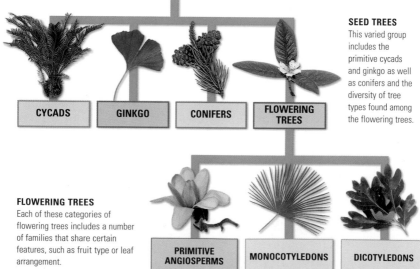

MAJOR DIVISIONS
This chart indicates the major groups and subgroups of trees described in this book. It does not imply any kind of evolutionary order. Trees are not equally divided between groups. The spore trees, the most primitive, are represented by only one living genus, although they were far more plentiful in prehistoric times. Seed trees include the most numerous group: the dicotyledons.

SPORE TREES

SEED TREES

SEED TREES
This varied group includes the primitive cycads and ginkgo as well as conifers and the diversity of tree types found among the flowering trees.

CYCADS

GINKGO

CONIFERS

FLOWERING TREES

FLOWERING TREES
Each of these categories of flowering trees includes a number of families that share certain features, such as fruit type or leaf arrangement.

PRIMITIVE ANGIOSPERMS

MONOCOTYLEDONS

DICOTYLEDONS

THE NORDMAN FIR IN CONTEXT

In the Linnaean system all species are classified within their major grouping by family and then by genus. Each species may include one or more subspecies. This example shows the classification of the Nordmann Fir (subspecies *borisii-regis*).

FAMILY

A family contains one or more related genera. The family name is always capitalized in roman type.

GENUS

A genus contains one or more species, and its name forms the first part of the species name. It is capitalized in italic type.

SPECIES

The species is the basic unit of classification. The name is made up of the genus and species names in italic type.

SUBSPECIES

Some species have subspecies that may differ in a minor way from the main species. The name has three elements.

Conifers

Pinaceae

Abies

Abies nordmanniana

Abies nordmanniana subspecies *borisii-regis*

which places plants into groups such as families and genera based on the establishment of a few shared defining characters (characteristics). Other classification systems place plants into an evolutionary order based on fossil records and comparative anatomy.

A MULTIPLICITY OF FORMS

The basic definition of a tree encompasses an astonishing variety of plant forms from the Grass-tree (below, left) to the Boojum (below, centre) and the Beech (below, right).

This book is arranged in the system accepted by the International Union for the Conservation of Nature (IUCN). The principal source is Kubitzki's *Families and Genera of Vascular Plants*. According to this system, trees fall into two main groupings: spore trees and seed trees. Seed trees are further divided between cycads, ginkgo, conifers (gymnosperms), and flowering trees (angiosperms). Flowering trees have three subdivisions: primitive angiosperms, monocotyledons and dicotyledons.

Tree Evolution

Plant life has existed on Earth for millions of years, with records of the first land plants dating from the Silurian period (350–320 million years ago). The huge success of trees in evolutionary terms is due to their ability to adapt to a wide variety of environments.

The earliest trees were conifers, which arose in the Permian period (220–195 million years ago), but it was not until towards the end of the Cretaceous period (140–70 million years ago) that forest vegetation had evolved into tree types that we would recognize today. By this time, forests contained trees that were similar to plane, magnolia, poplar, and fig. Such flowering plants were better equipped to spread to new areas than earlier flora. This spread was dictated by geographical and climatic changes. Another advantage of flowering trees was their association with pollinating insects such as bees; this enabled the plants to colonize a wide diversity of new sites.

PREHISTORIC FOREST
Prehistoric forests were dominated by tree ferns and giant horsetails creating areas of dense vegetation, as here in the Yarra Ranges National Park, Australia.

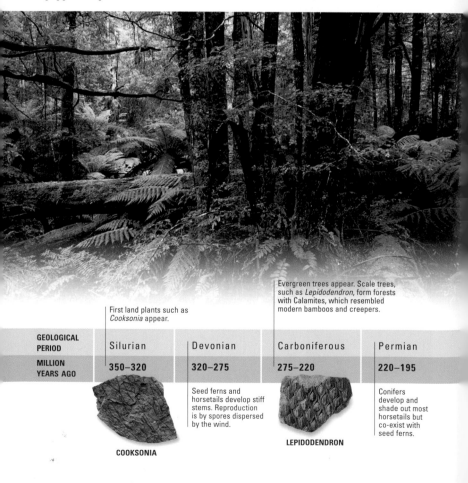

First land plants such as *Cooksonia* appear.

Evergreen trees appear. Scale trees, such as *Lepidodendron*, form forests with Calamites, which resembled modern bamboos and creepers.

GEOLOGICAL PERIOD	Silurian	Devonian	Carboniferous	Permian
MILLION YEARS AGO	350–320	320–275	275–220	220–195
	COOKSONIA	Seed ferns and horsetails develop stiff stems. Reproduction is by spores dispersed by the wind.	LEPIDODENDRON	Conifers develop and shade out most horsetails but co-exist with seed ferns.

CYCADS
This ancient family of tropical and subtropical plants is represented by about 100 living species.

GINKGOS
Only one living species (Maidenhair Tree) remains of this once extensive group of primitive plants.

TREE FERNS
Part of the Cycad family, these ferns from the Southern Hemisphere grow up to 10m (33ft) tall.

TREE MIGRATION

Trees respond to changes in conditions on the Earth by adapting their size and shape morphologically or by "moving". A tree population moves by successfully seeding in the direction of the most favourable conditions. In this way, modern trees have survived ice ages and global warming or global cooling for millions of years.

CONTINUING EVOLUTION

Tree evolution is a continuing process. Today there are species that are particularly unstable and prone to cross-breeding with near relatives. However, the resulting progeny are occasionally better suited to prevailing conditions than the original tree and are therefore more likely to survive and reproduce.

COAL

Coal is carbon from forest swamps of the Carboniferous period. Regular subsidence caused the forest to be flooded by fresh or salt water. Eventually mudstone, shale, or limestone sediments accumulated, compressing the remnants of forest and peat to form coal. In some areas, a long sequence of inundation and forest regeneration occurred causing "coal measures" – thin alternating bands of coal and rock. The layers below coal seams frequently contain fragments of tree roots.

COAL

MINING FOR COAL

	Triassic	Jurassic	Cretaceous	Eocene	Oligocene
	195–170	**170–140**	**140–70**	**70–45**	**45–35**

Conditions not favourable for tree growth until late in the period. Tree ferns (such as *Dicroidium*), cycads, and conifers are able to survive.

ARAUCARIA

Flowering plants (angiosperms), such as the birch-like *Betulites*, begin to appear. Most modern tree families have evolved by this time.

Grassland replaces large areas of forest. Forested swamps lay down brown coal (lignite). Modern trees have changed little since this period.

Cycads and conifers flourish. Maidenhair trees (*Ginkgo* and *Baiera*) and *Araucaria* conifers appear.

BETULITES

Flowering trees dominate. Palms appear. The deciduous conifer Dawn Redwood is first noted.

DICROIDIUM

Tree Structure

Like all living organisms, a tree is a complex structure composed of millions of cells, each with a distinct function. Unlike animals, however, trees are static and unable to seek out food so they make their own using sunlight and obtain water from the soil via their roots.

Trees need a reliable supply of essential nutrients for growth, reproduction, and immunity. They are distinct from many other plants in that they are designed for longevity. Most trees have the potential to live for decades and, in some cases, hundreds of years, and need to adapt themselves accordingly. Each year trees add a new layer of growth to their existing frames. To support this extra bulk, stiff wood is made in the stem and branches. Spreading roots develop to provide anchorage. These are subdivided into thousands of rootlets for maximum water- and mineral-absorbing capacity. In many species, flowers, followed by seeded fruits, are the means of reproduction.

PARTS OF A TREE
All trees have the same basic components of roots, trunk, branches, leaves, and flowers but there is huge variety between species.

a spreading base connects the tree to a circle of roots which anchor it in the ground

trunks grow longer and straighter when trees grow close together

bark becomes smoother higher up the tree

the bark at the base of a tree is more likely to be rugged and cracked

branches remain at the same height above ground as a tree grows, becoming thicker each year

ROOTS
The roots of all trees fix the tree into the ground so it is well supported and can grow upright, and enable it to seek out water and minerals to sustain growth and reproduction. Contrary to popular belief, root systems do not mirror the branches of a tree. They seldom reach very deep down into subsoil or bedrock; however, they do extend sideways well beyond the tree canopy.

TRUNK AND BARK
The trunk holds the tree upright so that the foliage can reach the light. Tissues within the wood conduct water and nutrients to the leaves, and sugars to all parts of the tree. The central heartwood confers strength and stiffness. Bark, which may be smooth, rough, or fissured, is the distinctive outer covering of the trunk that protects against the elements and invasion by insects, animals, and disease.

FISSURED BARK

corky layer

deep cracks

ROUGH BARK

leaf bud

BRANCHES

The aerial and lateral extensions of the tree, branches enable the canopy of leaves to exploit as much as possible of the sun's radiation. They extend from the trunk and have a similar structure internally and protective bark externally. Where lateral extensions are very wide, branches have the ability to buttress themselves by producing an extra layer of wood on the underside.

LEAVES

Green leaves (in broadleaf species) or needles (the specially adapted leaves in conifers and trees inhabiting extremely dry conditions) are the sites of photosynthesis (the manufacture of food using sunlight, carbon dioxide, and water) and transpiration (water loss by evaporation). Chlorophyll (the green component of leaves) converts minerals and water brought up from the soil and carbon dioxide from the air into sugars and starches using sunlight (see also pp.20–1).

CONIFER

needle-like shape

large surface area

BROADLEAF

leaves and flowers develop from buds each spring

in summer, deciduous trees have a dense canopy of leaves

female flower

male flower

FRUIT

Fruit develop from the fertilized female parts of the flower. Fruit may be soft and fleshy or hard and dry. In conifers the fruit is a seed-bearing cone. In all cases seed distribution is the goal and this takes place in different ways. Fruit may be eaten by birds and other animals, and the seeds dropped or released in the animal's droppings at some distance from the source; some fruits and seeds are dispersed by the wind, or by becoming attached to an animal's fur.

young fruit

PEACHES

FLOWERS

Flowers on trees are the sites of sexual reproduction. There is great variety in colour, appearance, and scent of the flowers, and many have specially adapted mechanisms for attracting pollinators. Pollen may be carried from one flower to another by insects, such as bees, or the wind. Male and female parts may form part of the same flower or they may be borne separately.

ALDER CATKINS

showy petals

MAGNOLIA

How Trees Work

Growth and reproduction are a tree's most important functions and to achieve this end the tree needs a constant supply of food and water that must be circulated to all parts of its structure. This is a complex process, the main component of which is photosynthesis.

Three fundamental stimuli govern tree growth: geotropism (response to gravity) makes shoots grow up and roots go downwards; phototropism (response to light) affects the direction of foliage growth and keeps roots away from light; hydrotropism (response to water in the ground) affects the direction and extent of root growth.

HOW TREES MAKE FOOD

The manufacturing of food for a tree – photosynthesis – takes place within the leaves. The end products are carbohydrates (starch and glucose) and cellulose formed from hydrogen, oxygen, and carbon derived from the air and minerals from the soil. Sunlight provides the energy for this process. Photosynthesis can only take place in the presence of chlorophyll,

a green pigment found within structures called chloroplasts in the leaf cells. The carbohydrates are transported to all parts of the tree. On arrival at the root tips, the sugar content builds up in the cells until it is greater than in the surrounding soil. To maintain a state of equilibrium, water

LEAF VEINS
A network of veins (sometimes called nerves) on the underside of a leaf transports the products of photosynthesis to and from all parts of the tree.

HOW PHOTOSYNTHESIS WORKS

The leaf is the main site of photosynthesis, which is the process by which carbon dioxide and hydrogen are converted into carbohydrates to feed the tree and the waste product oxygen is released into the atmosphere.

oxygen is released as a byproduct through stomata (pores)

sunlight activates chlorophyll inside leaf cells

chlorophyll inside leaf cells converts water and carbon dioxide into sugars

sugars are carried back into the tree to fuel growth

water and minerals are supplied to leaf cells

EUCALYPTUS STOMATA

carbon dioxide enters leaf through stomata

TREE CIRCULATION

The transportation of nutrients and water between leaves and roots is a complex process in a tree. The main components of the system (shown schematically below) are xylem vessels, which transport water and mineral salts, and phloem vessels, which carry mainly sugars. These vessels are situated in the veins of leaves and in the growing sections of the wood of the trunk and branches.

bark – the outer protective layer

phloem – the part of the wood that transports sugars from the leaves

heartwood – the oldest part of the trunk

xylem – the part of the wood that carries water and minerals from the roots

cambium – the growing layer that widens the trunk by adding to both phloem and xylem.

TREE RINGS

Each band in a cut trunk represents a new layer of xylem laid down annually during the growing season.

XYLEM VESSELS IN A PINE BRANCH

passes through cell walls into the root. The liquid is taken up by the tree, aided by a partial vacuum caused by the loss of excess water (transpiration) from foliage. Eventually the mineral-rich water reaches the leaves and is used in the food-manufacturing process.

USING EARTH AND AIR

A tree requires mineral salts, which are obtained by the roots in solution from the soil. Minerals go up through the xylem in the trunk (see Tree Circulation, above).

Excess water is expelled through pores on the surface of the leaf (stomata) and on young shoots (lenticels). These pores open or close in response to humidity and drying winds to maintain constant water pressure within the tree. The most important of the mineral salts is nitrogen. Leaves absorb hydrogen, carbon, and oxygen from the air, but nitrogen cannot be absorbed in this way. Electric storms cause nitrogen and oxygen to combine and dissolve in rain to form nitrous and nitric acids. In the soil, these combine with mineral salts and ammonia to form nitrites and nitrates, a process called the nitrogen cycle. A few plant species have nitrifying bacteria on their roots that convert nitrogen in the air into an absorbable form. Nutrients are recycled when dead leaves fall and rot, eventually being taken up again by the root system.

GNARLED BARK

The outermost layer of the trunk is composed of dead cells that impart a distinctive appearance. Bark is primarily protective, but it also contains tiny pores that allow gases to flow in and out.

Tree Reproduction

As in most other plants, many trees reproduce in three stages – pollen release, fertilization, and seed dispersal. Since trees are static, many devices have evolved over the years to increase the chances of successful reproduction. Trees also have other means of propagation.

POLLINATION

Most trees are either gymnosperms (conifers) or angiosperms (flowering plants). Conifers have separate, male and female flowers on the same tree; these are wind pollinated. The male flowers are small cone-like structures of bracts and stamens that produce vast clouds of pollen in early spring. The female flowers are miniature versions of the mature cones they will eventually become. Angiosperms have an elaborate array of flower types, some designed for wind pollination and others with fragrant petals and nectar to attract insects or other creatures. In some species, trees are exclusively male or female (dioecious). In others both male and female flowers, appear on the same tree; they may be combined (hermaphrodite) or they may be separate (monoecious).

DIOECIOUS
An example of a dioecious tree, Holly (*Ilex aquifolium*) is either exclusively male or, as in this case, female, which produces berries.

MONOECIOUS
The majority of conifers have both male and female flowers on the same tree, as in the Scots Pine (*Pinus sylvestris*).

male flower

female flower

HERMAPHRODITE
Apple (*Malus*) blossoms are hermaphrodite, with male and female parts.

BEE ON BLOSSOM
While penetrating the petals for nectar, pollen sticks to the insect and is transferred to the next flower.

BIRD DISPERSAL
In addition to receiving nutritional value from the berry, the feeding bird inadvertently spreads the seed.

WATER DISPERSAL
One of the largest and heaviest seeds, the coconut has evolved to travel hundreds of miles by water.

WIND DISPERSAL
When temperature and humidity are just right, the cone opens to release seeds that are carried by the wind.

SEED DISPERSAL

Conifer seeds are usually dispersed by the wind. Cones open in response to heat and humidity releasing the winged seeds over a long period to ensure that some of it has a chance of survival in ideal conditions. Some pines have seeds that stay in the cone until it drops to the ground and is carried away by an animal. Other conifers benefit from forest fires. The cones survive the heat of the fire then open to shed seed some hours later when the ash-enriched ground has cooled. Broadleaved trees employ a range of seed-distribution techniques. Some fruits have to be ingested by birds or animals before they will grow. Others are carried away and buried by animals or birds and may be abandoned or forgotten, allowing them to germinate. Winged seeds (keys) are carried away from the mother tree. Some, such as alder, are able to float in water. Many large seeds also float; some, such as the coconut, can travel great distances across oceans.

SELF-PROPAGATION

Some trees have the ability to layer, that is root into the soil when a branch rests on the ground. This is useful for trees prone to lightning strikes; the parent is destroyed but a ring of clones survives. Suckering is another successful survival technique. Surface roots send up new stems at a distance from the parent, eventually forming new trees. A few wetland trees propagate by breaking up. The Crack Willow (*Salix fragilis*) drops twigs, which eventually stick in wet mud and grow. Some forms of this species no longer reproduce sexually.

SUCKERING
With new shoots constantly springing up from the root system, this grove of aspens (below) is in fact comprised of multiple stems of a single parent tree.

LAYERING
The lower branches of some trees can take root if they make contact with the soil. The Red Mangrove (*Rhizophora mangle*), pictured above, provides an extreme example of this.

Forests of the World

The worldwide distribution of trees is the result of continuing evolution, with species settling into the most suitable climatic and geographic conditions. Broad zones provide a useful classification system, but there are many exceptions and borderline situations.

There are four broad forest zones (see panel, below), and within these there are numerous landforms and microclimates that affect vegetation. At the extremes of the zones, atypical habitats exist such as treeless swamps and fens, deserts, and mountains. In the Northern Hemisphere and equatorial regions, rainfall affects the distribution of trees. For example, in California rain falls mostly in winter; if it is absorbed by the soil and bedrock, trees can survive the summer months. If not, treeless desert will result. Snow on the Atlas Mountains in North Africa sustains coniferous forests that would not survive elsewhere in Africa. There is less conformity in the Southern Hemisphere, where zonal distribution is more complex. The huge expanse of southern oceans is broken by only three big landmasses each of which is diverse and mountainous and with excessively hot regions. Mountains and coastlines influence climate and therefore zones and species. So the broadleaf temperate zone in southern Australia is quite different habitat from that of the same zone in Europe.

WORLD FOREST ZONES
The world can be split very broadly into four main forest regions, interspersed by areas that are relatively treeless, such as mountains, prairies, and ice caps.

FOREST ZONES

CONIFEROUS FOREST
Covers huge swathes of Canada, Scandinavia, and Russia, and some mountain ranges. Conifers are well-adapted to harsh winters.

TEMPERATE BROADLEAF FOREST
Comprises species that tolerate seasonal cool conditions. Found further south than conifers in the Northern Hemisphere

TROPICAL BROADLEAF FOREST
Includes all tropical forest habitats except rainforest. This diverse category supports many species that also thrive in other zones.

TROPICAL RAINFOREST
Is home to evergreen plants that exist only in areas where humidity is 100 per cent, e.g. West Africa and parts of South America, Southeast Asia, and India.

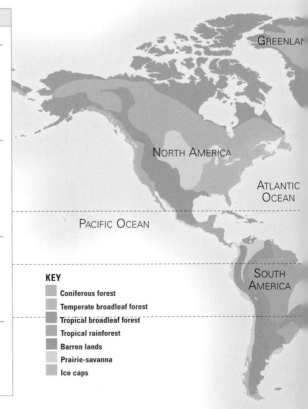

GREENLAN

NORTH AMERICA

ATLANTIC OCEAN

PACIFIC OCEAN

SOUTH AMERICA

KEY
- Coniferous forest
- Temperate broadleaf forest
- Tropical broadleaf forest
- Tropical rainforest
- Barren lands
- Prairie-savanna
- Ice caps

CONIFEROUS FOREST
Fir, pine, cedar, and spruce, species that are much exploited for their wood, are typical inhabitants of the coniferous forests of the world.

TEMPERATE BROADLEAF FOREST
A mix of deciduous and evergreen trees that have various adaptations to survive a cool season populate large areas in both Northern and Southern Hemispheres.

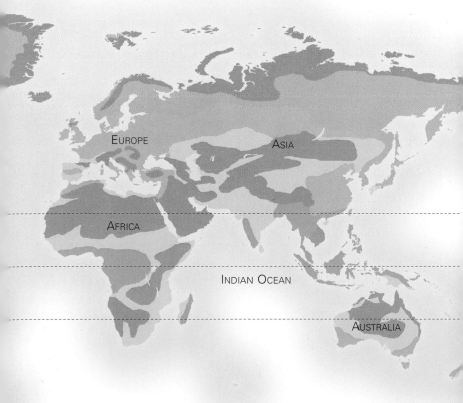

EUROPE

ASIA

AFRICA

INDIAN OCEAN

AUSTRALIA

Coniferous Forests

Conifers were once the dominant group of trees on the Earth but suffered from competition from broadleaved evergreens, which flourished in temperate and warm climates. Conifer forests now dominate only in cold, dry, mountainous regions.

SURVIVING THE COLD

Primitive conifers could not compete for light with the large, flat leaves of the new broadleaf species. They could grow tall, reaching above the canopy, but in so doing they provided shelter and incentive for the broadleaves to catch up. However, conifers had an advantage in that their narrow, often waxy foliage was good for conserving moisture. The only way for them to survive was to move by seeding into colder, drier areas. So conifers moved north towards the polar region and up into the mountains.

CONIFER NEEDLES
Cones of Tamarack (*Larix laricina*) on a long branchlet with needle-like leaves adapted for wintry conditions.

BLACK FOREST

Densely packed plantations of conifers characterize temperate conifer forests such as the Black Forest region in Germany, pictured here.

CONIFERS TODAY

In the cold Arctic tundra, the forest consists of thin, narrow-crowned spruces and low, bushy junipers. On mountains, dwarf pines hug the tree line stunted by snow and wind. In the vast wastes of Siberia and Canada, growth is slow but trees remain vertical with short

SURVIVAL THROUGH THE SEASONS
Massive forests of fir, spruce, and pine trees follow the winding path of the majestic Rocky Mountains in North America. They are able to survive the harsh winter conditions as far north as Alaska.

branches to shed snow easily. Dense forests of pine and Silver Fir (*Abies alba*) occur in the German Black Forest, the Caucasus, and Asia. Pine forests thrive in the northwestern USA and along the Pacific coast.

Conifers are genetically programmed to a particular climate. They must grow actively for about two months a year to survive, and many hardy species need a cold spell to rest, which ripens and stiffens the wood. In the south, Alpine trees fail by growing during brief warm winter spells only to be cut back by late frosts. Southern trees moved north start growing too late and do not complete their growth cycle before the winter.

ACID RAIN

Oxides of nitrogen and sulphur, produced by burning coal and oil, combine with raindrops to form solutions of nitric and sulphuric acids. In high concentrations, these acids can kill plants and animals and raise acid levels in soil and water. Conifer forests in Scandinavia have been particularly affected by acid rain.

ACID RAIN DAMAGE

FORESTS WORLDWIDE

THE AMERICAS
A huge belt of forest runs from Alaska to Labrador. Species of Redwood (*Sequoia*) populate conifer forests of the western USA. The Monkey Puzzle tree (*Araucaria araucana*) is a conifer species that occurs in the wild in Argentina and Chile.

ASIA
Vast areas of Russia are covered by dense spruce and pine forests, mainly Siberian Spruce (*Picea obovata*). **SEQUOIA**
The characteristic conifer species of Japan are the Japanese Cedar (*Cryptomeria japonica*) and Japanese Larch (*Larix kaempferi*).

EUROPE
Northern Europe is home to vast pine and spruce forests. Conifers extend south into the broadleaf zone, for example Maritime Pine (*Pinus pinaster*) close to the Mediterranean.

Temperate Broadleaf Forests

Temperate broadleaved trees evolved from tropical species. During dry periods, certain species on the fringes of tropical forests eventually became deciduous, that is, dropped their leaves in response to lack of rain as a strategy for survival.

BROADLEAVES WORLDWIDE

Since they first appeared, broadleaf trees have developed survival tactics, including dropping leaves. Some evergreen species evolved alternative ways of conserving moisture either by developing a waxy coating on the foliage (eucalyptus and hollies) or by reducing their surface area. Mixed deciduous woodland often has an underwood of evergreens including Box and Holly that absorb enough light during the winter months, when the leaves are off the larger trees, to survive. The zone of temperate broadleaf forest occupies the eastern USA, and Europe from Britain to Belarus and Russia.

BEECH FOREST
Where Beech predominates in a forest, it tends to shade out competitor species of tree so that eventually only mature Beech trees survive.

MAPLE LEAVES
In autumn, chemical changes in leaves as they are about to be shed produce a rich palette of warm colours.

Another large area of this type of forest exists in China and Japan. In the Southern Hemisphere, the zone includes temperate rainforest in Argentina and Chile, southern areas of Australia, and part of New Zealand's South Island.

FORESTS PRESERVED FOR GAME

In many parts of the world, particularly in northern European countries, tracts of broadleaf woodland have been preserved specifically as hunting forests and havens for game, such as deer and wild boar. Traditionally, pigs were kept in the woods and fattened on beech "mast" and acorns before being slaughtered.

ELK IN A FOREST CLEARING

BROADLEAVES AT HIGH ALTITUDE

In some tropical areas, isolated temperate broadleaved trees grow in the cooler conditions at high altitude. In southern Australia, eucalyptus forests typically consist of slender trees up to 60 metres (200ft) tall, and the forest is a light, airy environment because the leaves hang down and turn edgeways on to the sun keeping them cool but letting the light through.

AUTUMN GLORY

In New England, acre upon acre of mixed deciduous woodlands of maple, hickory, hornbeam, and aspen produce a fine display of autumn colour, which heralds the changing of the seasons every year.

FOREST TYPES

BEECH FOREST

Beech forest occupies warm temperate zones and is demanding of light. It suppresses other trees.

BIRCH–ALDER FOREST

Found in cold and poor soil conditions. Birch exists across the Northern Hemisphere up to the Arctic tundra. Alder colonizes wetland by making its own nitrogen fertilizer.

EUCALYPTUS FOREST

South of the tropical zone in Australia, cold-tolerant species form dense forests. In Tasmania some tolerate snow.

OAK FOREST

Many forests evolve into oak, with different oak species in America, Europe, and Asia. Other trees co-exist, creating a rich and diverse ecosystem.

SOUTHERN BEECH FOREST

In Chile and Argentina, Southern Beech (*Nothofagus* sp.) forms dense forests. Smaller forests occur in New Zealand.

Tropical Broadleaf Forests

One of the most diverse categories, tropical broadleaf forests are
found in all tropical habitats, except rainforest and barren lands.
The tree species that populate such forests have adapted in many
different ways to a wide range of habitats and climates.

TROPICAL BROADLEAF FOREST AREAS

CONTINENTAL TROPICAL FOREST

This type of forest is found in hot, dry places such as Australia and Africa.

MONSOON WOODLAND

Found in India, Myanmar, Laos, Thailand, Cambodia, Sumatra, and Java.

OCEANIC TROPICAL FOREST

These coastal forests are found in the Pacific Islands and northeastern Australia.

RIVERINE FOREST

Found in deep river valleys where there is waterfall spray and high humidity.

SUB-TROPICAL RAINFOREST

Found in Florida, the Brazilian Highlands, and The Great Divide in Australia.

THORN FOREST

Found in east Brazil, Paraguay, and coastal Texas and Mexico.

DIVERSE CONDITIONS

The climate that encourages growth of tropical
broadleaves is similar to that of tropical rainforests.
The difference is that a dry season occurs for part
of the year, which interrupts growth and forces trees
into a dormant phase. Deciduous species shed leaves in
response; evergreen trees enter a rest period as seen in
the wood by discernible rings of fast and slow growth.

Classification of this type of forest is difficult because
there are many transitional areas, particularly along the
cooler fringes of a tropical zone or where forest meets
the sea. Oceanic tropical forests are mainly evergreen,
forming an incomplete canopy, with further levels of
vegetation including a shrub layer and ground cover.
Lianas and epiphytes are frequent. Sea mist contributes
to alleviating the freshwater deficit. Red Mangrove
(*Rhizophora mangle*) swamps rapidly build up
a humid jungle of stems and roots.

SPARSE AFRICAN FOREST
In inhospitable parts of the world where extreme heat
and dry conditions prevail, tree life is sporadic with only
a few species, such as acacia, able to survive.

GIRAFFE BROWSING ON ACACIAS

DENSE TROPICAL EUCALYPTUS FOREST
Tight packing and flammable leaves make eucalyptus prone to forest fires but they have a built-in response: hidden buds in the stump regrow after the fire is out.

SURVIVING DROUGHT

Continental tropical forests have a very dry season that affects survival and natural selection. Many trees have small leaves protected by dense hairs. Others have drastically reduced their leaf area to conserve moisture. An example is the Beefwood (*Casuarina equisetifolia*), which resembles a horsetail with slender-jointed branches and scale-like leaves. Tropical forms of eucalyptus often grow alongside this species.

Monsoon woodland is a type of tropical forest that grows in tropical climates characterized by periods of very high rainfall. Typical species include Ebony (*Diospyros ebenum*) and Sago Palm (*Metroxylon sago*). Riverine forests occur in humid valleys where rainfall is less excessive.

Sub-tropical rainforest occurs at high elevation often above tracts of actual rainforest (see pp.32–3).

The mainly deciduous thorn forest occurs between dense tree cover and semi-desert in tropical zones. It is hot and dry for long periods. Adequate moisture is maintained in the soil and trees derive protection from their close proximity to one another. Species that thrive in these areas include Carob (*Ceratonia siliqua*) and Baobab (*Adansonia digitata*).

MOUNTAIN GUM LEAVES
The pale, grey-green waxy leaves of this species are an adaptation to prevent excess heat and moisture loss.

WILDLIFE IN EUCALYPTUS FOREST

Tropical forms of eucalyptus are among the most successful of trees with over 500 species and 150 varieties known. Almost all of these can be found in Australia where their aromatic leaves provide the staple diet for koalas. Eucalyptus leaves are not very nutritious, but these tree-dwelling marsupials have a low energy output, spending up to 18 hours a day resting in the branches.

KOALA EATING EUCALYPTUS LEAVES

Tropical Rainforests

Luxuriant tropical rainforest is a diverse evergreen plant community that exists in parts of the equatorial zone where there are conditions of high humidity and consistently warm temperatures. There is no dry season and growth of plants is continuous throughout the year.

UNIQUE ECOSYSTEM

An astonishing variety of plants live in the rainforest all with an ability to grow rapidly, an essential ingredient in the battle for light and survival. Rainforest trees typically have long, branch-free stems and smallish leafy tops packed into a continuous green canopy. Beneath this are smaller trees and shade-tolerant shrubs. Numerous climbing plants, such as lianas cling to trees, and orchids and ferns flourish on the dark forest floor. The rainforest habitat is perpetuated from within as well as by the climate. Reducing its size or making holes in it by felling trees changes the microclimate at great cost to the diverse species it supports.

SOUTH AMERICAN RAINFOREST

Larger than all the other rainforests combined, the Amazon Basin Rainforest (below and left) is home to almost half the world's bird species. Its trees release vast amounts of oxygen into the atmosphere.

TEAK
In the rainforest, species such as Teak (*Tectona grandis*) grow to great heights to reach the light.

MAHOGANY
Mahogany trees (*Swietenia* sp.) growing close together in the rainforest have few lower branches.

HOW A RAINFOREST WORKS

Transpiration of moisture from the trees supplements the natural rainfall in the forest. Massive quantities of life-giving oxygen are manufactured by the trees as a byproduct of photosynthesis and pumped into the atmosphere. The whole ecosystem is also a huge storeroom of fixed carbon. Although moisture is plentiful, rainforest soils tend to be poor. Evergreen foliage produces little leaf mould and the very high rainfall saturates unprotected soil so that nutrients not locked up in plants are soon leached away.

ORCHID
Orchids often share the rainforest, some growing on moist bark instead of soil.

AROUND THE WORLD

AFRICA

Equatorial rainforest occupies much of the Congo Basin and the Guinea coast. There are isolated areas in Zambia, near the Indian Ocean, and in eastern Madagascar.

INDIAN SUBCONTINENT

The western seaboard of India and Sri Lanka is tropical rainforest in the strict sense. Similar monsoon jungle and equatorial broadleaf forest obscure its eastern limits. Concentrations of rainforest also occur in Bangladesh.

SOUTH AMERICA

The world's largest area of rainforest occupies the Amazon Basin, extending from the Atlantic coast to the foothills of the Andes. It merges into savanna in the north and in the south, tropical broadleaf forest and grassland.

SOUTHEAST ASIA

Much of this area once supported rainforest, particularly Sumatra, Borneo, the Celebes, and the Philippines. In Myanmar, Teak (*Tectona grandis*) is still harvested commercially. It is sustainable only if replanted or allowed to regenerate.

RUBBER PLANTATION

Rainforests provide many of the raw materials for industry, including plants for the pharmaceutical industry and rubber. The Para Rubber Tree (*Hevea brasiliensis*) was first found in the Amazon rainforest; vast plantations now exist in India, Indonesia, Malaysia, and other equatorial regions. Latex is the sap of the tree and careful cutting of the bark (known as "tapping") releases the latex without causing damage. An individual tree can produce latex in economic quantities for up to 30 years.

RUBBER TYRE   **TAPPING RUBBER**

Barren Lands

Many situations exist in which trees survive against all the odds and it is remarkable how they can adapt to hostile places. Lands may be barren for many reasons including temperature extremes, boggy ground, and wind and salt near the sea.

TREE PIONEERS

Some groups of trees are specially adapted as pioneers, opening the way for others. Attributes of such trees include early maturity, massive seed production, rapid growth, and a relatively short lifespan. For example, the American Beach Pine (*Pinus contorta*) produces its first cones and fertile seed in just six years, and some poplars grow two metres (6½ft) a year. The ability to survive in close proximity to one another is another attribute of pioneer species such as the birch, which often grows in dense thickets, producing few branches and small, bushy tops. The birch plantation starts to decline and

ADAPTED FOR THE HEAT

The drooping leaves of many eucalyptus species have evolved to turn edgeways to minimize the area exposed to the heat of the sun.

break up after only 40–60 years, usually giving way to more robust species, such as oak, that require shelter as seedlings. Alder is an ideal wetland pioneer able to seed in sedge beds and other boggy places.

EXTREMES OF TEMPERATURE

Barren land often occurs where extremes of heat or cold provide a challenge to survival. In cold regions such as the Arctic sub-tundra, mountain snowlines, and bleak moorland, a number of hardy tree species exist just inside the limits of survival, waiting for a chance to venture into new, treeless territory. The trigger may be a run of slightly warmer winters or the arrival of rudimentary shelter. Even damage on hills by avalanche or erosion may provide an opportunity for seeding. Shelter is usually in the form of hardy alpine shrubs such as dwarf willows, Dwarf Birch (*Betula nana*), or shrubby junipers. Once established, these species provide additional shelter for larger woody plants and a progression to scrub and eventually forest occurs.

In hot conditions, migration into treeless semi-desert is triggered by a climatic anomaly, such as freak rainfall or temporary cooling. The activities of burrowing animals may also provide opportunities for seeds of acacia, thorn, or palm to germinate. Tree survival in hot conditions often depends on establishing a tight group that will provide mutual shelter from the sun. All desert trees rely on deep roots to seek out groundwater and on night-time condensation being trapped and dripping from the foliage.

DESERT TREES

Cacti show an extreme adaptation to a dry habitat. Their fleshy trunks conserve water, while their leaves have been reduced to spikes to reduce water loss.

ADAPTED TO COLD
In cold climates the tree species that survive tend to grow slowly and have small, hard needles. Chances of survival increase where trees grow close together.

CLINGING ON
Some trees require little soil, surviving in rock fissures and damp, peaty cavities. Here, an Acacia is clinging to the edge of the Waimea Canyon, Kauai Island.

TREES BY THE SEA

In coastal areas sea water leaching into the ground can make the land inhospitable to trees; most are killed by excessive soil salinity. Some plants, however, are salt resistant and rapidly move back into bare ground. Salt spray is limiting but not usually fatal. Young growth may be killed each year so trees take on a sculpted appearance leaning away from the sea. As in other hostile conditions, trees survive by making use of available shelter.

STONY GROUND
Frankincense Trees (*Boswellia sacra*) survive in stony deserts because small amounts of moisture condense between the hot surface and cold subsoil.

Identifying Trees

Many people can easily identify the trees that are common in the area in which they live. However, there are times, for example, when travelling or when confronted with an unfamiliar species that it is useful to be able to identify a tree in a more systematic way.

FIELD WORK

Reliable identification depends upon thorough observation. Gather as much information as possible in the form of notes, sketches, photographs and, with permission, small samples of foliage including a flower and fruit, even if it is old material picked up from the ground. As well as the items described in the panel below, a useful piece of equipment for field work is a pair of binoculars to see features that are out of reach. Many types of binoculars work as a powerful hand lens if used backwards.

You will also find it useful to acquire a detailed guide to the trees of the area in which you are interested. Some guides, known as keys, are designed to identify trees by a process of elimination. Trees are divided into groups according to certain distinguishing characters. Smaller groups are then sub-divided until finally the plant, or group to which it

VARIABLE HABIT
Each tree species has a characteristic overall shape when it grows unimpeded. However, the habit can be dramatically different if the tree is, for example, growing in close proximity to others, as can be seen in these photographs of Beech trees alone (above) and in a forest (left).

belongs, can be identified. It is important to always use a local key that refers to the region you are in. Photographs and illustrations are a valuable aid at every stage of the identification process.

TAKING FIELD NOTES

When you go out on a "tree spotting" trip, you will find it helpful to take a few items of equipment to aid identification. You will need a notebook, pencil, and a selection of coloured pencils to record your observations in words and pictures. You don't need to be an accomplished artist to make useful visual notes and annotations. A magnifying glass will enable you to see details on leaves, such as hairs and veins. With wax crayons and plain paper, you can take rubbings of bark texture. If you intend to bring samples of fallen leaves or fruit home, be sure to have a store of labels and bags to put them in. Lastly, bring a camera to take photographs of the tree.

A TREE DOSSIER
Detailed notes, sketches, photographs, bark rubbings, samples of leaves and fruit, should enable you to identify all but the most unusual trees.

SYSTEMATIC OBSERVATION

When faced with a tree that you are unable to recognize immediately, it is important to follow the process of identification systematically. Observe and take notes on each aspect of the tree's physical characteristics: bark, leaves, fruit, and flowers (see below). Take note, too, of the tree's size and habit (overall shape), although this is not necessarily a defining feature (see Variable Habit, opposite). Other important information to record could include the tree's location and the type of habitat in which it is growing –

for example, open parkland, barren mountainside, or dense forest. Note, too, other tree species growing nearby.

Many tree enthusiasts derive great satisfaction from keeping their own log of interesting trees they have seen. Notes, photographs, sketches, and bark rubbings can all contribute to a fascinating record of "meetings" with trees. A record of associated birds, insects, and other wildlife is also of interest. You might consider observing several trees close to your home through the seasons and over a number of years.

LEAVES

Observation of leaves should include taking note of its type, how it is arranged on the shoot, its overall shape, whether the leaf margins are smooth, lobed, or toothed, and what colour they are above and beneath. Use a magnifying glass to observe fine hairs and veining. (See Glossary for more information on leaf types.)

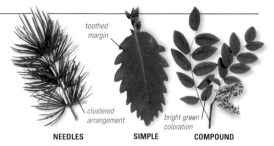

toothed margin

clustered arrangement

bright green coloration

NEEDLES   **SIMPLE**   **COMPOUND**

BARK

The bark of a tree often changes with age. Nevertheless it is an important feature to observe. Note the colour and the texture, whether it is smooth, flaking or peeling, or fissured. Make a bark rubbing with wax crayon for your records. You should also look for any resin visible from previous cuts in the bark. Do not make such cuts yourself.

FISSURED   **SMOOTH**   **FLAKING**

FLOWERS

The colour and shape of the flower are the most obvious features, but be sure to also look at their arrangement – whether they are solitary blooms or appear in a more complex inflorescence (see also Glossary). Some species have male and female flowers on the same tree. Others have male and female flowers on different trees.

CLUSTER   **SOLITARY**   **INFLORESCENCE**

FRUIT

Fruits appear after flowers and will only rarely be seen together. They may be several different types. Take note of the external colour, shape, and size. Then, if possible, open one and observe the number and arrangement of seeds within the fruit. Be aware that fruit often changes significantly in size and colour as it ripens on the tree.

DRUPE   **CONE**   **POD**

LIVING WITH TREES

Early People and Trees

More than ten million years ago, our ape-like ancestors lived in trees,
which provided their major needs of safety, food, and warmth.
By five million years ago, our human ancestors walked on the ground.
But we have still relied on trees through every phase of our prehistory.

Since humans first evolved from ape-like mammals, trees and forests have provided us with food, warmth, protection from the elements, and safety from predators. Trees were a source of plentiful and varied food, from succulent shoots to leaves, fruits, nuts, and berries. Many Neanderthal sites from 100,000 years ago are still littered with tree seeds and husks. Woods were also home to animals to hunt, from squirrels to deer and wild boar.

LIVING ALOFT
Our closest living cousins, the chimpanzees, still rely on trees for most of their requirements.

TREES FOR TRANSPORT
Dugout canoes (like this modern Dutch example) may date back over 8,500 years.

WOOD FOR FIRE
Early people probably noticed a wildfire's warmth, saw how the flames kept large predators at bay, and even tasted how the heat cooked carcasses. Early evidence for controlled fires at a specific site, using collected wood, comes from the charred animal bones and fossil ash layers at "Dragon Bone Hill", Zhoukoudian, near Beijing in China. These hearths date back more than 400,000 years. They were tended by representatives of the now-extinct human species, *Homo erectus*. By 100,000 years ago the also-extinct Neanderthal people were using wood-fuelled fires at various sites around Europe, to help keep them warm in the intense cold of the last Great Ice Age.

TREES FOR SHELTER
Prehistoric humans probably sheltered in woods, since conditions among the trees were preferable to the harsh sun or windy blizzards of open country. Some 400,000 years ago near Bilzingsleben, Germany, patterns of preserved holes suggest upright posts for purpose-built wooden shelters – again,

DEER-HUNT WITH WOOD BOWS AND ARROWS
This painting from Cavalls Cave near Valltorta, Spain dates back 12,000 years. Luckily, pigments of prehistoric art last longer than most wooden objects they depict.

probably the handiwork of *Homo erectus*. By 60,000 years ago Neanderthal people may have constructed hut-like shelters in Moldova. From 30,000 years ago Grimaldis and Cro Magnons – European groups of our own species *Homo sapiens* – made more complex dwellings from wood, mammoth tusks, and animal skins, at sites such as Dolni Vestonice, in the Czech Republic.

WOODEN WEAPONS

Before the Stone Age, ancient humans probably used branches to smash and stab. But unlike stone, wood decays. So evidence for wooden weapons and utensils comes mostly from associated stone artefacts such as axe-heads, spear-tips, or arrow-heads, and prehistoric art. *Homo erectus* may have thrown spears some 400,000 years ago near Schoningen, Germany. Nearby in Lehringen, the Mousterian tool culture of Neanderthal people probably included wooden spears. Early *Homo sapiens* left evidence of wooden spears 80,000 years ago at Mount Carmel, Israel. The notched spear-thrower or *atlatl*, for greater power and distance, dates from over 20,000 years ago; it may have led to the bow and arrow. Stone arrow-heads were known in Africa before 25,000 years ago, with European versions from 12,000 years ago. Danish bows of yew and elm date to 10,000 years ago. A frozen traveller, "Otzi the Iceman", who died 5,300 years ago in the European Alps, had 14 wooden arrows in his quiver.

ANASAZI AXE
This Aztec tool, almost 1,000 years old, has its original wooden shaft and willow twine binding.

ATLATL
Wooden spear-throwers probably preceded the bow and arrow.

FLINT-HEADED ADZE
A stone held in a wooden shaft was a basic tool for early humans.

Tree Myths and Spirits

Trees were the largest and oldest living things known to many early peoples. Their size and their importance in terms of providing shelter, sustenance, and a wide variety of materials have earned trees a prominent place in the world's myths and legends.

SPIRIT HOMES

Although ancient storytellers sometimes spoke of trees as spirits, in most mythologies trees are the homes of spirits. From North America to Africa, these spirits protect the trees they inhabit – they are said to attack anyone who tries to harm a tree or cut it down. If treated properly, tree spirits are usually seen as helpful to humans, but forests can be dark and intimidating places, and this is reflected in stories, common in Africa, of forest spirits that trap the unwary in their branches or eat human flesh.

Large baobabs are said to be home to many spirits. People are expected to warn these spirits well in advance – often in writing – before felling a baobab. The notice gives the spirits the chance to find another tree. If people need to cut down a tree for the timber, this has to be done with the correct respect and ritual. Repeating the appropriate spell or chant before felling a tree will bring good fortune to any objects that are made from the wood. In a similar way, a shaman must observe the correct rituals when cutting wood

YGGDRASIL
The great Ash tree of Norse mythology, Yggdrasil, was believed to support the world. Its branches and roots provided structure and protection.

and carving it to make a drum. Only then will the drum speak with the tree spirit's voice.

The ancient Greeks believed that each tree had its spirit, or hamadryad, who looked after the tree and tried to stop people cutting it down. Hamadryads, like the trees they inhabited, could live for hundreds of years and a hamadryad only perished when her tree met its death. In Japanese folklore, many trees are said to have spirits. One story tells how the spirit of

THE ENDURING BAOBAB
The capacity of the towering African Baobab to survive lightning strikes contributes to its link with the supernatural.

VOICE OF THE TREE
In Africa, people say that trees are the homes of powerful spirits. A shaman's drum is usually made from wood, and he hopes that the spirit of the tree speaks when he plays his instrument.

a plum tree defended a peasant who tried to stop a nobleman from transplanting the tree. When the nobleman drew his sword on the peasant, the tree moved so that the blow hit one of her branches, which then fell on the nobleman's head.

THE POWER OF ANCIENT TREES

Trees that are especially tall and old have always been given special respect and status. An especially ancient tree, such as some yews in English churchyards, are especially revered and are said to "ward off evil spirits". The world tree of Norse mythology, the ash called Yggdrasil, was

PRAYING BENEATH A BO-TREE

A Hindu devotee of Vishnu prays beneath a Bo-tree (or Bodhi Tree) in Sarnath's Deer Park. Both Hindus and Buddhists have special reverence for the Bo-tree, which Hindus regard as the eternal tree of life, and under which the Buddha achieved enlightenment.

SPRUCE TREE MYTH

Some Native peoples of the North American subarctic have myths of the Distant Time, when living things had a human form. Among these people were widows who pinched their skin and cried when told that their husbands had died. These women were believed to have become spruce trees, whose coarse, pinched bark was the result of this repeated pinching.

SPRUCE TREES IN WINTER

so huge that it linked together the entire Norse cosmos. The tree spread its canopy over the whole world and the sky, while its roots extended into the underworld. Stags grazed on its branches, a wise eagle lived in its canopy, and a squirrel carried messages between the eagle and the underworld. A sacred spring bubbled amongst its roots.

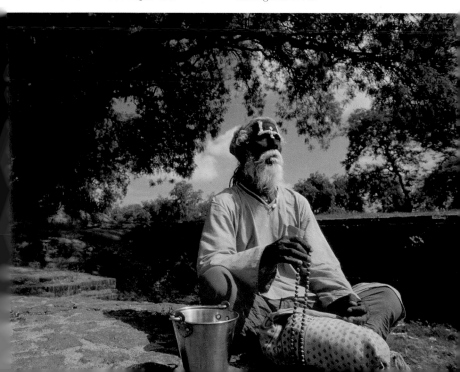

Trees for Sustenance

Early humans depended on natural woodlands for foods such as fruit and nuts, later learning to cultivate trees for these foodstuffs. In the modern world, vast businesses are based on edible tree products, from fruit and nuts to crops, such as coffee, that have to be processed.

FROM TREE TO TABLE

Fruit and nuts from trees are harvested worldwide: from hot climates come the date, papaya, pomegranate, olive, lychee, mango, avocado, coconut, pistachio, and brazil nut, among many others. Citrus fruits (lemons, oranges, among others) are an important group grown mainly in southern Europe and North Africa.

Cooler climes produce apples, pears, plums, damsons, cherries, walnuts, chestnuts, and almonds. Peaches, apricots, and figs are found in temperate regions.

Growing fruit and nuts commercially is a precise science. Orchards must be correctly managed, the right type of plants must be grown and, if grafted, put on the right rootstock. Irrigation and protection from extremes of weather are important considerations. Pests, diseases, and competition from grass or weeds must be anticipated and controlled before damage occurs. Pruning to control tree growth and improve crop yield is critical.

APPLE ORCHARD

With hundreds of varieties and rich in fibre and vitamin C, the apple is a deservedly popular fruit. Orchard trees (below) are often specially selected for small size to make the job of harvesting the crop (left) easier.

COCONUT
A giant among nuts, the versatile coconut provides a rich food source for humans and animals alike.

COFFEE BEANS
Coffee undergoes a long process of production before it can be roasted, ground, and savoured as a drink.

ALMOND
Grown in cool climes, the nut of the almond tree can be eaten raw, cooked, or made into confectionery.

PROCESSED CROPS

Many fruits and nuts that are eaten raw may be processed into other products to extend their life. Pineapple is canned, juiced, and pulped. Apples and oranges are turned into juice. Plums and apricots are made into jam, canned, or bottled. Coconut is shredded, creamed, or made into milk, and olives and many nuts are pressed to extract edible oils.

Other crops, notably coffee and cocoa, are transformed totally before they are fit for consumption. Coffee and cocoa beans are harvested by hand, and dried or roasted. The beans are then sold to manufacturers around the world where they are turned into a vast array of edible products and beverages.

HARVESTING COCOA BEANS

Cocoa beans are found in the seed pods of the Cocoa tree (*Theobroma cacao*). The pods are harvested at the peak of ripeness, split open, and the beans removed for fermentation and drying, before being made into chocolate.

SHELLING COCOA PODS

Trees for Wood and Building

In previous centuries, people depended entirely on wood to build fences, boats, dwellings, and furniture. Easy availability, sustainability, and variety made it a reliable choice. Although now replaced by other materials for many purposes, wood is still a valuable resource.

Wood is a sustainable commodity. Produced year by year in the stems of trees, it is made by the tree itself from nutrients from the soil and plant food manufactured in the leaves. Each type of tree produces wood with different qualities, making it useful for various functions. Some woods such as oak are hard and strong; others, such as yew and ash, are soft and flexible; poplar has fire retardant qualities; and many others are sought after for their colour or grain.

WOOD TYPES

SOFTWOOD

Softwoods come from coniferous trees. They have a more primitive cellular structure than hardwoods and often contain aromatic resins.

CEDAR

Softwoods can actually be heavier than hardwoods. Some are used mainly for construction (cedar, pine, larch, for example), others for paper or board manufacture (spruce, fir, hemlock, among others).

HARDWOOD

Timber from deciduous or evergreen broadleaved trees is called hardwood. The term does not refer to the physical hardness of wood but is a classification based on complex cell structures.

BEECH

Hardwoods range from very hard ebony to very soft balsa and are used mainly for building or furniture-making.

WOODEN DWELLING

In some parts of the world, a simple shelter made from cut branches provides an effective refuge from the elements for one or more families and their animals.

PRACTICAL USES

In former times, people relied on wood for shelters and boats. Often, thin rods of coppice wood (trees repeatedly cut back to produce material of a particular size) were used to build a basic shelter and confine domestic livestock. Early houses and barns tended to be built with small timbers squared up with an adze, or large cruck frames produced by splitting a whole tree trunk in half. Saw technology lagged far behind the axe, adze, or splitting wedge and therefore sawn wood was rarely used.

Wood was usually processed in the forest to avoid the problems of hauling heavy timbers great distances on poor roads. Choosing the right shape of tree or limb for a particular job was an important consideration, no more so than in shipbuilding, where naturally curved timbers were selected for frames and "knees" to support decks.

With the industrial age sawn wood came into its own. Baulks of timber

WOOD-FRAMED BOAT
Where handmade boats are still produced, naturally curved timbers are preferred for the frames because of their superior strength and durability.

were used for grand houses, sea defences, wharves, mill machinery, railway sleepers, and industrial buildings of every sort. Round wood was used extensively in coal mines to reinforce shafts and tunnels and for telephone and electricity transmission poles.

Today, wood in a building is likely to be a reconstituted constituent of manufactured board or glued laminated beams. Wood supplies now are much depleted and, increasingly, timber comes from carefully managed plantations rather than natural forests.

FURNITURE
Wood has been much prized over the centuries for making fine furniture.

WOOD-FRAMED HOUSE
A house with a wooden frame is rare today because of the prohibitive costs of timber. Any wooden elements are likely to be internal, and reconstituted or laminated.

Trees for Paper and Pulp

Wasps have been making paper for millions of years but for humans it started in the 3rd century BCE in Ancient Egypt. The Chinese were the first to use wood for paper. Their skills reached the Middle East in the 8th century CE, and Europe 300 years later.

WOOD PRODUCTS

ETHANOL

Volatile ethanol is a traditional fuel derived from wood. It is prepared by fermentation of sugars, but the process requires substantial amounts of energy.

ETHANOL BURNING

MODERN WOOD FUEL

Modern use of wood for fuel involves efficient self-feeding combusters, boilers, and heat exchangers that burn wood chips from sustainable low-grade woodland or sawmill waste. Such woodfuel heating is environmentally friendly, clean, and cost-effective.

BIOMASS

Some species such as poplar, willow, and eucalyptus can be grown like an agricultural crop, cut every two or three years. The end-product is wood chips that are suitable for fuel and other purposes such as mulching.

FIBREBOARD

FIBREBOARD

Pressed wood chips and pulp mixed with adhesives and hardeners produce various types of fibreboard for insulation, flooring, interior surfaces, and domestic fittings.

TRADITIONAL HANDMADE PAPER

Contemporary traditional papermaking techniques involve pouring prepared liquid pulp onto a mesh of finely woven cloth set in a wooden frame the size of the intended sheet. The water drains through leaving a flat film of fibres. Thickness of paper can be adjusted by adding more or less pulp. A second framed mesh (the deckle) is pressed onto the surface of the pulp expelling more moisture. Soon the fibres form a sheet that is turned upside down onto damp felt to dry. Colour, scent, and herbs can be added to the pulp. Various methods of pressing the paper are used to produce different surfaces.

INDUSTRIAL PROCESS

In 1840, Friedrich Keller invented an industrial process, still in use today, for reducing logs into paper pulp. Softwood made up of long fibres, such as spruce and poplar, is particularly suitable for making paper. It is sometimes used with hardwood, such as oak, to make paper for a particular purpose or quality.

Modern factory papermaking is a remarkable process that starts with vats of liquid pulp at one end (the wet end) of the milling machine and finishes with dry rolls of paper at the other end (the dry end). Pulp is usually made of waste, which is wood not reserved for lumber; it is chopped into chips that are broken down by steam and chemicals into a semi-liquid "soup" of fibres. A pump sprays a thin layer of liquid paper pulp onto a moving wire screen, which may be up to six metres (20ft) wide travelling at 95km/h (60miles/h). By the time pulp reaches the end of the screen it has partly solidified and the damp "paper" is fed onto the first of many pressing and heated drying rollers. Finally, rolls of paper, some around five metres (16ft) wide and weighing many tonnes, are removed from the machine. The process is continuous, with new rolls being started without breaking the cycle. Papermaking is a highly skilled and precisely co-ordinated job.

HANDMADE PAPER
Colouring and flowers can be added to the pulp to create special effects.

LOGGING
Trees are felled, floated downriver, and processed on a vast scale at this lumber mill in Sabah, Borneo.

OTHER PULP PRODUCTS

Wood pulp is naturally brown and has to be bleached to produce paper for printing. The brown pulp can be used to make cardboard, boxes, or brown paper. This and other packaging is made in much the same way as paper. Thick card is produced in individual sheets. Wet pulp is moulded to make shaped packaging.

Medium density fibreboard (MDF) and hardboard are pressed from hot pulp made from finely ground wood. Chipboard and thick reconstituted boards are pressed from coarse material bound by adhesive. These products require relatively low quality raw materials and can incorporate preservatives and insect repellent.

PAPER RECYCLING

Most waste paper can be recycled provided the print can be removed easily. Every tonne of recycled paper produces about as much usable wood pulp as an equivalent weight of logs. The quality of paper made from recycled paper can be greatly improved by mixing it with a quantity of new pulp.

RECYCLING LOGO

PAPER FOR PRINTING
Every day around the world, massive amounts of paper are used to print newspapers. Paper quality does not have to be high, so recycled paper is used, which helps to conserve resources.

Other Products from Trees

In addition to their vital role in producing wood, paper, and foodstuffs, trees are the sources of a wide variety of other products ranging from textiles to medicines. Each product is harvested from a particular part of the tree: bark, sap, leaves, flowers, or fruit.

MYRIAD USES

Before the advent of the modern pharmaceutical industry, most medicines came from trees and other plants. Today many trees are still exploited for their medicinal products, such as quinine from the bark of the Chinchona Tree (*Cinchona officinalis*), which is sometimes used to treat malaria. There are also many species still to be discovered that have potential medicinal value, particularly among the rich flora of the rainforests. It is important that these species are allowed to flourish as they may hold the key to conquering many diseases. Many poisons and mind-altering drugs, such as khat (*Catha edulis*), also come from trees.

All trees contain long, tensile fibres to give them strength and the ability to bend in the wind. These capabilities have been harnessed to make a range of everyday items such as cloth, rope, and baskets.

Rubber, cork, various resins, and tannin all come from the bark of trees, and many natural dyes are made from leaves, flowers, or crushed seeds. Trees are also the sources of many highly valued volatile oils that are used in perfumes, aromatherapy, and cooking; the oils may be extracted from the bark, leaves, flowers, or fruit.

WILLOW

Many types of willow tree (particularly *Salix purpurea*) have bark that is rich in salicin, a chemical that is the active ingredient of the painkiller aspirin.

SELECTED TREE PRODUCTS

Products from trees range from hard-wearing materials to delicate volatile oils. In most cases, a much larger quantity of raw material is harvested compared to the end product. Cork and fibrous matter are exceptions in that extraction is not required so the picked materials roughly equal the final wares.

FIBRE	Kapok Tree (*Ceiba pentandra*)	Seed pods are the source of kapok fibre
	Small-leaved Lime (*Tilia cordata*)	Inner bark used for rope and coarse fibre
	Raphia Palm (*Raphia farinifera*)	Twine for weaving and agricultural use
CORK	Cork Oak (*Quercus suber*)	Bark provides wine corks and flooring
LATEX, GUM	Para Rubber Tree (*Hevea brasiliensis*)	Sap (latex) is the raw ingredient of rubber
	Mastic Tree (*Pistacia lentiscus*)	Resin used for gum, varnish, medicines
TANNIN AND PRESERVATIVES	Oaks (*Quercus* sp.)	Tannin from bark for preserving leather
DYE	Anatto (*Bixa orellana*)	Colouring for food, cosmetics, fabric
	Henna (*Lawsonia inermis*)	Colouring for hair and skin decoration
RESIN, VARNISH, TURPENTINE	Maritime Pine (*Pinus pinaster*)	Resin used for varnishes and turpentine
MEDICINAL	Willows (*Salix* sp.)	Original source of chemical in aspirin
	Loquat (*Eriobotrya japonica*)	Leaf extract provides antibacterial agents
	Maidenhair Tree (*Ginkgo biloba*)	Extracts used to improve mental function
AROMATIC OIL	Clove (*Syzygium aromaticum*)	Oil for flavouring and toothache relief
	Italian Cypress (*Cupressus sempervirens*)	Oil used in perfumes and to repel insects
	Gum trees (*Eucalyptus* sp.)	Oil used in aromatherapy and inhalations

Trees for Amenity and Ornament

For thousands of years, trees have been planted to bring pleasure.
A rich history of gardening exists in China and Japan, particularly
near temples. In the West, the first gardens were cultivated in North
Africa, the Mediterranean area, and Mesopotamia before 2000BCE.

DESIGNING WITH TREES

Humans seem to have a need to surround
themselves with trees, and this is
especially important in the artificial
environment of a modern city. Planting
trees in a city or landscape involves
careful forward planning because results
may not be achieved
for over 50 years.
It involves an
understanding of
how trees evolve.
They grow larger,
change with the
seasons, and rapidly
fill up spaces. The
extended timescale
also means the
original purpose of the planted area may
change – for example, an area planned as
a park may be developed for housing.

THE RIGHT SPECIES

Care is vital when choosing tree species to
avoid the need for lopping and felling,
and to discourage unhealthy or dangerous
trees from growing. It is vital to know the
growth rate, and potential size and shape
of every species that is to be considered in
the plan. Various questions should be
asked, for example, is the tree broad,
narrow, spreading, weeping, columnar,
shrubby, evergreen, or deciduous? Does it
have any particular soil preference? Is it
tolerant of shade, strong sunlight, wind,
or pollution, either of the air or soil? Tree
breeding, especially in the United States,
has produced various cultivated forms of
trees that have been developed to fulfil
special requirements, particularly narrow-
crowned trees that are suitable for lining
streets. A species of Chinese Pear (*Pyrus
calleryana*) has provided a rich resource for
experiment, yielding not only a narrow
profile tree well suited to the urban
environment, but also a range of

attractive autumn foliage colour in
individual cultivars, such as 'Redspire',
'Trinity', and 'Autumn Blaze'.

The nature of the site will impose
limits on the types of tree that can be
planted. Grazing animals, conservation
constraints, recreation needs, landscape

STREET TREES
Palms are ideal street
trees in warm countries;
they cast shade, have
clear stems, and do not
drop slippery leaves or
block street lights.

enhancement, shade, and screening traffic require trees with different kinds of tenacity. Regular maintenance is essential to ensure that beauty, function, and longevity can be prolonged.

CITY TREES

The urban environment is harsh and the lifespan of a city tree is short compared to the same species in the country. Screening, one of the main uses of trees in a city, is best achieved by mass planting but this may not be appropriate where people feel threatened in dark confined places. Thickly planted trunks may also form a litter trap.

CENTRAL PARK, NEW YORK
Tree-filled parks in the centre of major cities not only provide much needed leisure space, but also create a "green lung" that helps to improve air quality in areas of high pollution.

JAPANESE GARDEN
The Japanese are masters of garden design. They are famous for thoughtful planting of trees to provide a good succession of spring blossom and autumn foliage.

TREES IN GARDENS

Garden trees can form an eye-catching focus or a pleasing background. Size is crucial; small gardens need small trees, and some species should not be planted near to houses because of the risk of damage from invasive roots. Dense foliage can be used to advantage, providing shade and blocking nasty views. You can create striking contrasts and accents by planting trees with copper or red foliage. Features such as glossy leaves, an unusual undersurface colour, or coloured bark, can add interest in a garden, as do trees with conspicuous flowers, although tree blossom is often short-lived.

BONSAI TREES

The ornamental value of trees has been taken to the extreme in the Japanese art of bonsai, in which miniature versions of trees are cultivated. Maple and juniper are commonly grown species. The art of bonsai lies in producing aesthetically appealing shapes by prescribed techniques of growing, pruning, and training, and by choosing a base or container that perfectly complements the tree. More art than horticulture, bonsai is a very popular pastime.

BONSAI LARCH AND PINE TREES

Planting and Caring for Trees

The act of planting a tree is the final and least difficult stage in a process that involves consideration of many factors ranging from the season to the type of tree. Assessing the physical attributes of the site, such as soil type and position is also a key element.

CHOOSING AND PLANTING A TREE

Every tree has ecological and physical needs that should ideally match the location. Exposure, drainage, soil type, drought, and disease must all be considered. In urban sites, in addition, there are problems of whether the tree is liable to block light, break into underground services, or damage cables, walls, and foundations. Expert advice on the choice of tree is essential.

Having chosen the species, the next consideration is the optimum time for planting. Temperate trees should be planted in the dormant season; evergreens shortly before they start to grow in spring. Prepare the site by removing rubbish or diseased roots. The ground surrounding the tree should be treated or covered to stop weeds and grass growing. Plastic mulch mats work well and can be disguised with composted wood chips. Only add fertilizer to deficient soil. Do not add uncomposted mulch as this can cause oxygen and nitrogen deficiencies.

PLANTING A TREE

The hole should be freshly dug so it does not dry out, flood, or lose beneficial soil organisms. Keep the tree in the shade, roots covered, until you are ready to plant. When you have finished planting, support the tree with a stake.

1 Place the tree to be planted in the centre of the chosen site and mark out a circle about 90cm (3ft) in diameter.

2 Dig a hole in the marked area; mix the soil with well-rotted organic compost before partly re-filling the hole. Water if dry.

3 Remove the tree from the pot and gently ease the compacted roots apart and remove any that are damaged.

4 Drive a short stake off-centre and put the tree next to it; the root collar should be level with the ground. Backfill with soil.

PRUNING A BRANCH
Using a sharp saw, secateurs, or loppers, cut unwanted branches or competing leading shoots close to the collar. Do not cut into the trunk.

PRUNING CONSIDERATIONS

In general, once a tree is established it requires minimal maintenance. Pruning should be kept to a minimum in the early years, bearing in mind that every scrap of green top growth is needed to feed the tree. However, dead or diseased twigs can be safely cut off. Once the tree is more mature, pruning and training can begin, especially by removing competing leading shoots and wayward branches that may eventually turn into weak dangerous forks. Wound painting is not recommended unless there is a serious risk of infection locally from airborne diseases.

PEST AND DISEASE CONTROL

Pest and disease damage is best prevented right from the start by a good choice of species. A tree that is not naturally suited to its site is always more vulnerable than one that is. Protection from air pollution, salt spray, and gales can best be achieved by choosing a hardy species and a protected site. Browsing animals have to be kept out with tree shelters or fencing. Squirrels and small rodents can be a difficult problem that may require specialist control. Avoid watering if at all possible in order to promote root growth, but if it is essential, water liberally and continue watering until the end of the growing season. It is preferable to use rain water that has collected in a butt rather than tap water, which contains many chemicals that are potentially harmful to a growing tree.

SPOTTING PROBLEMS

HOLES IN LEAVES

This damage is often caused by sawfly. The larvae will strip whole branches. Holes in leaves can also be caused by weevils and fungal or bacterial canker.

WEBBER MOTHS

Leaf damage along with the appearance of a dense white webbing over the affected leaves and shoots may be the result of infestation by the caterpillars of various moths. Mild cases can be treated by careful pruning. In more serious cases, it may be necessary to use chemical pesticides.

RUST DAMAGE

Summer foliage covered with orange-coloured crusts, is usually the result of fungal disease. If the tree is small enough it can be treated with a commercial fungicide following the instructions on the label.

BARK DAMAGE

Splits in the bark may be caused by drought and made worse by irregular watering. Bark damage can also be caused by rodents or by diseases such as stem canker.

Forest Practice

The aim of a well-run commercial forest is to produce timber, while also conserving wildlife and providing an amenity. For success, the long process depends on careful planning in the early stages and expert management throughout the life of the forest plantation.

Forest management begins with the selection of new sites or suitable existing woodlands for regeneration. Preparation of the ground may involve clearing and draining, cultivating bare sections, and fencing the area to keep out animals. Vehicle access may need upgrading but often not until it is time to harvest.

TREE SHELTERS
Plastic tubes called tree shelters are used to protect young trees from attack by rodents and sometimes deer. They are removed once the trees are well established.

COMMERCIAL PLANTING

Forest nurseries grow seedlings in raised beds and these are dug up and transplanted after a year. These young trees grow to around 30 centimetres (12in) tall in two to three years depending on species. This technique encourages a dense root system and a well-balanced plant. Hardwoods with long taproots, such as oak, often have the main root shortened to promote fibrous growth; this improves the tree's survival chances. Planting is still generally done by hand except in open sites, such as farm woodlands, where an adapted agricultural planting machine may be used. To plant a tree, a slot is cut in the ground and opened up by a transverse slot and some leverage with the spade. The tree is lowered into the hole then firmed in with a boot. After the first year or two, failed trees are replaced. Planting takes place at the start and end of winter in order to avoid periods of severe weather, particularly frost.

COPPICING
This ancient and sustainable system of woodland management involves harvesting the shoots from an established root system every 7–15 years.

GROWING IN ROWS

Managed forests are usually planted in neat rows that allow for easy access for forest-maintenance work, as in this plantation of young conifers in Scotland.

FOREST MAINTENANCE

Young plantations survive best where competition from natural vegetation is minimal. This is achieved by hand weeding, herbicides or the use of tree shelters. Pest control may be required as young trees are vulnerable to attack from rodents and insects. Fertilizer may be applied if the soil shows deficiencies. In order to produce single, straight trees some pruning, training, and sometimes staking may be necessary.

Thinning may be carried out either for the benefit of the remaining trees or to produce small trunks for a particular market. Mixed forests can also be thinned to favour particular species, usually those best suited to the site. Silvicultural thinning is a painstaking process that looks at the situation and prospects of every tree and marks those for removal. A more common and cheaper option is to remove single lines of trees; usually one in four. The advantage is that

machines can easily access the site to cut and remove the trees. A disadvantage is that this thinning method results in the indiscriminate removal of healthy and unhealthy trees.

FELLING

Final felling may involve total clearance using machinery. Continuous cover forestry is a more aesthetic method in which some trees are left until new ones planted in between have taken. Natural regeneration, if of good quality, may be encouraged. Commercial management of natural forests usually works in this way.

Coppicing is a form of forest management in which a single species is regularly cleared from small areas of a larger wood. It may also involve frequent removal of underwood from a forest of a slower-growing species. This is a sustainable system that provides a regular supply of timber.

PLANTING IN COSTA RICA

Environmentalists and farmers work together planting trees by hand as part of a reforestation programme in the Puriscal region, Costa Rica.

Trees and the Environment

A delicate and complex balance exists between the environment and trees and, at the most basic level, one cannot survive without the other. Environmental problems impact on the health of trees, and if large numbers of trees die or are removed, the environment suffers.

THE CARBON CYCLE

Central to the relationship between trees and the environment is the carbon cycle (see facing page). Carbon exists in the atmosphere in the form of carbon dioxide. Leaves absorb this during photosynthesis (see page 20). A byproduct of this process is oxygen, which is released into the air. Animals take in oxygen and release carbon dioxide when they breathe. They also release carbon when their dead bodies decompose. Another source of carbon in the air is from burning fuels such as wood, oil, and coal. The net result is an increase in atmospheric carbon above the amount that can be reabsorbed, and the equilibrium is upset.

SOIL STABILIZATION
In the African state of Niger, trees are planted to form wind breaks as part of a project to stabilize sand dunes.

ENVIRONMENTAL CHANGES

Pollution and climatic changes are the factors most likely to endanger tree species. Firstly, chemicals released by industry and other human activities are polluting the atmosphere. In some areas this pollution goes beyond the tolerance of native trees; sulphur dioxide poisoning is an extreme example. In some polluted areas, however, trees have benefitted in the short term because insect predators and fungal diseases tend to succumb first, allowing the trees to grow more vigorously. But there may also be undesirable effects, such as the loss of immunity to disease.

The major climatic change is global warming – heating up of the planet by polluting (greenhouse) gases: carbon dioxide, nitrous oxide, and methane. Many modern trees that have evolved with a particular climate will have to adapt, migrate, or perish.

The last substantial rise in global temperature was about 6,000 years ago. If human activities force the temperature up this high again, trees will be affected. Conifers, such as juniper and spruce, and broadleaved species of birch and beech will become extinct or will need to migrate to higher and cooler regions. Eucalyptus and fan palms will colonize new areas. Fungi, bacteria, and insects will also evolve and could unleash epidemics of disease and infestation on an unprecedented scale.

RAINFOREST DEFORESTATION

The destruction of huge areas of rainforest, most seriously in South America (far right), is going to cause untold problems for mankind. Short-sighted commercial interests risk depriving the world of many plant and animal species, and destroying the planet's largest living "lung",

SUSTAINABLE

carbon dioxide in the atmosphere is absorbed by leaves

leaves fix carbon from carbon dioxide in the form of wood

living creatures exhale carbon dioxide

carbon from plants, faeces, and decomposed bodies of animals remains in the soil

UNSUSTAINABLE

high levels of carbon dioxide in the atmosphere add to the "greenhouse" effect

carbon from burning wood, oil, and coal is released into the atmosphere as carbon dioxide

carbon fixed in the earth from plants in prehistoric times is extracted for fuel in the form of oil and coal

BENEFICIAL EFFECTS OF TREES

The presence of trees around us is something we often take for granted, failing to appreciate the many vital functions that they perform. Tree roots provide infinitely better erosion control than any artificial substitute. Not only do the roots stop soil from being washed away, the trunk and branches above ground can trap silt and debris until the ground level rises above the flood plain. Salt-tolerant species such as mangroves can even do this close to the sea. Shelter

CARBON CYCLE

The diagram above shows the contrast between sustainable carbon levels in which emissions roughly equal absorption, and unsustainable, where carbon release far exceeds the ability of trees to absorb it.

from wind is another benefit provided by trees. Shelterbelts of trees can modify a microclimate so that crops and domestic animals can be raised on land that was once too bleak to use. In the southern United States, magnolias are used to protect homes; often the lower branches are layered to increase stability.

Tree Conservation

Trees and forests are vulnerable. A tree may take hundreds of years to grow to maturity and be replaced, but only a few hours to be destroyed. Technology has produced an arsenal of lethal weapons that have increased the ease with which trees can be removed.

Trees have been exploited for thousands of years and some people feel that as long as communities rely on logging and societies demand the produce, the forestry industry cannot be abandoned. Commercial pressures can certainly help to maintain certain tree species, but this is not always possible in the case of rare trees that grow only slowly. However, unless sustainable forest management strategies are implemented certain types of forestry will die out because the resource will be gone.

NATURAL THREATS

Although many individual species of trees are threatened with extinction due to over-exploitation, trees in general are not threatened to the same degree. Species that we know and rely on may go, but others will take their place. Volcanoes, asteroids, continental drift, sea-level fluctuations, and ice ages have failed to exterminate trees completely. Trees have a long history of survival but they have to evolve. Where there is bare earth or a great tree is cut down, scores of new seedlings will move in. An oak may go but ash, elder, and birch will replace it.

RED-FAN PARROT
Habitat loss threatens this vulnerable South American species.

EDEN PROJECT
Honed out of a redundant clay pit in Cornwall, England, the Eden Project comprises a series of domes in which a botanical garden and conservation centre flourishes.

GENE POLLUTION
In some cases new alien introductions will accidentally cross breed with native trees until no pure progeny exist. Goat Willow (*Salix caprea*), pictured above, is a species that has been affected by this phenomenon.

HABITAT CONSERVATION

Conserving tree habitats is one of the cornerstones of any conservation programme. When a forest is cut down, the plant and animal community is modified and partly destroyed. Animals leave and the biological and genetic diversity of the site is altered. Any change to a natural habitat will divert it from its evolutionary path. It will become a different kind of habitat. In areas where the landscape is "artificial", past human activities are considered a valid biological contribution. If "alien" species were planted 300 years ago and they have hybridized with native plants, the aliens are considered indigenous.

ARBORETA AND SEED BANKS

Saving today's trees is the business of botanical gardens and arboreta, and seed banks play a vital role in preserving our tree heritage. However, it is doubtful if many saved trees will ever be returned to the wild; there may not even be a habitat to return to. There is also a danger that new trees released into an existing habitat might endanger resident species. Many rescued plants stand the best chance of survival in an artificial plantation containing as many diverse individuals as possible. Biodiversity is essential for vigorous trees and to avoid threats from disease and predators.

ENDANGERED TREE SPECIES

DIOSPYROS EBENUM
In demand for its black wood, this species is threatened by over-exploitation.

ARAUCARIA ARAUCANA
The genetic diversity of this species has been severely depleted by over-harvesting.

SORBUS LEYANA
This whitebeam was at one time reduced to only nine specimens in Wales, UK.

DENDROSICYOS SOCOTRANUS
The Cucumber Tree is threatened by human activity and climatic changes.

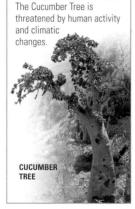

CUCUMBER TREE

MILLENNIUM SEED BANK

Part of Britain's Royal Botanic Gardens, Kew, and based in West Sussex, the Millennium Seed Bank is an international plant conservation programme and centre. This global initiative aims to safeguard the future of 24,000 plant species in an effort to prevent them from worldwide extinction. Started in 2000, the scheme has already secured the future of most of the UK's flowering plants. The seed bank also aims to provide a world-class resource facility.

SEED STORAGE

TREES OF
THE WORLD

SPORE TREES

Spore trees belong to the families Cyatheaceae and Dicksoniaceae and are also known as tree ferns. They are the most primitive trees, reproducing by means of spores, which form tiny plants that produce sperm or eggs. The fertilized eggs then grow into new ferns.

S pore trees are natives of tropical rainforests, where they may exceed 20 metres (66ft) in height. Persistent roots that form a dense buttress support the stem, which is rarely branched. Spore trees do not form wood. Instead, the tall trunk of tree ferns

A YOUNG FROND UNCURLS

is strengthened by deposits of a material called lignin. The trunk supports a crown of pinnate leaves that may reach four metres (13ft) in length. During every growing season some adult ferns form two types of fronds; sterile fronds that lack sporangia (spore sacs) and fertile fronds that bear sporangia. In some species, fronds formed by a juvenile fern are very different to those formed when the same plant reaches maturity.

wood-like stem   leaf bases or stipes

STEM CROSS-SECTION
The fronds of the Black Tree Fern (*Cyathea medularis*) are attached to the stem by leaf bases, seen here arranged around the stem.

Dicksonia antarctica

Soft Tree Fern

HEIGHT up to 15m (50ft)
TYPE Evergreen
OCCURRENCE Australia
(S.E. Queensland, New South Wales,
Victoria coast, Tasmania)

The Soft Tree Fern is very slow-growing, but can live for up to 400 years. It grows at a rate of about 3.5–5cm (1½–2in) per year and does not start producing spores until it is at least 20 years old. A thick mass of brown fibrous roots form on the trunk, which is covered with soft brown hairs on top, and large fronds form a spreading canopy. In the wild, this species thrives in damp places and is usually found in moist gullies and sheltered forests. However, it is also tolerant of frost and drought. The pith can be eaten, either cooked or raw, and is a very good source of starch. **BARK** Dark brown, with leaf scars. **LEAF** Dark green, roughly textured, arching fronds, about 3m (9¾ft) long, with tiny pointed leaflets, frond stalks very hairy at the base. **FLOWER** Flowerless. **FRUIT** Small round groups of spore capsules or sporangia (sori).

frond
stalk

reddish
brown
hairs

bark covered
with roots
and old leaf
bases

frond
segments

BARK

FROND BUD

SEED TREES

Seed trees are vascular plants (plants with a circulatory system) that transport water and nutrients by means of tissue called xylem and phloem. Seed plants first appeared some 350 million years ago. They were plants with fern-like leaves that bore seeds on their leaves.

P roducing seed bypasses the need to have water in the environment for fertilization to occur, because the pollen, which contains the male germ cells, is transported to the female parts by wind or insects, so the sperm does not have to swim to the egg. Another advantage of seeds is that they have an outer layer that protects the embryo and incorporates a food reserve for it.

GROUPS OF SEED TREES

Seed trees can be divided into gymnosperms and angiosperms. Cycads, Ginkgo, and conifers are all woody gymnosperms. All of these produce seeds that are covered by a seed coat, but are not true fruit. The angiosperms (flowering trees) are the largest and most diverse group. They all produce seeds within a fruit. Angiosperm flowers may have some or all of four structures: a stalk; a perianth (petals and sepals); stamens (male pollen-bearing structures) and/or carpels (female ovule-bearing

ADAPTED FOR SURVIVAL
The enormous range of adaptations of seed trees has helped them to colonize all areas of the earth.

structures). Gymnosperm "flowers" never have a perianth or bear ovules or pollen on the same plant. They are wind pollinated. Angiosperm flowers have more means of becoming pollinated (wind, insects, birds, and bats). Many angiosperms have evolved alongside the insects that pollinate them.

JAPANESE MAPLE
Flowering trees have a wide variety of seed dispersal methods. The seed of this maple is enclosed in a winged key.

CYCAD SEED CONES
Female cycads are fertilized by free-swimming sperm that are carried by wind from a male plant.

seed cone of a female cycad

CYCADS

Cycads are woody plants that produce seeds and resemble ferns and palms. They are, however, unique and unrelated to any other group of living plants. Cycads were at their peak some 150 million years ago in the Jurassic period. Today there are around 185 species of cycads in 11 genera, native to warm, subtropical regions.

The main roots of cycads are thickened and fleshy. All species also produce upright-growing, branched roots, known as coralloid roots. These roots contain symbiotic blue-green algae, which can fix nitrogen from the atmosphere. The woody stems of cycads may grow entirely below ground or emerge from the ground to form a trunk-like structure. The leaves of most species are pinnate and often develop a palm-like crown. A plant is either male or female. Cycads reproduce by producing cones. Woody growths on the cones, called sporophylls, bear the sexual parts.

new shoots

FOSSIL CYCAD FROND
A frond of the fossil cycad *Nilssonia compta* from the Jurassic period, approximately 180 million years ago.

FIRE ADAPTED
Shoots that will develop into palm-like fronds emerge from the top of a *Cycas media* following a forest fire.

old leaves

Cycas circinalis

False Sago

HEIGHT up to 5m (16ft)
TYPE Deciduous
OCCURRENCE India (Karnataka, Kerala, Tamil Nadu, Maharashtra)

FOLIAGE

The False Sago (not to be confused with the Sago Palm) occurs in dense, dry, scrubby woodland in hilly areas and sheds its foliage in extremely dry seasons. It is valued for its beauty and is widely planted as an ornamental. Its trunk contains an edible, starchy material.
BARK Brown, covered in old leaf bases.
LEAF Pinnate, glossy bright green, 1.5–2.5m (5–8ft) long, with 170 opposite leaflets, flat, on hairy stalks.
FLOWER Males: narrowly ovoid,

orange pollen cones, covered in matted woolly hairs; females: cones arranged in a ring around the shoot tips.
FRUIT Yellow, nearly round seeds that can float.

feather-like leaves

female cone

CAROLUS LINNAEUS

Carolus Linnaeus (Carl von Linné) (1707–1778) was a Swedish physician and botanist who introduced the taxonomic system for grouping and categorizing organisms. He established *Cycas circinalis* as a single species, but his description was based on earlier work that covered at least three distinct species.

GINKGO

The ginkgos are a group of seed trees that appeared about 250 million years ago and reached their maximum diversity 100 million years ago. By about 40 million years later, the number of species in this group had been reduced to a single, very variable species known as *Gingko adiantoides*, which is similar to the only species of ginkgo in existence today, *Ginkgo biloba* (Maidenhair Tree).

parallel veins

golden coloration in autumn

LEAF SHAPE
The bright green leaves of the Maidenhair Tree *(Ginkgo biloba)* have a distinctive two-lobed shape with a deep cleft in the centre.

Often thought of as a "living fossil", *Ginkgo biloba* is a large woody tree, with branched stems and small simple leaves. There is considerable doubt that any ginkgo trees still exist outside cultivation, although specimens in the wild have been reported in eastern China. This plant might only exist today because of the efforts of Buddhist monks in Japan and China. They adopted *Ginkgo biloba* as a sacred tree and cultivated it in their temple gardens. Subsequently its worldwide popularity as a garden tree has secured its survival. It is a highly adaptable plant, growing in almost any temperate or Mediterranean climate. It is also unusually resistant to pollution and pests. These attributes have made ginkgos very popular in cities. The females are not as sought after as the male trees for gardens or street trees because of the unpleasant smell of their seeds.

MALE FLOWERS
Male ginkgo flowers produce pollen containing motile (free-swimming) sperm that are among the largest in the plant kingdom. Fertilization is usually by wind pollination.

Ginkgo biloba

Maidenhair Tree

HEIGHT up to 30m (100ft)
TYPE Deciduous
OCCURRENCE E. China

A primitive and ancient species, the Maidenhair Tree is held sacred by Buddhists and it is often seen around Buddhist temples. It symbolizes longevity, hope, and unity, and is now widely cultivated around the world, especially in the USA. Its wood does not decay quickly, is fire-resistant, and has a fine grain and silky shine. It is used for carving, furniture, chessboards, and tubs for brewing "saké", among other items. The leaves and seeds are used in herbal medicine. The rotting fruit has a particularly unpleasant odour. **BARK** Pale brown, roughening into corky fissures.

LEAVES | *cleft between lobes*

LEAF Fan-shaped, bright green turning golden yellow in the autumn, two-lobed, notched; with parallel veins, dividing into two, about 8 cm (3¼ in) wide. **FLOWER** Males and females on separate trees; males: in small green catkins, females: in pairs, stalked, small, green, and round. **FRUIT** Greenish yellow plum-like fruit with a fleshy coating, and edible kernel.

FRUIT

— silvery bloom

up to 4cm (1½ in) long

SEEDS

MEDICINAL LEAVES

People in China began using the seeds of this species for medicinal purposes over 1,000 years ago. Its leaves have traditionally been used for treating circulatory and respiratory ailments. In the West, in recent years, Ginkgo has become popular as a natural remedy to improve mental performance and boost short-term memory.

GINKGO SUPPLEMENTS

GINKGO
The Ginkgo's unusual fan-like leaf shape, with two lobes (hence its species name *biloba*) and parallel venation, is easily identified. The leaves are used in traditional Chinese medicine to treat a variety of ailments, including high cholesterol and angina.

CONIFERS

The conifers are so called because they bear seed in distinctive cones. They first appeared in the fossil record in the Permian period over 200 million years ago and they are still abundant today. There are seven families of living conifers, containing over 600 species. They are widely distributed, dominating forest habitats in the earth's colder, drier regions in which other trees cannot survive.

The leaves of conifers vary widely. In many conifer genera, such as spruce (*Picea*), fir (*Abies*), and pine (*Pinus*), the leaves are long and narrow, and are called "needles". In others, the leaves are very small and scale-like – for example, junipers (*Juniperus*), incense cedar (*Calodcedrus*), and cypresses (*Cupressus*). Conifer leaves are usually covered in a waxy layer and the stomata (tiny pores) lie beneath the leaf surface. These leaf characteristics prevent water loss and help conifers resist drought. In most conifers the leaves develop on long shoots, and are arranged spirally and alternately.

Conifers produce distinct male and female cones on the same or separate trees. These function as flowers. Female cones tend to be much larger

FEMALE CONES AND MALE FLOWERS
Male Beach Pine (*Pinus contorta*) flowers (right) appear on the same tree as females. The female develops into a seed-bearing cone (left).

than males. Male conifer flowers may appear in the leaf axils or on new shoots. They usually wither away after the pollinating period has ended.

Conifers are wind pollinated. After pollination, the scales of the female cone close tightly, until the developed seeds are released from the mature cones (now serving as the fruit). In the "closed-cone pines", the heat produced by a forest fire is usually needed to liberate the seeds. The Taxaceae (yew family) do not have cones: each seed is enclosed by a fleshy coating, known as an aril.

SCALE-LIKE LEAVES
Some conifers such as the Hinoki Cypress (*Chamaecyparis obtusa*) have leaves that resemble scales rather than needles.

leaves arranged in flattened sprays

GIANT CONIFERS
Conifers are known for attaining enormous heights. Giants of the conifer world include Wellingtonia (*Sequoiadendron giganteum*), pictured right, and the White Fir (*Abies grandis*), which may reach a height of 60 metres (200ft).

Abies alba

Silver Fir

HEIGHT up to 46m (150ft)
TYPE Evergreen
OCCURRENCE C. Europe

The branches at the top of this tree often divide, giving it a "stork's nest" appearance. Its resin is a constituent of turpentine. **BARK** Grey, smooth, cracking with age. **LEAF** Flat needles, dark green above with two silver bands below. **FLOWER** Males: yellow, grouped on undersides of shoots; females: green. **FRUIT** Erect, cylindrical brown cone.

FLOWERS

needle 1.5–3cm
(½–1¼in) long   **LEAVES**

Abies grandis

White Fir

HEIGHT up to 75m (240ft)
TYPE Evergreen
OCCURRENCE W. North America

Also called the Grand Fir, this tree thrives in moist areas. **BARK** Grey-green, smooth with resin blisters. **LEAF** Flat needles, on either side of shoot, 2–6cm (¾–2¼in) long, dark green above with two silver bands below. **FLOWER** Males: small and purple, beneath shoots; females: green. **FRUIT** Erect, resinous, cylindrical brown cone, 5–12cm (2–4¾in) long.

Abies nordmanniana

Nordmann Fir

HEIGHT up to 46m (150ft)
TYPE Evergreen
OCCURRENCE N.E. Turkey W. Caucasus

This popular Christmas tree, also known as the Caucasian Fir, has thick foliage and a conical shape. **BARK** Grey, smooth, but developing fissures with age. **LEAF** Flat, notched needles, shiny dark green above, two silver lines beneath. **FLOWER** In separate clusters. Males: red; females: yellow-green. **FRUIT** Erect, greenish brown cone.

needle 2–3cm
(¾–1¼in) long

male flower
clusters

LEAVES AND FLOWERS

Abies koreana

Korean Fir

HEIGHT 9–18m (30–60ft)
TYPE Evergreen
OCCURRENCE Korea

This fir is shrubby or broadly pyramidal. **BARK** Purple-grey, smooth, with resin blisters, furrowed in plates. **LEAF** Narrow, notched needles, in dense spirals, 1.5–5cm (½–2in) long, green above, underside keeled with blue-green lines. **FLOWER** Males: broad, oval, red to yellow or green, tinted with violet-brown; females: rounded, blue-grey. **FRUIT** Cone, ripens to dark violet; red-brown bracts.

YOUNG CONES

Abies procera

Noble Fir

HEIGHT up to 50m (160ft)
TYPE Evergreen
OCCURRENCE W. North America

Tolerant of wind, snow, and poor soil, this tree has light but strong timber, which is used for interiors. **BARK** Silver-grey, smooth, cracking on older trees. **LEAF** Flat needles with rounded tips, blue-green on both sides. **FLOWER** Males: deep red, beneath shoot; females: yellow, above shoot. **FRUIT** Erect, barrel-shaped cone, 12–25cm (4³/₄–10in) long.

needle 1–3.5cm
(³/₈–1¹/₂in) long

LEAVES

Cedrus atlantica

Atlas Cedar

HEIGHT up to 60m (200ft)
TYPE Evergreen
OCCURRENCE North Africa

The Atlas Cedar has a stout trunk and its branches are angled upwards. The blue form, *Cedrus atlantica* 'Glauca' has blue-white needles and is planted as an ornamental in parks. **BARK** Silver-grey, becoming grooved with age. **LEAF** Green or blue-green needles, 1–3cm (³/₈–1¹/₄in) long, arranged in tufts. **FLOWER** Males: pinkish; females: bright green. **FRUIT** Egg-shaped cones, 5–8cm (2–3¹/₄in) long, with hollowed tips.

Cedrus deodara

Deodar

HEIGHT up to 60m (200ft)
TYPE Evergreen
OCCURRENCE Himalayas

Like the Atlas Cedar, this tree has a stout trunk with a triangular crown, but with downswept branches, and a drooping leading shoot. Its oil was once used to treat skin diseases. **BARK** Grey-brown and smooth when young, rough and grooved when mature. **LEAF** Pale green needles, up to 5cm (2in) long, in tufts of about 15–20 on spur shoots. **CONE**
FLOWER Males: yellowish, in clusters, often curving; females: greenish, in upright clusters. **FRUIT** Erect, barrel-shaped cones that turn brown as they ripen.

to 12cm
(4³/₄in) long

LEAVES WITH YOUNG CONES

Cedrus libani

Cedar of Lebanon

HEIGHT up to 40m (130ft)
TYPE Evergreen
OCCURRENCE Middle East

A slow-growing tree, this cedar has a conical shape when young. When mature, it has a massive trunk and large, tiered branches with dense foliage. It is very long-lived; those in the Taurus Mountains in Turkey are up to 1,000 years old. There are over 18 references to this tree in the Bible and the timber is said to have been used to construct King Solomon's Temple. It is now used for veneers or drawer linings.

EMBLEM TREE

Some cultures hold the Cedar of Lebanon in special esteem. The green cedar, symbolizing immortality and fortitude, is placed in the middle of the Lebanese flag. Between two horizontal red stripes, the tree stands out against a white background that is reminiscent of snow on the mountains of Lebanon.

LEBANESE FLAG

BARK Red-brown, finely fissured between shallow ridges. **LEAF** Dark green needles, borne singly on long shoots and in tufts of about 10–20 on short side shoots. **FLOWER** Males: yellow-brown when open, up to 6cm (2¼in) long; females: bright green with purple tinge, 7–15cm (2¾–6in) long. **FRUIT** Erect, barrel-shaped cones with rounded tops, ripening from purple to pink-brown.

cone 7–15cm (2¾–6in) long

needle 2–3cm (¾–1¼in) long

LONG SHOOT WITH CONE

spreading branches

Larix decidua

Larch

HEIGHT up to 38m (125ft)
TYPE Deciduous
OCCURRENCE C. Europe

The Larch is one of the first trees to burst into leaf in spring. Its timber is strong and durable. **BARK** Grey-brown, cracking with age. **LEAF** Flat, soft needles, blunt or short-pointed tips, bright green. **FLOWER** Males yellow; females pink-red. **FRUIT** Brown, egg-shaped cones, with smooth scales and visible bracts.

up to 4cm (1½in) long

scaly bark on mature trees

1.5–3cm (½–¼in) long

YOUNG CONES   **BARK**

Larix kaempferi

Japanese Larch

HEIGHT up to 35m (115ft)
TYPE Deciduous
OCCURRENCE Japan

Also known as the Money Pine, this tree is used in Japan for bonsai growing. It is a popular species for timber because it grows faster than other larches and is more disease-resistant. **BARK** Red-brown, cracking with age. **LEAF** Flat, soft needles with blunt or short-pointed tips, blue-green with two grey-white bands on underside, mostly in rosettes of 30–40. **FLOWER** In clusters. Males yellow; females green-yellow. **FRUIT** Small brown cones, with hidden bracts.

needle to 4cm (1½in) long

upright cone 3cm (1¼in) long

CONE

Larix laricina

Tamarack

HEIGHT up to 25m (80ft)
TYPE Deciduous
OCCURRENCE North America

needle 1–2.5cm (⅜–1in) long

LEAVES AND CONE

cone 1–2cm (⅜–¾in) long

Mostly found on upland, loamy soils, this hardy tree also grows in cold, poorly drained areas like sphagnum bogs. Its wood is used for fence posts, railway ties, and for building boats. **BARK** Red-brown, scaly, and thin. **LEAF** Flat, soft needles with blunt or short-pointed tips, light blue-green, turning yellow in autumn. **FLOWER** Males: yellowish and very small; females: deep red, small. **FRUIT** Small, egg-shaped cones, with rounded, overlapping scales, rose-red turning to pale brown.

CEDAR OF LEBANON
Over the centuries, forests of Cedar of Lebanon
(*Cedrus libani*) have been depleted as a result of
felling. However, this tree is a popular specimen
planting in many temperate parklands, such as this
garden in Sussex, England.

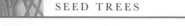

Picea abies

Norway Spruce

HEIGHT up to 40m (130ft)
TYPE Evergreen
OCCURRENCE N., C., and E. Europe

The wood of this popular Christmas tree is used for building work, packing cases, paper pulp, and for making sounding boards and posts for violins. **BARK** Orange-brown, turning grey-brown with age and developing small scales. **LEAF** Stiff, prickly, four-sided needles, dark green on all sides. **FLOWER** In separate, upright clusters. Males: red; females: dark red. **FRUIT** Pendent cylindrical cones have scales that are notched at the tip, 12–16cm (4³/₄–6¹/₂ in) long, tapered at each end, like a cigar.

LEAVES

needle 1–2cm
(³/₈–³/₄ in) long

LEAVES AND CONES   red-brown cones

Picea sitchensis

Sitka Spruce

HEIGHT up to 80m (260ft)
TYPE Evergreen
OCCURRENCE North America

Named after the Sitka Sound in Alaska, this tree thrives in moist conditions, and is found only within 80km (50 miles) of the coast. Its strong, but light wood is used for pulp. **BARK** Grey, becoming purple-grey and peeling with age. **LEAF** Thin, sharp needles, dark green and shiny above, two broad white bands below. **FLOWER** In clusters. Males: red; females: green-purple. **FRUIT** Pendent, slightly tapered, pale brown cones.

needle 2–3cm
(³/₄–1¹/₄in) long

cone 7–8 cm
(2³/₄–3¹/₄in) long

LEAVES AND FRUIT

Pinus banksiana

Jack Pine

HEIGHT up to 27m (90ft)
TYPE Evergreen
OCCURRENCE North America

This species is the northernmost pine in the world. It grows on poor, dry soil and depends on fire to release the seeds from its cone. **BARK** Orange-red to red-brown, scaly. **LEAF** Twisted, yellow-green needles, with fine lines on both surfaces, in pairs. **FLOWER** Males: orange to yellow; females: green-yellow. **FRUIT** Cones, lance-shaped, pale brown, ripening after two years.

cone 3.5–5cm (1½–2in) long

needle 2–5cm (¾–2in) long

CONES AND LEAVES

Pinus pinea

Stone Pine

HEIGHT up to 25m (80 ft)
TYPE Evergreen
OCCURRENCE S. Europe

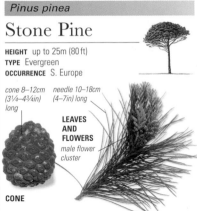

cone 8–12cm (3¼–4¾in) long

needle 10–18cm (4–7in) long

LEAVES AND FLOWERS

male flower cluster

CONE

This pine has a broad, domed crown, a tall, bare trunk, and branches that radiate upwards. **BARK** Pale brown, cracking into long, flat plates. **LEAF** Needles, in pairs, grey-green, with fine lines on each side. **FLOWER** Golden males and green females in separate clusters at the ends of shoots. **FRUIT** Cones, ripening from green to brown, containing edible "pine nuts".

Pinus parviflora

Japanese White Pine

HEIGHT up to 20m (65ft)
TYPE Evergreen
OCCURRENCE Japan and Korea

A common ornamental, this pine has a wide, low crown and a massive, straight trunk, which sometimes splits into two or more branches. **BARK** Smooth, grey, becoming rough and fissured, peeling off into scales. **LEAF** Twisted needles, triangular in cross-section, dark green above, pale green beneath, borne densely around shoot in fives. **FLOWER** Males: clustered around shoot; females: at end of shoot, pink-purple. **FRUIT** Cones, 6–8cm (2¼–3¼in) long, ripen from green to purple.

yellow or brown male flowers

needle 3–6cm (1¼–2¼in) long

LEAVES AND FLOWERS

Pinus pinaster

Maritime Pine

HEIGHT up to 30m (100ft)
TYPE Evergreen
OCCURRENCE W. Mediterranean, N.W. Africa

This pine thrives on sandy soil and was used to reclaim sand dunes in southern France. **BARK** Dark with red, brown, black, and buff tones; thick, scaly, and fissured. **LEAF** Needles, usually in pairs, green to yellow green, with fine lines. **FLOWER** Males: yellow, at base of shoots; females: red, in clusters at the ends of shoots. **FRUIT** Long, oval, glossy brown cones, in small clusters.

needle 12–25cm (4¾–10in) long

cone 9–18cm (3½–7in) long

LEAVES AND CONES

STONE PINE
The broad, domed crown and graceful, slender trunks of the Stone Pine (*Pinus pinea*) are a characteristic feature of many Mediterranean landscapes. However, prized for its edible nuts, it has also been widely planted elsewhere.

Pinus cembra

Arolla Pine

HEIGHT up to 22m (70ft)
TYPE Evergreen
OCCURRENCE Europe, Russia (Urals, Siberia)

*needles
5–8cm
(2–3¼ in)
long*

LEAVES

This tree grows at higher altitudes than any other pines. **BARK** Pale brown, with resin blisters when young. **LEAF** Stiff needles, in fives, shiny green above, whitish beneath. **FLOWER** In clusters. Males: yellow; females: red. **FRUIT** Erect, egg-shaped cones.

Pinus caribaea

Caribbean Pitch Pine

HEIGHT up to 30m (100ft)
TYPE Evergreen
OCCURRENCE Caribbean Islands, Mexico, Nicaragua

This invasive pine forms dense stands.
BARK Grey, forms plates later. **LEAF** Needles, in bundles of 3–5. **FLOWER** In clusters. Males: stalkless; females: conical. **FRUIT** Pale brown or reddish cone.

*yellow-green
needles
15–25cm
(6–10in)
long*

LEAVES

Pinus contorta

Beach Pine

HEIGHT up to 50m (160ft)
TYPE Evergreen
OCCURRENCE North America

The cones of this pine stay closed for years, opening up only in the heat of forest fires. **BARK** Red- or yellow-brown; old trees have deep fissures and dark scales. **LEAF** Needles in pairs, 4–5cm (1½–2in) long, blue-green turning yellow-green in winter. **FLOWER** Males: yellow; females: green. **FRUIT** Elongated brown cone.

LEAVES AND CONES *cone to 5cm (2in) long*

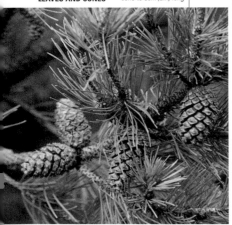

Pinus longaeva

Bristlecone Pine

HEIGHT up to 16m (50ft)
TYPE Evergreen
OCCURRENCE North America

The largest tree in the subalpine zone, this pine can be very long-lived. The oldest specimen is the 4,789-year-old "Methuselah" tree in the White Mountains of California. **BARK** Red-brown, fissured. **LEAF** Deep yellow-green, needles in fives. **FLOWER** Males: purple-red; females: purple. **FRUIT** Red-brown, drooping cone, 6–9cm (2¼–3½in) long.

LEAVES AND FLOWERS

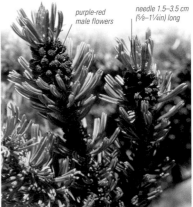

*purple-red
male flowers*

*needle 1.5–3.5 cm
(⅝–1¼in) long*

Pinus nigra
Corsican Pine

HEIGHT up to 50m (160ft)
TYPE Evergreen
OCCURRENCE W. Mediterranean mountains

With its straight trunk, thick bark, and slender branches, this pine is a useful source of timber. It needs plenty of light. **BARK** Grey, thick. **LEAF** Twisted, slender, rigid, dark green needles in pairs, 10–15cm (4–6in) long, with pointed tips. **FLOWER** Males: 1–1.5cm ($^3/_8$ $^5/_8$in) long, yellow, in clusters at base of shoots; females: red, at shoot tips. **FRUIT** Cone, 5–8cm (2–3$^1/_4$in) long, green, ripening to grey- or yellow-buff, falling intact from the tree when ripe.

Pinus patula
Mexican Pine

HEIGHT up to 30m (100ft)
TYPE Evergreen
OCCURRENCE Mexico

needles 15–25cm (6–10in) long   cone 7–10cm (2$^3/_4$–4in) long   **LEAVES AND CONES**

The Mexican Pine prefers acid soil and plenty of moisture. Its timber is used for pulp. **BARK** Red-orange, becoming grey-brown and vertically ridged. **LEAF** Pale green to yellow-green needles, in threes or fives. **FLOWER** Males and females on same plant; females appearing a year later than males. **FRUIT** Brown or yellow-brown cones in groups of 3–6.

Pinus strobus
White Pine

HEIGHT up to 65m (215ft)
TYPE Evergreen
OCCURRENCE E. North America

Also called the Weymouth Pine, this tree was once extensively logged to construct ships' masts. **BARK** Grey, becoming furrowed with purple-tinged rectangular plates. **LEAF** Needles, in bundles of five. **FLOWER** Males: yellow, in clusters at the base of shoots; females: pinkish, in pairs at the end of shoots. **FRUIT** Banana-shaped, pale brown cones, in clusters.

LEAVES AND CONES   cone 8–20cm (3$^1/_4$–8in) long   needle 6–10cm (2$^1/_4$–4in) long

Pinus roxburghii
Chir

HEIGHT up to 55m (100ft)
TYPE Evergreen
OCCURRENCE Himalayas

The timber of this tree is a rich source of resin. **BARK** Dark red to brown, resinous, thick, scaly, fissured. **LEAF** Needles, in bundles of three, 20–30cm (8–12in) long. **FLOWER** Males and females on same plant. **FRUIT** Elongated cones, 10–20cm (4–8in) long.

BRISTLECONE PINE

Bristlecone Pines (*Pinus longaeva*) are typically found in barren landscapes such as this on the slopes of Mount Washington, Nevada, USA. The wood of this pine decays extremely slowly; some wood on the ground may be over 10,000 years old.

Pinus sylvestris

Scots Pine

HEIGHT up to 40 m (130 ft)
TYPE Evergreen
OCCURRENCE Europe, N. Asia

The Scots Pine is one of only three conifers native to the British Isles, although it is distributed in many other parts of the world. It grows well on poor sandy soil, and it tolerates a remarkably wide range of climatic conditions, from the warm summers of southern Europe, to the bitterly cold winters of Siberia.

LIVING ON PINE SEEDS

The Scottish Crossbill, an endangered species, is restricted to the highlands of Scotland, and depends heavily on Scots Pine seeds for its food. Its curved mandibles cross over when the bill is closed, enabling the bird to pry open pine cones and get at the seeds. The female is dull greenish, while the male is bright orange-red in colour.

CROSSBILL

LEAVES, FLOWERS, AND CONES

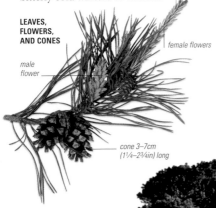

female flowers

male flower

cone 3–7cm (1¼–2¾in) long

Its wood is strong, yet easily worked, and is used to make saw logs, veneers, and telegraph poles. **BARK** Red-brown, turning purple-grey, with deep fissures. **LEAF** Blue-green twisted needles, 5–7.5cm (2–3in) long, in pairs, with white waxy lines on both surfaces. **FLOWER** Males: yellow, in clusters at the base of shoots; females: crimson, in pairs at the ends of shoots. **FRUIT** Small egg-shaped cones, with broad scales, each ending in a raised peak; glossy green, ripening to brown in the second autumn.

Pinus wallichiana

Blue Pine

HEIGHT up to 50m (160ft)
TYPE Evergreen
OCCURRENCE Himalayas

The hard, durable wood of this conifer is used for buildings and to make tea chests. **BARK** Orange or pink-brown, cracks with age. **LEAF** Needles in fives, 15–20cm (6–8in) long, green on top, bluish white lines below. **FLOWER** Males: yellow, in clusters; females: green-yellow in groups of up to six. **FRUIT** Long cones, mature from green to pale brown.

wide-tipped scales

LEAVES AND CONE

Pseudotsuga menziesii

Douglas Fir

HEIGHT up to 100m (325ft)
TYPE Evergreen
OCCURRENCE North America

female flowers in clusters

cone 5–8cm (2–3¼in) long

Named after plant collector David Douglas, this tall fir is valued for its fine timber. **BARK** Dark grey or purple, fissured. **LEAF** Soft, green needles; two white bands beneath. **FLOWER** Males: yellow, beneath shoots; females: red, on shoot tips. **FRUIT** Pendent cone, pale brown.

CONE

three-pronged bracts

Tsuga canadensis

White Hemlock

HEIGHT 30m (100ft)
TYPE Evergreen
OCCURRENCE E. North America

Cultivated as an ornamental, with many bushy dwarf forms, the White Hemlock grows well on chalky soil. Its timber is used for pulp. **BARK** Grey, ridged, flaking. **LEAF** Twisted needles on yellow stalks, in three ranks, minute teeth on edges, especially near tip; dark green above, narrow silvery bands beneath; fruity smell when crushed. **FLOWER** Males yellow; females green. **FRUIT** Small, oval cones on short stalks.

needle to 2cm (¾in) long

LEAVES AND CONES

cone 1.5–2.5cm (⅝–1in) long

Tsuga heterophylla

Western Hemlock

HEIGHT up to 60m (200ft)
TYPE Evergreen
OCCURRENCE W. North America

The wood of this hemlock is used for building and making boxes. The bark has a high tannin content. **BARK** Red-brown, turning purple-brown, flaking. **LEAF** Blunt-tipped needles, dark green above, with two blue-white bands below; unpleasant smell when crushed. **FLOWER** Reddish; males: under shoot, turn pale yellow when pollen is shed; females: at shoot tips. **FRUIT** Small, bronze green to brown oval cones, with rounded scales.

Agathis australis

Kauri

HEIGHT up to 50m (160ft)
TYPE Evergreen
OCCURRENCE New Zealand

This tree has a rounded, flat crown when it grows above the forest canopy. The Maoris used its wood for making canoes. **BARK** Sheds thick flakes. **LEAF** Alternate, strap-like. **FLOWER** Clustered. Males: cylindrical; females: spherical, grey-green. **FRUIT** Cone.

thick green foliage

BARK   grey to purple mottled bark

Agathis robusta

Queensland Kauri

HEIGHT up to 50m (160ft)
TYPE Evergreen
OCCURRENCE Australia (Queensland)

This tree grows on the margins of rainforests. **BARK** Orange- to grey-brown, smooth to flaky. **LEAF** Stiff, linear to elliptic adult leaves, 5–13cm (2–5in) long. **FLOWER** Males cylindrical; females pear-shaped. **FRUIT** Cones, 9–15cm (4–6in) long, that release winged seeds.

Araucaria bidwillii

Bunya-bunya

HEIGHT up to 50m (160ft)
TYPE Evergreen
OCCURRENCE Australia (S.E. and N. Queensland)

Sacred to Aboriginals, this tree is valued for its large, hard-shelled, edible nuts. **BARK** Dark brown to black. **LEAF** Oval adult leaves, overlapping on branchlets. **FLOWER** Males cylindrical; females round. **FRUIT** Huge cone, weighing 10kg (5½lbs), dark green, with 50–100 seeds.

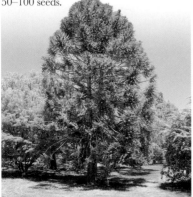

Araucaria columnaris

Cook Pine

HEIGHT up to 60m (200ft)
TYPE Evergreen
OCCURRENCE South New Caledonia Loyalty Islands

This tree is also known as the Coral Pine. **BARK** Dark brown to black. **LEAF** Needle-like juveniles; adults more triangular. **FLOWER** Male cone: single, oblong, 20cm (8in) long; females: 10–15cm (4–6in) long. **FRUIT** Large, egg-shaped seed cone.

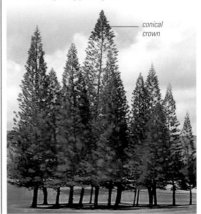

conical crown

Araucaria araucana

Monkey Puzzle

HEIGHT 30–40m (100–130ft)
TYPE Evergreen
OCCURRENCE S. Chile, S.W. Argentina

This species is now protected in the wild, and is mainly used as a popular ornamental in cool temperate regions. **BARK** Grey-brown and resinous. It is smooth and marked by rings from old branch scars. **LEAF** Scale-like, persisting for 10–15 years, even on the trunk; broadly triangular, 0.8–2.5cm ($^5/_{16}$–1in) wide, shiny green on both sides, with sharp spines.

FLOWER Male cones are erect, yellow-brown, 7–15cm ($2^3/_4$–6in) long and 5cm (2in) wide, with 20 whorled scales that have outwardly curved points; female cones are globe-like, green, 10–18cm (4–7in) long and 8–15cm ($3^1/_4$–6in) wide. **FRUIT** Spherical seed cone has overlapping spiny bracts, ripen to brown in 2–3 years.

rounded crown

developing flower cluster

leaf with sharp spines

old male flower

THE PEHUENCHE

The Pehuenche people of Chile consume the seeds of the Monkey Puzzle tree as a staple food. The nuts are rich in nutrients and delicious when cooked. These seeds are also used as animal fodder. The tree is important in the harvest and fertility ceremonies of the Pehuenche people.

MONKEY PUZZLE
This ancient stand of Monkey Puzzle trees (*Araucaria araucana*) is in the Malacahuello National Reserve, Chile. Trees of the *Araucaria* family are now found only in the Southern Hemisphere, although they were once widespread in the Northern Hemisphere as well.

Araucaria cunninghamii

Hoop Pine

HEIGHT up to 60m (200 ft)
TYPE Evergreen
OCCURRENCE Australia (N. Queensland to New South Wales), W. New Guinea

This conifer is used as an ornamental and plantation tree in Australia. The quality of its white to light brown timber is excellent, especially for plywood.
BARK Grey-brown, rough, with horizontal bands; flakes in fine circular bands.
LEAF Juvenile leaves arranged spirally on branches, grey-green to green, with smooth edges; adult leaves overlapping on branches, keeled on both sides, scale-like, 0.8–2cm (5/16–3/4 in) long. **FLOWER** Males: cylindrical, 2–3cm (3/4–1 1/4 in) long; females: more oval, 8–10cm (3 1/4–4in) long. **FRUIT** Oval cone up to 10cm (4in) long, releases seeds with narrow wings when mature.

Araucaria hunsteinii

Klinki Pine

HEIGHT up to 85m (275ft)
TYPE Evergreen
OCCURRENCE Papua New Guinea

A pyramidal tree when young, the Klinki Pine becomes flat-topped with age. It is an endangered species. **BARK** Dark brown, resinous, flakes in corky plates.
LEAF Juvenile leaves awl-shaped; adult leaves lanceolate, 6–15cm (2 1/4–6in) long, flat. **FLOWER** Males: narrow, cylindrical; females: oval. **FRUIT** Oval cone up to 20cm (8in) long.

Araucaria heterophylla

Norfolk Island Pine

HEIGHT 50–70m (160–230ft)
TYPE Evergreen
OCCURRENCE Norfolk Island (east of Australia)

This ornamental tree has branchlets in whorls of 4–7. **BARK** Grey-brown.
LEAF Awl-shaped juvenile leaves; scale-like mature leaves. **FLOWER** Males: in clusters, 4cm (1 1/2 in) long, yellow-brown or reddish; females: broader than long, with triangular scales and a bract. **FRUIT** Cone, releasing winged seeds.

bright green mature leaves

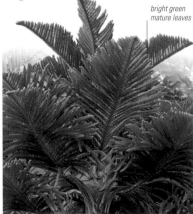

Podocarpus macrophyllus
Kusamaki

HEIGHT up to 15m (50ft)
TYPE Evergreen
OCCURRENCE China, Japan

The fruit of the Kusamaki has a fleshy, foot-like base, giving rise to the genus name, *Podocarpus*, which means "foot" and "fruit" in Greek. **BARK** Grey, red, and brown, long flakes. **LEAF** Alternate, lanceolate, green above, grey-green below. **FLOWER** Males: in cone-like catkins, 3cm (1¼in) long; females: solitary. **FRUIT** Round green or purplish cone, 1cm (⅜in) wide, with an outer fleshy layer.

Cephalotaxus harringtonia
Plum Yew

HEIGHT up to 12m (40ft)
TYPE Evergreen
OCCURRENCE China, Japan

Used as an ornamental, this spreading tree can be shrubby. It grows at altitudes up to 900m (3,000ft). **BARK** Greyish, flakes in strips. **LEAF** Needles in two rows, curving upward to a V-shaped trough, glossy green above, two light bands beneath. **FLOWER** Yellow; females larger than males. **FRUIT** Oval, plum-like cone.
FEMALE FLOWERS
male flowers
yellow flowers
LEAVES

Sciadopitys verticillata
Parasol Pine

HEIGHT 20–30m (65–100ft)
TYPE Evergreen
OCCURRENCE Japan

An attractive ornamental, this tree is sacred in Japan. Its wood is water-resistant. **BARK** Red-brown, thick, soft, and stringy. **LEAF** Brown scale leaves on stem; fleshy needles in clusters of 10–30 at shoot nodes, glossy green above. **FLOWER** Males: yellow, in dense clusters; females: oval, green, solitary. **FRUIT** Fragile cone, ripens to brown; orange-brown seeds.

CONE   **LEAVES AND FLOWERS**

3.5–6.5cm (1½–2½in) long
male flower

Taxus brevifolia
Californian Yew

HEIGHT up to 20m (65ft)
TYPE Evergreen
OCCURRENCE North America (N.W. Pacific coast)

This yew was used by Native Americans to make weapons and implements. Its foliage, seeds, and bark are poisonous but are also a source of taxol, an anticancer drug. **BARK** Scaly, purplish brown outer scales and reddish purple inner scales. **LEAF** Whorled, linear, 0.8–3.5cm (⁵⁄₁₆–1½in) long, green, two yellow-green bands beneath. **FLOWER** Males: pale yellow; females: tiny green globes. **FRUIT** Oval seed in fleshy red coating.

Taxus baccata

Yew

HEIGHT up to 25m (80ft)
TYPE Evergreen
OCCURRENCE Europe, W. Asia

Also known as the English Yew, this tree has poisonous bark, leaves, and seeds. It is a symbol of eternal life in several religious traditions, perhaps because it is evergreen, exceptionally long-lived, and resistant to decay, thus uniting death (by poison) to eternal life. It thrives on chalky soil. **BARK** Smooth, red-brown with patchy flakes that reveal purple-red underbark. **LEAF** Needles, in two ranks on horizontal branches but in spirals on upright shoots, linear, glossy dark green above with two grey-green bands below, ridged midrib. **FLOWER** Catkins, males

THE LONGBOW

The close-grained wood of the yew has elastic properties and was valued for making longbows in the Middle Ages. The English used these bows, capable of piercing armour, to defeat French forces in the Battle of Agincourt in 1415. Yew wood was in such demand for bow-making that local supplies were soon exhausted.

and females on separate trees. Males: spherical, beneath shoots; females: like tiny buds, near shoot-ends. **FRUIT** Aril enclosing a single brown seed.

needle 1–3cm (³⁄₈–1¹⁄₄in) long

pale yellow male flowers

bright red ripe fruit

RIPE AND UNRIPE FRUIT

yellow fruit

T. BACCATA 'LUTEA'

MALE FLOWER CLUSTERS

Torreya californica

Californian Nutmeg

HEIGHT up to 20m (65ft)
TYPE Evergreen
OCCURRENCE USA (California)

This prickly tree thrives in moist places. Its leaves exude a strong odour when crushed. **BARK** Grey to grey-brown. **LEAF** Needles, shiny green above, two white grooves beneath. **FLOWER** Males: yellowish white; females: green. **FRUIT** Seed in fleshy aril.

spherical male flowers

FLOWERS AND LEAVES

vertical fissures

BARK

Calocedrus decurrens

Incense Cedar

HEIGHT 18–46m (60–150ft)
TYPE Evergreen
OCCURRENCE W. USA, Mexico

This tree is named for its aromatic leaves. **BARK** Pale reddish brown. **LEAF** Shiny green and scale-like, in flattened, vertical sprays. **FLOWER** Males red-brown to pale brown; females red to golden brown. **FRUIT** Cone, with up to four seeds.

mature open cone

leaf to 3mm (⅛in) long

BRANCH WITH CONES

Chamaecyparis lawsoniana

Lawson's Cypress

HEIGHT up to 50m (160ft)
TYPE Evergreen
OCCURRENCE USA (S.W. Oregon to N.W. California)

Cultivated as an ornamental, this tree is also valued for its versatile timber. **BARK** Reddish brown, stringy. **LEAF** Tiny, overlapping scales in sprays, in four ranks, dark green above, paler beneath. **FLOWER** Males: red to purple with red pollen sacs; females: green, bud-like. **FRUIT** Cones, dull purple to red-brown, with 8–10 scales in pairs, each scale containing 2–4 seeds.

leaf 2–3mm (1/16–⅛in) long

cone 8–12mm (5/16–4¾in) wide

BRANCH WITH RIPE CONES

Chamaecyparis pisifera

Sawara Cypress

HEIGHT up to 20m (65ft)
TYPE Evergreen
OCCURRENCE Japan

This cypress is an important timber tree in Japan and a common ornamental elsewhere. **BARK** Reddish brown, fibrous. **LEAF** Scales with sharp tips, in overlapping rows, glossy green above, white marks beneath. **FLOWER** Males pale brown; females green. **FRUIT** Round cone.

vertical strips

BARK

Cryptomeria japonica

Japanese Cedar

HEIGHT up to 50m (160ft)
TYPE Evergreen
OCCURRENCE Japan, China

In Japan, this is the most important timber tree and is widely planted around temples. **BARK** Reddish brown to dark grey, peeling in strips. **LEAF** Pale green needles in spirals. **FLOWER** Males: plum-red, in racemes; females: green, rosette-like, in groups of 1–6. **FRUIT** Spherical cone.

cone ripens to brown

RIPE CONE

male flowers 5mm (³⁄₁₆in) long

Cupressus lusitanica

Mexican Cypress

HEIGHT up to 30m (100ft)
TYPE Evergreen
OCCURRENCE Mexico, Guatemala, Honduras

This narrowly conical tree has an open, sometimes weeping, habit. **BARK** Reddish or greyish brown, thick. **LEAF** In four ranks, bluish green. **FLOWER** In clusters; **LEAVES AND CONES** males yellow-brown; females blue-white. **FRUIT** Cone.

tiny, scale-like leaves

rounded in shape

RIPE CONE

BARK

longitudinal fissures

Cupressus macrocarpa

Monterey Cypress

HEIGHT up to 30m (100ft)
TYPE Evergreen
OCCURRENCE USA (California)

This unusual tree is a rarity in the wild where it is stunted. It often grows tall in cultivation. **BARK** Yellowish brown. **LEAF** Scale-like, in sprays. **FLOWER** Males: yellow, egg-shaped; females: green, oblong. **FRUIT** Spherical cone.

grey-brown when ripe

MATURE CONES

Cupressus sempervirens

Italian Cypress

HEIGHT up to 30m (100ft)
TYPE Evergreen
OCCURRENCE Mediterranean region

A common ornamental, planted around the world, this tree grows well on alkaline and acid soil. Its wood is durable and easily worked. **BARK** Grey, smooth, turning grey-brown and furrowed with age. **LEAF** Scale-like, tiny, less than 1mm (¹⁄₂₄in) long, dull green. **FLOWER** Males yellow-brown; females green. **FRUIT** Short-stalked, glossy brown to grey cone, with 8–14 wavy edged scales in pairs, brown seeds.

cone 2–3cm (³⁄₄–¹⁄₄in) long

FOLIAGE AND CONES

x *Cupressocyparis leylandii*

Leyland Cypress

HEIGHT up to 40m (130ft)
TYPE Evergreen
OCCURRENCE Britain

Widely planted as garden hedges and screening, this fast-growing conifer is a hybrid between the Nootka Cypress (*Chamaecyparis nootkatensis*) and the Monterey Cypress (*Cupressus macrocarpa*), trees from different genera. The first seedlings were planted in Britain by C. J. Leyland, after whom this tree was named. This species has ascending, nearly vertical branches. **BARK** Reddish brown, with shallow fissures. **LEAF** Densely packed, overlapping on shoots, scale-like, in sprays, up to 2mm ($1/16$in) long; green, yellow, or greyish. **FLOWER** Both in clusters at the tips of shoots; males yellow and females green. **FRUIT** Spherical cone, with four scales in pairs.

cone 2cm (³/₄in) wide

LEAVES AND YOUNG CONES

Juniperus communis

Juniper

HEIGHT up to 6m (20ft)
TYPE Evergreen
OCCURRENCE North America, Europe

conical crown

6–9mm (¼–1¹/₃₂ in) wide

RIPE FRUIT

needles 0.5–2cm (³/₁₆–³/₄in) long

sharp tips

Juniper oil was used with cedar oil by the ancient Egyptians for embalming. In medieval times, the berry-like fruit were used medicinally and are still used to flavour gin. When crushed, the leaves smell of apple or gin. **BARK** Red-brown, with papery sheets that peel in strips. **LEAF** Flattened, awl-shaped needles, in whorls of three; concave, blue-green above, with a broad, waxy band; pale grey beneath, with a blunt keel. **FLOWER** Males and females on separate plants. Males yellow; females green, bud-like in leaf axils. **FRUIT** Spherical, fleshy berry-like cone, taking three years to ripen from green to blue to black.

Juniperus virginiana

Red Cedar

HEIGHT up to 18m (60ft)
TYPE Evergreen
OCCURRENCE E. North America

— conical to columnar habit

Also called the Pencil Cedar because its wood was used to make pencils, this tree has a slender profile and is the tallest of the junipers. Its wood is light, soft, and aromatic. It is durable and resists attack by insects. For this reason it has been used to make moth-proof linings for cupboards. **BARK** Reddish to greyish brown, peeling vertically. **LEAF** Juvenile leaves: needle-like, up to 6mm (1/4in) long, in threes at shoot tips; mature leaves: scale-like, 1–3mm (1/32–1/8in) long, overlapping, below shoot tips. **FLOWER** Yellow males and green females on separate shoots. **FRUIT** Smooth, oval cone, ripens to violet-brown.

cone 3–5cm (1/8–3/16 in) long

peels in long strips

LEAVES AND CONES   **BARK**

Metasequoia glyptostroboides

— conical habit

Dawn Redwood

HEIGHT up to 45m (150ft)
TYPE Deciduous
OCCURRENCE China

This tree was only known from fossil records until specimens were found in China in 1941. **BARK** Peels vertically in stringy flakes. **LEAF** Soft, needle-like, flat, borne on deciduous branchlets; bright green at first, turning dark green, and later red-brown in autumn. **FLOWER** Males: catkin-like in pairs on stalks, yellow, tiny, oval; females: in hanging clusters, green, rounded. **FRUIT** Pendent cones, turning woody and dark brown when ripe.

leaf up to 2.5 cm (1in) long

LEAVES

orange-brown

unripe cone

BARK   **FRUIT**

Sequoia sempervirens

Californian Redwood

HEIGHT up to 110m (360ft)
TYPE Evergreen
OCCURRENCE USA (S.W. Oregon, N.W. California)

The world's tallest tree, the Californian Redwood can live up to over 2,000 years. It is named after a Cherokee Indian, Sequo-yah. **BARK** Red-brown, tough, fibrous, deeply furrowed with broad, scaly ridges. **LEAF** Sharp-pointed needles, shiny dark green above with two white bands beneath. **FLOWER** In separate clusters on the same tree; males: yellow-brown, rounded; females: red-brown, bud-like. **FRUIT** Diamond-shaped seed cone.

SHOOTS WITH FLOWERS ⟍ *flowers at ends of shoots*

Sequoiadendron giganteum

Wellingtonia

HEIGHT up to 90m (300ft)
TYPE Evergreen
OCCURRENCE USA (California)

The largest tree in the world, although not the tallest, this conifer can weigh up to 2,000 tonnes. In the Sierra Nevada, it has a lifespan of up to 3,000 years. **BARK** Up to 50cm (20in) thick, fibrous, with ridges. **LEAF** Sharp-pointed, scale-like, 5–8mm ($^{3}/_{16}$–$^{5}/_{16}$in) long, grey-green. **FLOWER** Males: pale green, round to oval, at tips of shoots; females: green, oval, at stem tips. **FRUIT** Barrel-shaped pendent cone.

red–brown

male flower buds

LEAVES AND BUDS

5–8cm (2–3¼ in) long

UNRIPE CONE

BARK

WELLINGTONIA
These giant redwoods (*Sequoiadendron giganteum*)
photographed at the Jedediah Smith State Park,
California, USA, are among the world's tallest trees.
Their lofty canopy casts dense shade, but shafts of
sunlight penetrate gaps where trees have died.

Platycladus orientalis

Chinese Arbor-vitae

HEIGHT up to 20m (65ft)
TYPE Evergreen
OCCURRENCE China, Korea, E. Russia

This usually quite shrubby tree, has several main branches emerging from the base. It has been extensively cultivated in the past in its native regions. It is long-lived; some trees in China are believed to be over 1,000 years old. **BARK** Red-brown to pale grey-brown, thin, flaking in long strips. **LEAF** Scale-like, with blunt tips, overlapping in four ranks on shoots. **FLOWER** Males and females on the same tree. Males: yellow-green, oval, 2–3mm ($^{1}/_{16}$–$^{1}/_{8}$in) long; females: at end of shoots, blue-green, round, 3mm ($^{1}/_{8}$in) wide. **FRUIT** Cones, red-brown when ripe, flat, thick, woody, with 6–8 scales; seeds wingless, grey to purple-brown, with ridges.

SHOOT — cone to 2cm ($^{3}/_{4}$ in) long

conical habit

Taxodium distichum

Swamp Cypress

HEIGHT up to 50m (160ft)
TYPE Deciduous
OCCURRENCE S.E. USA

Freshwater swamps are this tree's native habitat. **BARK** Pale brown, furrowed, stringy, peeling at base. **LEAF** Alternate, 80–100 in two ranks on each branchlet; slender, short, flattened. **FLOWER** Males: yellow, in hanging catkins; females: green, in small clusters on the same plant as males. **FRUIT** Rounded cone with small spines, green ripening to purple.

FOLIAGE

Tetraclinis articulata

Alerce

HEIGHT up to 15m (50ft)
TYPE Evergreen
OCCURRENCE S.E. Spain, Morocco, Malta, Algeria, Tunisia

This medium-sized conifer is tolerant of hot conditions, and is often seen on dry, rocky hillsides. It is renowned for its resin and "Thuya Burls", outgrowths formed on the roots of the tree due to fungal infection. These are golden red and are highly valued in Morocco. The wood is aromatic, heavy, and oily, turns well, and has a high shine. **BARK** Peeling in long, slender strips. **LEAF** Scale leaves in whorls of four on vertical, dull green branchlets, with horizontal bands. **FLOWER** Males yellow and females green; inconspicuous. **FRUIT** Cones with two pairs of smooth scales containing eight red-brown seeds.

unripe cone

FRUIT

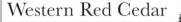

Thuja occidentalis

White Cedar

HEIGHT up to 20m (65ft)
TYPE Evergreen
OCCURRENCE E. North America

leaf 2–5 mm
(¹/₁₆–³/₁₆ in)
long

**FLATTENED
LEAF SPRAY**

scale-like
leaves

Found in swampy areas, this conical, multi-stemmed tree is grown as an ornamental. **BARK** Red-brown, fissured. **LEAF** In four ranks, dark green above, yellow-green beneath, apple-scented. **FLOWER** Males: red-brown, on shoot tips; females: green or purple, on tips of branchlets. **FRUIT** Oval brown cone.

Thuja plicata

Western Red Cedar

HEIGHT up to 50m (160ft)
TYPE Evergreen
OCCURRENCE W. North America

This tree is valued for its soft, durable wood. **BARK** Red- or grey-brown, fibrous. **LEAF** Scale-like, in four ranks, dark green above, pale beneath. **FLOWER** Males red; females yellow-green. **FRUIT** Oval cone.

open cones on branchlet

Thujopsis dolobrata

Hiba

HEIGHT up to 15m (50ft)
TYPE Evergreen
OCCURRENCE Japan

Also known as False Arborvitae, the Hiba is one of the five sacred trees of Japan. **BARK** Red-brown, peeling in strips. **LEAF** Scale-like, 4–7mm (¹/₈–¹/₄in) long and 2mm (¹/₁₆in) wide, shiny, broad patch beneath. **FLOWER** Males: cylindrical, blackish green; females: blue-grey. **FRUIT** Oval cone, with 6–8 scales.

**LEAVES
AND
CONES**

white patch on
underside of leaf

dense,
pyramidal
habit

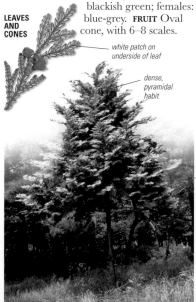

Xanthocyparis nootkatensis

Yellow Cedar

HEIGHT up to 40m (130ft)
TYPE Evergreen
OCCURRENCE W. North America

This tree is well-adapted to its snowy habitat with its hanging foliage that allows heavy snow to slide off. **BARK** Greyish brown, fissured irregularly. **LEAF** Scale-like, dark green above, yellow-green beneath, overlapping. in four ranks, thick. **FLOWER** Males grey-brown; females green. **FRUIT** Dark red-brown, waxy cone, with 4–6 scales.

drooping
branches

SWAMP CYPRESS
This large tree grows in the freshwater swamps of southeastern USA. In its natural habitat oxygen is scarce in the water. Swamp cypress (*Taxodium distichum*) thrives because it pushes up aerial roots from its root system.

FLOWERING TREES

Flowering trees belong to the angiosperm group of plants. They first appeared about 100 million years ago in the Cretaceous period. They are diverse in form and habitat – from spreading oaks, in temperate forests to leafless, desert-loving cactii. This diversity, alongside other factors could account for their undoubted success.

The term angiosperm is derived from the Greek for vessel (*angeion*) and seed (*sperma*) and refers to the fact that all the trees in this group produce seeds, which are enclosed in a "vessel", known as a carpel, to form a fruit. Although commonly called flowering plants, the fact that all angiosperms have flowers is not the main distinction between them and the gymnosperms.

A major difference between angiosperms and gymnosperms such as conifers is the origin of the food source for the seed. In angiosperms two sperm are released from the pollen tube. One fertilizes the egg, the other enters the central cell, which develops into a structure known as the endosperm. This provides nourishment for the seed

FROM FLOWERS TO FRUIT
Angiosperms all produce fruit, but some species such as the Sweet Orange (*Citrus sinensis*) and have been selectively cultivated for the sweet edible pulp that surrounds the seeds.

after germination. In gymnosperms, the tissue that surrounds the egg nourishes the seed before it is fertilized. Angiosperm seeds are enclosed in fruits. The fruits can be dry or succulent. Dry fruits take the form of follicles, capsules, or pods. Succulent fruits include berries, drupes, or pomes. There are three types of angiosperm: primitive angiosperms (page 112), monocotyledons (page 123), and dicotyledons (page 141).

VENATION
The leaves of angiosperms are veined: those of monocotyledons have parallel venation; those of dicotyledons have a branching network of veins.

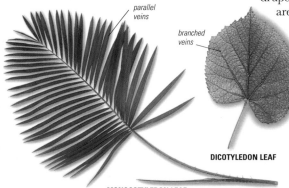

parallel veins

branched veins

DICOTYLEDON LEAF

MONOCOTYLEDON LEAF

JACARANDA IN BLOSSOM
A colourful and often fragrant display of flowers serves the vital purpose of attracting pollinating insects, birds, or bats.

PRIMITIVE ANGIOSPERMS

This small group represents the earliest flowering trees.

These angiosperms first appeared in the Cretaceous Period. Primitive angiosperms are often evergreen and woody; their often simple, leathery leaves may be arranged in a spiral or alternately, as in Nutmeg (*Myristica fragrans*). Some plants in this group have no vessels in the xylem. Many are aromatic, such as Pond Apple (*Annona glabra*) and Winter's Bark (*Drimys winteri*).

The flowers of the primitive angiosperms are showy and tend to be radially symmetrical with petals and sepals that are difficult to differentiate (called tepals). The evolution of flowering plants closely paralleled that of insects. "Primitive" flowers, like those of magnolia trees, are often pollinated by "primitive" insects such as beetles.

numerous stamens

PRIMITIVE FLOWER
Bull Bay (*Magnolia grandiflora*) flowers are typical of this group in that they have tepals and many stamens.

large tepals

Illicium verum

Star Anise

HEIGHT up to 8m (26ft)
TYPE Evergreen
OCCURRENCE S. China, Vietnam

This aromatic tree is valued for the oil obtained from its fruit. This is mainly used as a culinary spice and has medicinal properties. **BARK** White to grey. **LEAF** Alternate, lanceolate, glossy dark green above, dull paler green beneath. **FLOWER** Pale yellow, with more than 15 strap-shaped petals. **FRUIT** Star-shaped, with 5–10 rust coloured seed pods containing hard seeds.

LEAVES

untoothed margins

FRUIT

boat-shaped seed pods

glossy brown seeds

Canella winterana

Canella

HEIGHT up to 10m (32ft)
TYPE Evergreen
OCCURRENCE S. USA (Florida)

A salt-tolerant species, the Canella tree is used as an ornamental for its showy flowers. It has rich, dense foliage, which provides pleasant shade. The trunk grows straight up through the centre of the canopy and develops thin branches that grow no more than 1.2m (4ft) long. The aromatic inner bark and leaves are used in tonics and condiments. The leaves are also used as a medicinal tea. The berries are peppery when dried and crushed. **BARK** Grey-brown. **LEAF** Opposite, olive green, thick, obovate, up to 20cm (8in) long. **FLOWER** Red to purple and white. **FRUIT** Bright red, round, fleshy berry, less than 1cm (³/₈in) wide.

FLOWERS

yellow stamens

purplish buds

Drimys winteri

unripe fruit

whitish green underside

FLOWERING TREE

LEAVES AND FRUIT

Winter's Bark

HEIGHT up to 15m (50ft)
TYPE Evergreen
OCCURRENCE Argentina, Chile

This tree is named after Captain William Winter who sailed with the English seaman Sir Francis Drake in the 16th century. The bark is used to treat digestive ailments. The leaves have a peppery odour when crushed. **BARK** Reddish brown, smooth, aromatic. **LEAF** Alternate, oval, leathery, up to 20cm (8in) long, bright glossy green above, paler beneath. **FLOWER** In clusters of up to 10 on branch tips; 5–7 white to cream petals, red sepals. **FRUIT** Small, round, green seed pod, ripening to purple-black, in clusters at the ends of long stalks; black seeds.

flowers in branched clusters

FLOWERS

Myristica fragrans

Nutmeg

HEIGHT up to 18m (60ft)
TYPE Evergreen
OCCURRENCE Molucca Islands
(otherwise known as Spice Islands)

The spices nutmeg and mace are both
produced by this tree. Middle Eastern
traders brought these products to
southern Europe in the 6th century.
By the 12th century, these spices were
well known throughout Europe. The
Portuguese found Nutmeg trees in the
Molucca Islands and dominated the
trade until the Dutch gained ascendency
in the 17th century. **BARK** Greyish;
exudes yellow juice. **LEAF** Alternate, oval,
pointed, dark green, shiny above, 2–7cm
(³/₄–2³/₄in) wide, leaf stalks 1cm (³/₈in)
long. **FLOWER** Pale yellow, waxy, fleshy,
and bell-shaped; usually unisexual with

6–9cm (2¹/₄–3¹/₂ in)
long

**FRUIT AND
LEAVES**

5–15cm
(2–6in) long

BARK

smooth texture

LEAF

male and female flowers found on
different trees; males, up to 5–7mm
(³/₁₆–⁷/₃₂in) long, are in groups of
one to ten; females, up to 1cm (³/₈in)
long are in groups of three.
FRUIT Drupe, which is similar to an
apricot, fleshy, yellow, and smooth, with a
longitudinal ridge. When ripe, it splits in
half, revealing a purplish brown oval seed
(nutmeg), 2–3cm (³/₄–1¹/₄in) long encased
in a red covering (mace).

A VERSATILE SPICE

Nutmeg, a spice with a sweet smell, comes from the
hard seeds of the nutmeg fruit. It is used to flavour
cakes, puddings, and some drinks.
The oil is used to make perfume and   **NUTMEG**
to flavour tobacco. The nutmeg also   **AND**
contains a thick, yellow fat called   **MACE**
nutmeg butter, used to make candles,
and is an important ingredient in
salves and medicines.
Medicinally, nutmeg has
been used for thousands of
years for headaches and
fever, and as a digestive
aid and aphrodisiac.

Liriodendron tulipifera

Tulip-tree

HEIGHT up to 30m (100ft)
TYPE Deciduous
OCCURRENCE E. USA

This tree has a pyramidal crown with a straight trunk. **BARK** Pale grey-green with white grooves or patches. **LEAF** Alternate, palmately veined, and four-lobed. **FLOWER** Showy, with six petals, pale green at the edge and deep orange at the centre. **FRUIT** Cone-like group of woody, one-seeded fruit with one wing.

LEAVES WITH FLOWER

flower 4–5cm (1½–2in) wide

leaf 10–20cm (4–8in) long

Magnolia champaca

Champak

HEIGHT up to 33m (110ft)
TYPE Evergreen
OCCURRENCE S.E. Asia, India

Essentially a timber tree, the Champak is also grown in India as an ornamental, where its flowers are used for adornment. The aromatic orange blooms appear nearly all year round. Essential oil extracted from the flowers is used in expensive perfumes. **BARK** Pale grey, smooth, 2cm (¾in) thick. **LEAF** Alternate, lanceolate, glossy above and dull beneath with a 2–3cm (¾–1¼in) leaf stalk. **FLOWER** Yellow with three sepals, six strap-shaped petals, and an elongated receptacle. There is also a white variety. **FRUIT** Oval, greenish, containing angular seeds.

FRUIT

CROSS-SECTION OF FRUIT

LEAF

fleshy seed covering

13–25cm (5–10in) long

Magnolia grandiflora

Bull Bay

HEIGHT up to 27m (90ft)
TYPE Evergreen
OCCURRENCE USA coast (from North Carolina to Florida and east to Texas)

This magnolia is the state flower of Mississippi and Louisiana. Its timber is sometimes used for veneers. **BARK** Brown to grey, thin, smooth, later developing scales. **LEAF** Alternate, pinnately veined, leathery, dark glossy above, with a rusty, velvety underside. **FLOWER** Showy, fragrant white flowers, 20–30cm (8–12in) wide. **FRUIT** Bright red, kidney-shaped seeds that hang from a red-brown cone-like structure that is 5–10cm (2–4in) long.

LEAVES WITH BUD

leaf 13–20cm (5–8in) long

immature fruit receptacle

Annona cherimola

Cherimoya

HEIGHT up to 9m (30ft)
TYPE Deciduous
OCCURRENCE Central America

The fleshy, creamy fruit of this tree is considered a delicacy. **BARK** Grey-brown, smooth. **LEAF** Alternate, oval to lanceolate, 7.5–15cm (3–6in) long. **FLOWER** Stalked, three green outer petals, three pinkish inner petals. **FRUIT** Pale green, spotted berry, with black, glossy seeds.

FRUIT　　　　　　　10–20cm (4–8in) long

Annona muricata

Soursop

HEIGHT up to 9m (30ft)
TYPE Evergreen
OCCURRENCE South America, Caribbean, introduced in S.E. Asia

LEAVES

glossy dark green

6–20cm (2¼–8in) long

All parts of this tree are used for traditional remedies. **BARK** Red-brown. **LEAF** Alternate, oval to elliptical, pointed at ends. **FLOWER** Single, three yellow-green outer petals, three pale yellow inner petals. **FRUIT** Heart-shaped berry, 10–30cm (4–12in) long.

Annona glabra

red inner base

SOLITARY FLOWER

Pond Apple

HEIGHT up to 15m (50ft)
TYPE Semi-deciduous
OCCURRENCE Americas, W. Africa

The Pond Apple is one of the few trees that is equally at home on riverbanks, in freshwater wetlands, and in brackish coastal mud. Its fruit and seeds both float – a feature that helps to make it a highly invasive species in some parts of the tropics. **BARK** Grey and flaky. **LEAF** Alternate, 7.5–12.5cm (3–5in) long, leathery, bright green above and paler below, aromatic. **FLOWER** Solitary, 2.5cm (1in) wide, creamy white to pale yellow, with three leathery outer petals and three smaller inner petals. **FRUIT** Berry that looks like a green apple, broad at the base; aromatic and fleshy when mature, containing about 140 pumpkin-like seeds.

7.5–12.5cm (3–5in) long　　**RIPE FRUIT**　　oval to elliptical leaf

Asimina triloba

YOUNG FRUIT WITH LEAVES

leaf 12.5–27.5cm (5–11in) long

purplish brown petals

FLOWER

fruit 6–10cm (2¼–4in) long

RIPE FRUIT

Pawpaw

HEIGHT up to 12m (40ft)
TYPE Deciduous
OCCURRENCE North America

Valued for its fleshy, nutritious fruit, this tree is also known as Papaw. The fruit has a short shelf-life, but does not require toxic chemicals for cultivation as it contains a natural insecticide. **BARK** Grey-brown, smooth, with wart-like lenticels. **LEAF** Alternate, pale green, oval to kite-shaped, 5–7.5cm (2–3in) wide. **FLOWER** Bell-shaped, 5–7.5cm (2–3in) wide, with six petals, appearing slightly before or with the leaves. **FRUIT** Green berry that resembles a banana, ripening to yellow and brown.

Cananga odorata

Ylang-ylang

HEIGHT up to 21m (70ft)
TYPE Evergreen
OCCURRENCE Indonesia, Malaysia

Also called the Perfume Tree, the Ylang-ylang is famous for the fragrant oil made from its flowers. The oil is used in perfumes and in aromatherapy; it is said to have a calming effect. Coco Chanel introduced Chanel No. 5, a cologne redolent of the scent of this tree, in 1923. Various parts of the tree are used in traditional medicine to treat malaria and fevers. **BARK** Pale grey. **LEAF** Alternate, oval, green. **FLOWER** Fragrant, in dense clusters in leaf axils, with six narrow yellow petals. **FRUIT** Small, oval, black berry that resembles a grape; contains 6–12 seeds.

FOLIAGE AND FLOWERS

FLOWER

trailing petals

LEAF

pointed leaf tip

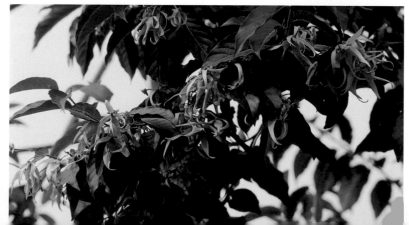

Polyalthia longifolia

Indian Willow

HEIGHT up to 15m (50ft)
TYPE Evergreen
OCCURRENCE India

The Indian Willow, also known as the Weeping Ashoka, is often confused with the sacred Ashoka tree (*Sarca indica*). The Indian Willow is a common roadside tree in India and is widely used as an ornamental for its weeping branching habit. It can be seen lining the avenue leading to the Taj Mahal. A popular variety is *Polyalthia longifolia* 'Pendula', which has a very narrow, columnar shape. The parts of this tree are valued for their antimicrobial properties.
BARK Brownish, smooth. **LEAF** Alternate, lanceolate, up to 20cm (8in) long, glossy green, with wavy margins. **FLOWER** Star-shaped, pale green. **FRUIT** Round black berry, 2.5cm (1in) wide.

wavy margins

slender, glossy leaves

FOLIAGE

UNRIPE FRUIT

berries in clusters

immature berries

KEEPING THE AIR CLEAN

Indian cities have become increasingly choked with traffic in recent years. This has greatly increased air pollution, especially the concentration of lead, which is highly toxic, in the air. The Indian Willow is especially useful because it readily absorbs lead from the air, thereby reducing lead pollution. This makes it a useful bioindicator, as analysis of the leaves can indicate the levels of atmospheric lead.

Chlorocardium rodiei

Greenheart

HEIGHT up to 39m (130ft)
TYPE Evergreen
OCCURRENCE Guyana, French Guiana, Suriname, Brazil; introduced in Vietnam

This very large and dense forest tree is the most important timber species in Guyana and has a high commercial value. Its wood is durable when in contact with seawater and is used for building ships, docks, piers, and wharves. Since the mid 20th century, the number of trees has declined due to over-exploitation of natural reserves and limited success in establishing plantations, since the tree fruits only once every 15 years. **BARK** Ash grey, smooth, dense. **LEAF** Smooth, leathery, 10–15cm (4–6in) long. **FLOWER** Small, whitish. **FRUIT** Nut with a large, hard, and brittle pericarp, containing a single large, fleshy seed.

Cinnamomum verum

Cinnamon

HEIGHT up to 18m (60ft)
TYPE Evergreen
OCCURRENCE Asia

Cinnamon is cultivated in southern India for its inner bark, which is used as a spice. Once more valuable than gold, this pale brown, aromatic spice was the most profitable spice in the Dutch East India Company trade. **BARK** Pale, pinkish brown. **LEAF** Opposite, linear-oval, waxy, 10–15cm (4–6in) long, and 4–8cm (1½–3¼in) wide, with three parallel veins. **FLOWER** Yellow-green, in axillary clusters. **FRUIT** Oval drupe, 1cm (³⁄₈in) long.

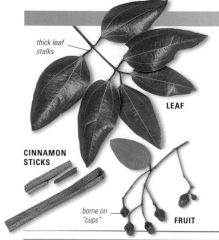

thick leaf stalks

LEAF

CINNAMON STICKS

borne on "cups"

FRUIT

Cinnamomum aromaticum

Cassia Bark

HEIGHT up to 15m (50ft)
TYPE Evergreen
OCCURRENCE S. China

Cassia, a spice derived from the bark of this tree, is used as a flavouring agent, similar to cinnamon, though less prized. It is also used to combat vermin. The oil, which is distilled from the leaves, has a strong, penetrating smell and was valued in biblical times.

BARK

nearly parallel veins

to 1.5cm (½ in) thick

LEAF

BARK Grey, smooth. **LEAF** Long, lanceolate, leathery, reddish when young. **FLOWER** White, borne in loose umbels. **FRUIT** Elliptic, aromatic black drupe.

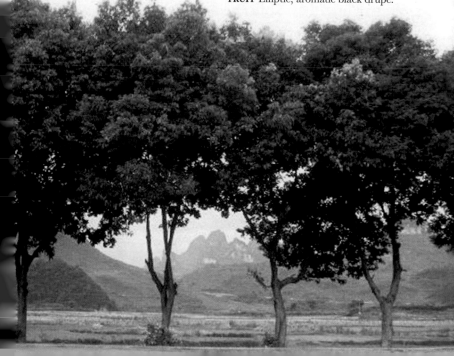

Cinnamomum camphora

Camphor Laurel

HEIGHT up to 30m (100ft)
TYPE Evergreen
OCCURRENCE China, Japan

Widely planted as an ornamental, this sturdy tree is resistant to fire and air pollution and also acts as an effective windbreak. It is easily distinguished by its leaves that smell of camphor when crushed. The leaves, twigs, and wood are a source of camphor, which has been used to treat ailments ranging from parasitic infections to toothache. The wood is also prized for its red and yellow stripes.

BARK Bright green, tinged with red, smooth, maturing to dark grey-brown, with an uneven surface.
LEAF Alternate, oval, up to 12.5cm (5in) long, leathery, dark green and glossy above, green and whitish beneath, with three distinct veins, aromatic.
FLOWER Creamy yellow and tiny, in panicles that are smaller than the leaves.
FRUIT Numerous, round black berries, less than 1cm (3/8in) long, attached to panicles by cup-like green cones.

wavy margins

LEAVES

shallow fissures / **BARK**

green tinged with red

YOUNG SHOOT

glossy green leaves

FOLIAGE

Endiandra palmerstonii

Queensland Walnut

HEIGHT up to 35m (115ft)
TYPE Evergreen
OCCURRENCE Australia (N. Queensland)

Also called the Black Walnut, this large tree has a spreading canopy and grows in the lowland and upland rainforests of northern Queensland. Its timber is used to make furniture and veneers. The seed of the fruit, although poisonous, is an important traditional food for Aboriginal peoples. After processing and cooking, it is said to taste like bread. **BARK** Silver-grey, smooth. **LEAF** Shiny green, ovate.

FLOWER Creamy yellow and small, with six segments, hairy, scented.
FRUIT Green to red, ribbed drupe that is about 6cm (2¼in) wide, containing a single large, round seed.

buttressed base

TRUNK

Laurus nobilis

Bay Tree

HEIGHT up to 18m (60ft)
TYPE Evergreen
OCCURRENCE N. Asia, Mediterranean

The Bay Tree is the true laurel of Greek and Roman mythology. Considered sacred to the god Apollo, it symbolized victory and merit. It was an honour to be crowned with a garland of fruiting laurel leaves and even today, a baccalaureate (*baca lauri*, Latin for "laurel berry") signifies achievement. The tree is now grown commercially for its aromatic leaves, which are used in cooking.
BARK Shiny grey, smooth.
LEAF Alternate, shiny dark green, leathery, 7.5–10cm (3–4in) long, with wavy margins, pointed tips, tapered base; red leaf stalks.

FLOWER Males and females on separate trees, in clusters on leaf axils; small, yellow, with six petals, males with numerous stamens.
FRUIT Black to purple, rounded, fleshy berry, up to 1.3cm ($\frac{1}{2}$in) long, on female plants.

yellow stamens

MALE FLOWERS

elliptic leaves

broadly conical habit

berries ripen from green to black

BRANCH WITH RIPE FRUIT

Persea americana

Avocado

HEIGHT up to 18m (60ft)
TYPE Semi-evergreen
OCCURRENCE S. Mexico

A fast-growing tree, the Avocado was first cultivated in Central America, but it is now grown throughout the tropics. Its egg-shaped or pear-shaped fruit have yellowish flesh, with a buttery texture, which is exceptionally rich in proteins and oils. In its native habitat, the tree sheds its leaves briefly during the dry season, when it flowers. **BARK** Dark grey-brown, smooth.
LEAF Alternate, glossy dark green above, whitish below, variable in shape. **RIPE FRUIT**
FLOWER Pale green to yellow-green, three petal-like lobes, with nine stamens; in racemes. **FRUIT** Yellow to black drupe, speckled with yellow dots or raised spots.

round to oval seed

dense foliage

pear-shaped drupe

FRUIT-BEARING BRANCHES

Sassafras albidum

Sassafras

HEIGHT up to 20m (65ft)
TYPE Deciduous
OCCURRENCE E. USA

This broadly spreading tree has aromatic leaves. The bark, twigs, and leaves provide food for wildlife, particularly deer, and can be used to restore depleted soil. The orange timber is used for making barrels, buckets, and other items. Tea is brewed from its roots and the leaves are used for thickening soups. Its oil is used for making perfume. **BARK** Dark grey-brown, thick. **LEAF** Grey-green above, whitish beneath; juveniles with toothed margins, adults mitten-shaped or three-lobed. **FLOWER** Green-yellow, petalless, borne in drooping, few-flowered, axillary racemes; males and females on separate trees. **FRUIT** Dark blue, single-seeded drupe with pulpy flesh; thick red stalk.

three-lobed adult leaf

yellow anthers

unlobed juvenile leaf

LEAVES

BARK

deeply furrowed

downy young shoots

MALE FLOWERS

Umbellularia californica

lanceolate leaf

BUDS

unopened flower buds

Pepperwood

HEIGHT up to 30m (100ft)
TYPE Evergreen
OCCURRENCE USA (California, Oregon)

Often multi-stemmed, the Pepperwood has a broadly spreading habit and is found in forests and scrub in canyons and valleys. It is valuable for its pale brown timber. It has an attractive finish and is used as a veneer in furniture, panelling, and cabinetwork. **BARK** Grey-brown, thin, smooth, becoming reddish brown, scaly with age. **LEAF** Alternate, dark green, leathery, glossy above, peppery aroma when crushed. **FLOWER** Yellow-green, 6–10 on each flowering stem, in leaf axils. **FRUIT** Drupe, green at first, ripening to bluish black, up to 2cm ($^3/_4$in) wide, on yellow stalk.

FLOWERS AND FOLIAGE

MONOCOTYLEDONS

About a quarter of all flowering plants.

Monocotyledons are so called because their seeds only have one cotyledon (seed leaf), which emerges from the soil during germination. The flower parts (sepals and petals) are in multiples of three and the major leaf veins are parallel to each other and the leaf edge. The vascular bundles are scattered throughout the stem and the roots are adventitious (arising from the stem). They do not produce true wood, but have successfully evolved tree-like forms. Overlapping leaf bases, thickened and enlarged cells, and prop roots are some of the strategies they use to support massive frames. Some species of *Yucca*, *Dracaena*, and *Aloe* have a thick central trunk, which may bear leafy branches. Other species, such as palms, have leaves attached at their base.

PALM TREE
Palms have a trunk that supports the leaves directly, without branches. Some species of palm can reach great heights.

MONOCOT SEEDLING
When a monocotyledon seed germinates, it sends out a root and a single seed leaf. The young plant is nourished by the food reserves (endosperm) within the seed.

single seed leaf

seed covering

seed

root

GROUPS OF THREE
The petals of the flowers of the Yucca tree are arranged in groups of three, one of the defining characters of the monocotyledons.

Pandanus tectorius

Screw-pine

HEIGHT up to 9m (30ft)
TYPE Evergreen
OCCURRENCE Tropical Pacific

This tree has stout "root props" that grow from the bottom of the trunk and firmly anchor the tree in loose soil. They are salt-tolerant and ideal for binding sand and preventing erosion on seaward dunes. The fruit and root tips are a major food source, eaten either raw or cooked. The leaves are used for thatching and woven into mats and baskets. Regarded as the Nature Spirit (Kupua) in ancient Hawaii, this tree has been revered for centuries by Pacific people. **BARK** Prickly, with leaf scars, bearing aerial support roots. **LEAF** In spirals, pale green, usually 0.9–1.5m (3–5ft) long and 5–7cm (2–2¾in) wide, with small upturned spines along the edges. **FLOWER** Borne on separate

TRUNK WITH ROOT PROPS

woody segments   **FRUIT**

trees; males: in clusters, 30cm (12in) long, of tiny, fragrant flowers, surrounded by white or cream bracts; females: in flowerheads that develop into fruit. **FRUIT** Resembles a pineapple, consisting of many woody segments fused together; can remain on the tree for up to 12 months.

Kingia australis

Black Gin

HEIGHT up to 8m (26ft)
TYPE Evergreen
OCCURRENCE S.W. Australia

A tree-like perennial, which grows from a thick rhizome or underground stem, this tree is now listed as a threatened species. Fire plays an important role in its regeneration and stimulates flowering; as many as 100 flowers may bloom after the tree is exposed to fire. It is common for them to have fire-blackened trunks, which is why they are often called "blackboys". The trunk is valued for the resins it yields. Fibres from its stem pith were used to make cricket balls. **BARK** Greyish or blackish (from fire) and covered with persistent leaf bases. **LEAF** Alternate, long, linear, grass-like, near the top of the "trunk"; bunched together, appearing rather like a skirt; blue to blue-green with a silky, silvery sheen. **FLOWER** Yellowish, round, papery inflorescences, at the tip of a stout stalk that resembles a drumstick. **FRUIT** One-seeded capsule.

Xanthorrhoea australis

Grass-tree

HEIGHT up to 2m (6ft)
TYPE Evergreen
OCCURRENCE Australia (New South Wales, Victoria, Tasmania)

Grass-trees are unique to the Australian bush. They are very slow-growing and can survive for many hundreds of years. Some plants may branch and have two or more heads, unlike the Black Gin, which has only one. The tree flowers in spring, blooming prolifically after a bush-fire. Grass-trees were a staple plant for the Aboriginals, providing food, drink, fibre, and materials for making implements and weapons. They are now valued as garden specimens. **BARK** Thick, corky, covered with leaf bases. **LEAF** Long, narrow, green, crowded at the top of the trunk.

spear-like flower spikes

spike 3m (9¾ft) tall

"skirt" of leaves

ABORIGINAL GLUE

A hard, waterproof resin, extracted from the leaves of the Grass-tree, was used by Aboriginals in Australia as an adhesive. It was used to glue shafts and tips to spears, which had butt ends made out of the straight flower stalk.

CRAFTING SPEARS

FLOWER Very small, clustered together, in tall, straight, cylindrical spikes that arise from the leaves, with six white or cream petals, and white stamens; they contain copious amounts of nectar.
FRUIT Capsule, with hard, black seeds.

Aloe dichotoma

Quiver Tree

HEIGHT up to 8m (26ft)
TYPE Evergreen
OCCURRENCE S. Namibia, N.W. South Africa

The branches of this desert species repeatedly divide into two, which explains its name "dichotoma" (forked). The name "Quiver Tree" comes from the lightweight branches, which can be easily hollowed out and were once used by the hunters of the San tribe in southern Africa as quivers. The tree has a rounded crown topped with rosettes of leaves. The bark and fleshy leaves can store water. **BARK** Pale brown, corky and smooth, with large plates that peel off. **LEAF** Grey-green, narrow, pointed, with triangular-toothed margins. **FLOWER** Bright yellow, nectar-filled, up to 3cm (1¼in) long, on branched spikes. **FRUIT** Smooth, shiny capsule with narrow seeds.

Aloe bainesii

Tree Aloe

HEIGHT up to 18m (60ft)
TYPE Evergreen
OCCURRENCE Southern Africa

This multi-branched tree is well adapted to its dry habitat. Its prickly leaves protect it from grazing animals and their waxy coating reduces water loss. **BARK** Pale grey, smooth. **LEAF** Succulent, long, narrow, deeply grooved. **FLOWER** Rose-pink or apricot-orange, three-branched inflorescences. **FRUIT** Spherical capsule.

cylindrical racemes

YOUNG PLANT

leaves in dense rosette

Cordyline fruticosa

Ti

HEIGHT up to 3m (10ft)
TYPE Evergreen
OCCURRENCE S.E. Australia, tropical Pacific Islands

A popular container plant, Ti is believed to have originated from Papua New Guinea. The Hawaiians use its leaves to make "hula" skirts. **BARK** Grey, shiny, with horizontal leaf scars. **LEAF** Spirally arranged in tufts, at the ends of branches. **FLOWER** Yellow or red, sweetly scented; in large pendent panicles up to 30cm (12in) long. **FRUIT** Small red berries.

up to 75cm (30in) long

LEAF

glossy green

Cordyline australis

Palm Lily

HEIGHT up to 20m (65ft)
TYPE Evergreen
OCCURRENCE New Zealand

Also known as the Cabbage Tree, this popular ornamental has sweetly scented flowers. It can withstand drought and can grow in coastal habitats. **BARK** Shallowly fissured. **LEAF** Long, strap-shaped, green, in tufts at the ends of branches. **FLOWER** White, small, in pendent panicles 30cm (12in) long. **FRUIT** Small pale lilac to green berries.

pale grey bark

Dracaena cinnabari

Dragon Tree

HEIGHT up to 15m (50ft)
TYPE Evergreen
OCCURRENCE Island of Socotra (Indian Ocean)

The Dragon Tree, with its stout trunk and dense crown, has been popular since antiquity for medicinal purposes and alchemy. It gets its name from its red resin, once believed to be dragon's blood. The resin is used as a varnish for violins. **BARK** Silvery, rough, thin. **LEAF** Stiff, broad-based spiky leaves, in tufts at the end of branches. **FLOWER** Pale yellow, in clusters. **FRUIT** Yellow berry, to 2cm (³⁄₄in) wide, blackening with age.

Joshua Tree

HEIGHT up to 15m (50ft)
TYPE Evergreen
OCCURRENCE USA (California, Arizona, Nevada, Utah), Mexico

A characteristic plant of the Mojave Desert, this tree favours high desert plains. It relies on the Yucca moth for pollination, but can sprout from its roots and stumps to form new plants. **BARK** Pale brown, covered with dead leaves, becoming irregularly ridged and furrowed with age. **LEAF** Strap-shaped, stiff, 15–30cm (6–12in) long, with sharp-pointed tips and fine-toothed edges, blue-green. **FLOWER** Bell-shaped, cream, yellow, or green, about 4cm (1½ in) long, in upright clusters at ends of branches. **FRUIT** Fleshy capsule, pale to red-brown, 6–12cm (2¼–4¾ in) long, 5cm (2in) wide, with six segments.

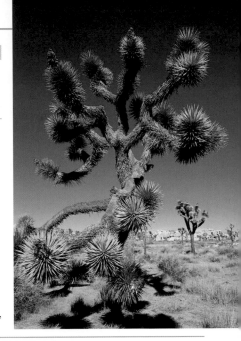

Betel

HEIGHT up to 15m (50ft)
TYPE Evergreen
OCCURRENCE S.E. Asia

The Betel has a narrow, upright habit and is popular in many tropical countries for its chewable seeds, called nuts. These contain an alkaloid that acts as a stimulant. It is said to aid digestion and combat intestinal parasites and infections. **BARK** Dark green, ringed. **LEAF** Pinnate, 5–9 leaves, 30–50 dark green leaflets. **FLOWER** In horizontal stalks; males at the end and females at base of stalk. **FRUIT** Red or orange berry, up to 5cm (2in) long.

egg-shaped berry

UNRIPE FRUIT

Sugar Palm

HEIGHT up to 18m (60ft)
TYPE Evergreen
OCCURRENCE India, S.E. Asia

Sap from this single-stemmed tree is used to make sugar, vinegar, wine, and alcohol. **BARK** Black, fibrous, spiny. **LEAF** 20–25, pinnate, with many upright leaflets, very dark green above, silvery green beneath. **FLOWER** Yellow and showy, on long stalks. **FRUIT** Round to oval purple berry, with three seeds.

leaf to 12m (40ft) long

DRAGON TREE
Found only in the Socotran Archipelago, the Dragon Tree (*Dracaena cinnabari*) is one of many plant and animal species unique to these islands, located off the coast of Somalia. Its characteristic canopy is thought to be typical of early trees.

Borassus flabellifer

Palmyra Palm

HEIGHT up to 20m (65ft)
TYPE Evergreen
OCCURRENCE India, Sri Lanka, S.E. Asia, New Guinea

The Palmyra Palm is cultivated for its edible fruit and for its sap. Palms provide an important income for farmers during the dry season, when there are no crops in the field. **BARK** Dark grey-brown, with the remains of the bases of leaves, especially near the bottom; in older trees the upper trunk is greyer and smoother.
LEAF Pointed, palmately lobed, stiff and green with a sheath and a spiny leaf stalk. **FLOWER** Males and females separate, bunched at base of oldest leaves; small, 3mm (1/8 in) long, 5mm (3/16 in) wide, with three sepals and three petals and either three stamens or three stigmas.
FRUIT Rounded, smooth, reddish black when ripe, contains hard-shelled seeds within soft, fibrous, yellow pulp.

leaf 1–1.3m (3¼–4¼ft) long

LEAVES

10–12cm (4–4¾in) wide

FRUIT

SUGARY SAP

Also known as the Toddy or Wine Palm, the Palmyra Palm is tapped for its sap, which has a sugar content of 14 per cent. This can be boiled and made into syrup. The syrup is then left to cool and harden into lumps of sugar. It is also fermented into palm wine (toddy) or vinegar. **COLLECTING SAP**

Caryota urens

Kitul Palm

HEIGHT up to 30m (100ft)
TYPE Evergreen
OCCURRENCE India, Myanmar, Sri Lanka

This tree is a source of fibres known as kitul. Its sap contains a significant percentage of sugar and is used to make an alcoholic drink. The seeds contain oxalic acid and are toxic if eaten. The fruit also needs to be handled with care since the juice can burn the skin. **BARK** Grey, covered with regularly spaced leaf scars. **LEAF** Bipinnate, 3–6m (9³/₄–20ft) long, with wedge-shaped, dark green leaflets, resemble the lower fin of a fish.

FLOWER Cream-coloured, on inflorescences up to 6m (20ft) long, produced at the end of the tree's life and appearing first at the highest leaf level, then lower down. **FRUIT** Red drupe that is 2cm (³/₄in) wide, containing one or two dull grey seeds.

LEAVES

hanging inflorescence

"fishtail" leaflets

3–6cm
(1¼–2¼in)
long

FLOWERING PLANT

Ceroxylon alpinum

Wax Palm

HEIGHT up to 20m (65ft)
TYPE Evergreen
OCCURRENCE South America (Colombia, Venezuela)

A tall palm with a narrow trunk, the Wax Palm grows in the cloud forests of the Andes mountains in South America. It is found at altitudes of 1,500–2,000m (5,000–6,500ft). The tree is endangered in Colombia because its habitat is prime coffee-growing country. **BARK** Grey and smooth, with fine horizontal leaf scars and a thin coating of wax. **LEAF** Pinnate, long, dark green above and powdery white beneath. **FLOWER** Males and females on separate trees, in loose panicles; both males and females small and greenish. **FRUIT** Bright, orange-red drupes, clustered together so that they look like a large bunch of grapes; each drupe contains a hard, dark brown seed.

Cocos nucifera

Coconut Palm

HEIGHT up to 30m (100 ft)
TYPE Evergreen
OCCURRENCE S. and S.E. Asia, Central and South America, tropical Africa

Widely distributed in the tropics, this tree provides many natural products. The leaves are used for thatching, the trunk for building supports, the sugary sap makes an alcoholic drink, and its white flesh is edible.
BARK Grey, marked by leaf scars.
LEAF Pinnate, with stiff, strap-shaped leaflets. **FLOWER** In shoots at leaf axils; males at tip, females at base; both with six stamens and yellow-orange, lance-shaped petals. **FRUIT** Drupe composed of green outer layer (exocarp) that ripens to grey-brown, fibrous middle layer (mesocarp), hard inner layer (endocarp), surrounding a seed composed of white flesh (copra), coconut milk (endosperm), and an embryo.

ridged leaf scars

TRUNK

MATURE SEED

mesocarp 4–8cm (1½–3¼in) long

FRUIT

COIR FROM THE SEED

Mature coconuts weigh 1–3kg (2¼–6½lbs). Each one has a fibrous outer layer, up to 8cm (3¼in) thick, which helps the seed to float and protects it from damage. When coconuts are harvested, the fibre, known as coir, is separated from the nut, before being cleaned and packed into bales. Coir is used to make mats and ropes.

SPINNING COIR

Copernicia prunifera

Carnauba Wax Palm

HEIGHT up to 9m (30ft)
TYPE Evergreen
OCCURRENCE Brazil

The heat-resistant wax harvested from the leaves gives this tree its name, and is a vital Brazilian export. Each of its approximately two dozen leaves provides about 7kg (15lb) of wax. **BARK** Grey, leaf bases in a spiral pattern. **LEAF** Fan-shaped, waxy, blue to green, divided into 30–60 segments. **FLOWER** Brown, on stalk. **FRUIT** Round brownish drupe, 2–5cm (¾–2in) wide.

LEAVES

deeply divided leaf

Corypha umbraculifera

large, fan-shaped leaves

Talipot Palm

HEIGHT up to 24m (80ft)
TYPE Evergreen
OCCURRENCE S. India, Sri Lanka

The largest of the fan palms, the Talipot has a dramatic life history. It blooms only once in its lifetime of 30–80 years, raining down millions of flowers and fruit, but dies soon after. **BARK** Grey. **LEAF** Palmate, up to 4.5m (15ft) wide, 30–40 in number; the rachis extends halfway up the leaf, bearing 110–130 spiny leaflets with split, blunt ends. **FLOWER** Cream, on tall, branched flower stalk. **FRUIT** Olive green, waxy drupe, with a round seed.

divided base

LEAF STALKS

COCONUT PALM

The slender and delicate-looking *Cocos nucifera* is deceptively robust, surviving for up to 100 years. It is able to withstand high winds in the stormy coastal areas in which it grows because of its strong network of roots that anchor it to the soil.

Elaeis guineensis

Oil Palm

HEIGHT up to 20m (65ft)
TYPE Evergreen
OCCURRENCE W. Africa, introduced in S.E. Asia

Found in tropical rainforests, the Oil Palm produces the highest oil yield of any oilseed crop. **BARK** Grey, ringed with leaf scars. **LEAF** Pinnate, green leaf stalks with saw-toothed edges, with 100–150 pairs of green leaflets that are 0.6–1.2m (2–4ft) long and 3.5–5cm (1½–2in) wide. **FLOWER** Inflorescences, 10–30cm (4–12in) long; males: borne on short, furry branches; females: borne close to the trunk on short, heavy stalks. **FRUIT** Plum-like drupes, in large bunches, ripening to black; fleshy white mesocarp surrounds seeds that are enclosed in fibrous husk.

fruit to 3.5cm (1½ in) long

UNRIPE FRUIT

3.5–5m (11–17ft) long

prominent midrib

PALM FROND

HARVESTING PALM OIL

Two kinds of oil are extracted from the palm nuts. Palm oil, which has a high unsaturated fat content, is taken from the fleshy, ivory white mesocarp while the seeds yield palm kernel oil. Both are used as cooking oils.

Hyphaene thebaica

Doum Palm

HEIGHT up to 9m (30 ft)
TYPE Evergreen
OCCURRENCE Coastal N. and E. Africa

Unusually for a palm, this grassland and desert species has a branching trunk. **BARK** Grey, smooth lower down, leaf scars higher up. **LEAF** Pinnate, stiff, blue-green. **FLOWER** Long-branched, purple and yellow inflorescences. **FRUIT** Oval drupe, yellow-orange fibrous layer surrounding a hard seed that is 4cm (1½in) wide.

65–75cm (26–30in) long

FAN-SHAPED FRONDS

Jubaea chilensis

Chilean Wine Palm

HEIGHT up to 25m (80 ft)
TYPE Evergreen
OCCURRENCE C. Chile (coastal areas)

Found in dry gullies and ridges with scrub, this tree has the largest trunk of all the palms. **BARK** Grey, marked with leaf scars. **LEAF** Pinnate, feathery, dull green above, grey below. **FLOWER** Purple, small, and numerous, in groups of two males to every female. **FRUIT** Round, yellow drupe, 5cm (2in) wide; seed, called "coquito", is like a tiny coconut.

Metroxylon sagu

Sago Palm

HEIGHT up to 15m (50ft)
TYPE Evergreen
OCCURRENCE S.E. Asia (probably originated in Papua New Guinea)

The starch from the Sago trunk is a staple food. Trees are harvested after 12 years. **BARK** Chestnut brown, patterned with leaf bases. **LEAF** About 24, pinnate, feathery 5–8m (17–26ft) long; 100–190 leaflets. **FLOWER** Terminal, branched inflorescence, 3m (10ft) tall. **FRUIT** Straw-coloured drupe.

Lodoicea maldivica

Double Coconut

HEIGHT up to 34m (110 ft)
TYPE Evergreen
OCCURRENCE Seychelles

The seeds of this palm, the largest in the world, are very rich in fats, oils, and protein. **BARK** Grey-brown, prominent leaf scars. **LEAF** Fan-shaped, palmate veins, fringed edges, 4.5m (15ft) wide. **FLOWER** Male catkins at 1m (3¼ft) long are the longest known. **FRUIT** Large, two-lobed drupe, weighing 20kg (44 lb).

Phoenix dactylifera

Date Palm

HEIGHT up to 30m (100ft)
TYPE Evergreen
OCCURRENCE Native to N. Africa, but introduced elsewhere

The Date Palm grows in many climates but only sets fruit in warm areas of low humidity. All parts of the palm are used, although it is best known for its sugary fruit. It has great historical, economic, and cultural importance and features in ceremonies of Judaism, Christianity, and Islam. **BARK** Grey-brown, covered with remains of leaf bases in a spiral pattern. **LEAF** 20–30, pinnate, up to 6m (20ft) long, ascending upper leaves, downward curving lower leaves; sharply pointed leaflets. **FLOWER** Males and females on separate trees in axillary, pendent clusters up to 1.2m (4ft) long; small, whitish, fragrant. **FRUIT** Oblong drupe, up to 4cm (1½ in) long, dark orange when ripe, containing one woody seed.

pendulous clusters

FRUIT

DATES IN MILLIONS

Evidence suggests that the Date Palm was cultivated in 4000BCE. According to the World Food and Agricultural Organization, of the 90 million trees in the world, 64 million are in Arab countries. Iraq is the top producer and exporter of dates, followed by Saudi Arabia, Egypt, and Algeria.

PACKAGED FOR EXPORT

ascending upper leaves

rigid, linear leaflets

FROND

Phoenix canariensis

Canary Palm

HEIGHT up to 20m (65ft)
TYPE Evergreen
OCCURRENCE Canary Islands

One of the most grown ornamentals of the world, this tree has a rounded crown. **BARK** Brown, thick, with prominent leaf scars. **LEAF** Pinnate, up to 5.5m (18ft) long, deep green, shading to yellow at stalk. **FLOWER** Males and females on separate trees; small, off-white, on stalks up to 2m (6½ft) long. **FRUIT** Orange drupe.

LEAVES AND FRUIT

Raphia farinifera

Raphia Palm

HEIGHT up to 10m (33ft)
TYPE Evergreen
OCCURRENCE Madagascar, E. Africa

This imposing African palm has the largest leaves of any tree. They are the source of raffia, a natural fibre. Its flowers are borne in clusters of thousands, on a drooping shoot that looks like a large rope. **BARK** Pale grey or brown, with leaf scars. **LEAF** Pinnate, to 20m (66ft) long. **FLOWER** Borne on the same inflorescence; males: on top, large, tubular; females: at bottom, small. **FRUIT** Oval, scaly brown drupe.

Roystonea regia

Royal Palm

HEIGHT up to 20m (66ft)
TYPE Evergreen
OCCURRENCE Native to Cuba and Honduras, but introduced in Florida

This graceful palm is notable for its salt-resistance and rapid growth. **BARK** Pale grey, smooth. **LEAF** 15–20, pinnate, bright green, with linear leaflets. **FLOWER** Males and females on same flowering shoots, both small, white. **FRUIT** Round drupe, green ripening to purple-black, with small seed.

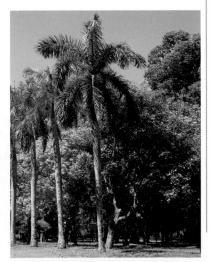

Trachycarpus fortunei

Chusan Palm

HEIGHT up to 10m (33ft)
TYPE Evergreen
OCCURRENCE China

The hardiest palm, this ornamental tree occurs in mountainous regions that are often covered with snow in winter, and can survive without its leaves. Its trunk tends to be narrower at the base. **BARK** Grey or brown, coarse, becoming smooth with age. **LEAF** Unevenly divided, split halfway to leaf stalk, dark green above, silvery below, 1.2m (4ft) wide. **FLOWER** Males and females in branched clusters on separate trees. **FRUIT** Round to oblong, blue-black berry.

FLOWERS AND FRUIT

fruit 1.3cm (⅜ in) wide

bright yellow flowers

prominent leaf scars

BARK

fan-shaped

FROND

Washingtonia

HEIGHT up to 18m (60ft)
TYPE Evergreen
OCCURRENCE USA (S.E. California, W. Arizona), Mexico (Baja California)

A native of deserts and semi-arid areas, this tree is also known as the Petticoat Palm because its old leaves hang around the trunk like a petticoat. **BARK** Pale red-brown, smooth. **LEAF** Palmate, grey-green, with cotton-like threads; dark brown, shiny leaf base.

FLOWER White or yellow, on stalks that emerge between the leaves. **FRUIT** Black, spherical, fleshy berry up to 12.5cm (5in) wide, containing small, glossy red seeds.

dead leaves

BARK

FOLIAGE   *fan-shaped leaves*

Traveller's Palm

HEIGHT up to 12m (40ft)
TYPE Evergreen
OCCURRENCE Madagascar, widely planted in tropical areas

Traveller's Palm is not a true palm and has been described as being part banana and part palm. In young plants, the trunk is underground. In mature plants, it emerges above the ground, elevating the crown. It gets its common name from the fact that when it rains, water collects in the flower bracts and leaf folds, providing a drink for travellers. **BARK** Green, with distinctive leaf scar rings. **LEAF** Up to 4m (13ft) long and 25–50cm (10–20in) wide, long stalks, arranged symmetrically on the trunk, like a giant fan. **FLOWER** Small, numerous, creamy white, held in bracts and borne in clusters 30cm (12in) long. **FRUIT** Brown berry, containing blue seeds.

DICOTYLEDONS

Most flowering plants, including trees.

Dicotyledons are so called because the embryo within the seed has two cotyledons (seed leaves). The leaves of dicotyledons have a complicated branching network of leaf veins. This is called reticulated or net venation. The dicotyledons have a vast range of flower forms, but the parts of the flower (petals and sepals) are mostly arranged in fives. Flowers with parts arranged in fours are less frequent, but an example is Beech (*Fagus sylvatica*). In dicotyledons the vascular bundles that contain xylem (water-conducting tissue) and phloem (sugar-transporting tissue) are arranged in a ring. Hardwood trees in this group have xylem that contains cells called tracheids and wood vessels, plus tightly packed, thick-walled fibre cells. This makes the wood hard. An example is Ebony (*Diospyros ebenum*), which has wood so dense that it sinks in water.

stamens

petals in fives

FLOWERING IN FIVES
Almond (*Prunus dulcis*) flowers have five petals. Most dicotyledons have their flower parts arranged in fives.

seed leaf

DICOTYLEDON SEEDLING
When seeds germinate, the embryonic root emerges from the seed first. The paired seed leaves emerge later.

seed covering

ANNUAL RINGS
The vascular bundles formed in spring are much larger than those formed in summer. This difference produces "annual rings" seen in a cross-section of the trunk.

annual ring

Grevillea robusta

Silky Oak

HEIGHT up to 30m (100ft)
TYPE Evergreen
OCCURRENCE E. Australia

Mostly planted in Australia as a shade tree for coffee and tea plantations at high altitudes, this tree is valued for its timber. It is cultivated as an ornamental for its spectacular flowers and feathery foliage. **BARK** Pale grey. **LEAF** Alternate, fern-like, 15–30cm (6–12in) long, grey-green above, silvery beneath. **FLOWER** Bright yellow-orange, stalked; on terminal bottlebrush-like flowering shoots that are 8–15cm (3¼–6in) long. **FRUIT** Brown-black, leathery seed capsules, with one or two flat winged seeds.

flower 2–3cm (¾–1¼in) long

long, protruding stigma

FLOWER WITH LEAF

capsule to 2cm (¾in) long

IMMATURE FRUIT

PATTERNED TIMBER

The timber of the Silky Oak is immensely valued for its decorative lace-like pattern. Once marketed as "lacewood", it was a leading face veneer. The heartwood is pale pink, darkening to red when dry. The timber is of medium strength and easily worked. It is used for furniture, packing cases, flooring, and panelling.

CABINET

Macadamia integrifolia

Macadamia

HEIGHT up to 20m (65ft)
TYPE Evergreen
OCCURRENCE New South Wales, Queensland, E. Australia

Cultivated for its nuts, the Macadamia is the only Australian native plant to be grown as a major food crop. It grows in coastal rainforests and is very productive, flowering and fruiting for 3–12 months of the year. Its timber is also useful and it is also cultivated as an ornamental. The Macadamia nut is used to make a bland salad oil, but it is usually too valuable as a dessert nut to be used in this way. **BARK** Brown, rough, but unfurrowed. **LEAF** Whorls of three, pale green or bronze when young, later green and oblong, 10cm (4in) wide, on leaf stalks about 1.5cm (1/2in) long, margins may be waxy, with a few spines. **FLOWER** Small, creamy white, petalless, borne in groups of three to four in a long axis, in racemes. **FRUIT** Round nut, hard green outer layer, and hard inner shell that protects the white kernel.

LEAVES, FLOWERS, AND FRUIT

mature leaf 10–30cm (4–12in) long

glossy green leaf

raceme

nut to 2.5cm (1in) wide

whorls of leaves

spreading crown

THE MACADAMIA NUT

Considered one of the best-tasting nuts in the world, the Macadamia nut has a rich oil content of 75–80 per cent. The nuts mature six to seven months after flowering and fall to the ground when ripe. After harvesting, they are dehusked, washed, and dried. The shells are cracked for processing; the shelled kernels are then vacuum packed and shipped for sale.

PACKAGED NUTS

FRESH NUTS

Platanus x *hispanica*

London Plane

HEIGHT up to 45m (150ft)
TYPE Deciduous
OCCURRENCE S. Europe

A handsome ornamental with a spreading to broadly columnar crown, this tree is planted in many cities and towns. It is particularly suited to urban environments because its bark has the ability to renew itself by peeling off in plates to prevent its pores from getting clogged by pollution. **BARK** Smooth and grey, peeling to reveal yellow or green inner bark. **LEAF** Alternate, with three, five, or seven pointed lobes cut about halfway to the base, toothed margins; leathery, shiny green above, pale matt green with downy hairs beneath. **FLOWER** Petalless; males and females in separate spherical clusters on the same tree; males yellow, females reddish. **FRUIT** Burr-like, pendent achenes, covered with brown bristles, green ripening to brown.

AN ACCIDENTAL HYBRID

The London Plane is a cross between *P. orientalis* (Oriental Plane) and *P. occidentalis* (Buttonwood). According to one story, the hybrid arose in the garden of the British botanist John Tradescant. It is more likely, however, that it originated by accident in Spain or France in the mid 17th century.

15cm (6in) wide

PALMATE LEAF

up to four achenes on single stalk

FRUIT

peels in jigsaw-like pieces

BARK

Platanus occidentalis

Buttonwood

HEIGHT up to 30m (100ft)
TYPE Deciduous
OCCURRENCE E. North America

Also known as the American Plane, this massive tree has a heavy, spreading crown and zigzag branches. Its spherical fruit are used to make Christmas tree ornaments. **BARK** Thin, mottled brown, green, and white; older stems are grey-brown and scaly. **LEAF** Alternate, palmately veined, oval, with 3–5 lobes and toothed margins; veins below may be hairy. **FLOWER** Deep red; males and females in separate dense, spherical heads, about 1cm (³⁄₈in) wide. **FRUIT** Achene, hanging from a 7.5–15cm (3–6in) long stalk, with a winged seed.

FOLIAGE | 10–20cm (4–8in) wide

Buxus sempervirens

Box

HEIGHT up to 9m (30ft)
TYPE Evergreen
OCCURRENCE S. Europe, N. Africa, W. Asia

Well known as a garden hedge and shrub, this tree prefers lime-rich soil. **BARK** Pale brown, later cracks into small, grey, corky squares. **LEAF** Opposite, borne on squarish stems, elliptic to oblong, notched at tip, dark green above, paler or yellow-green beneath, with creamy yellow mid-veins.

FLOWER In small clusters of 5–6 stalkless males surrounding one short-stalked female; pale yellow, petalless, fragrant. **FRUIT** Capsule with three split horns; green becoming brown and papery, releasing glossy black seeds.

leaves
12–25cm
(4¾–10in)
long

urn shaped
capsule

FRUIT AND LEAVES

TOPIARY FAVOURITE

Widely used in topiary, the art of clipping trees into ornamental shapes, the Box makes a beautiful clipped hedge. Its foliage can be easily trimmed to form pyramids, cones, spirals, or rounded shapes.

POTTED ORNAMENTALS

LONDON PLANE
Platanus x hispanica is the archetypal city tree; it provides a pleasing dappled shade and is tolerant of both pollution and vigorous pruning. In a less restricted environment, a mature tree can reach a great size, with widely spreading branches.

Triplaris weigeltiana

Long Jack

HEIGHT up to 5m (16ft)
TYPE Evergreen
OCCURRENCE South America

This tree dominates forests in Surinam and old plantations in east Guyana. It is fairly invasive. **BARK** Pale grey. **LEAF** Dark green and glossy, 10–22cm (4–9in) long, 4–6cm (1½–2¼in) wide, pointed at the tip, with a prominent mid-vein, many pairs of side veins, and untoothed margin. **FLOWER** Males and females borne on separate spikes, each 6–10cm (2¼–4in) long.

cream flowers in spikes

MALE FLOWERS

Males: tiny, cream; females: with three enlarged red-purple sepals that are about 3cm (1¼in) long and 5mm (³⁄₁₆in) wide. **FRUIT** Dry nut, 1cm (³⁄₈in) long.

FLOWERING BRANCHES

Charpentiera densiflora

Papala

HEIGHT up to 12m (40ft)
TYPE Evergreen
OCCURRENCE Hawaiian Islands (Kauri)

Moist forests located in valleys and gulches are the native habitat of this tree. It is an endangered species; fewer than 400 mature trees exist. **BARK** Smooth, greyish brown. **LEAF** Elliptic to oval, leathery, 13–40cm (5–16in) long. **FLOWER** Numerous, borne in panicles 22–48cm (9–19in) long. **FRUIT** Not described.

minute flowers

INFLORESCENCE

leaf 13–40cm (5–16in) long

Haloxylon persicum

Saxaul

HEIGHT up to 7m (22ft)
TYPE Evergreen
OCCURRENCE W. Asia (Russia to Iran to China)

Found in the desert, the Saxaul has a large root system that helps to stabilize sand. Its heavy, durable wood is used in carpentry and is highly valued as fuel. **BARK** Grey-white. **LEAF** Triangular, scale-like, pressed to stem, with straw-coloured cusp at tip. **FLOWER** Pale yellow, solitary, 4–7mm (⁵⁄₃₂–⁷⁄₃₂in) long; males and females on the same plant, in scale-like bracts on dwarf side spurs of previous year's branches. **FRUIT** Round, winged nut, 2.5mm (⅛in) wide.

grass-like foliage

Carnegiea gigantea

Saguaro

HEIGHT up to 15m (50ft)
TYPE Evergreen
OCCURRENCE S.W. USA (Sonora desert), Mexico

The Saguaro is the world's largest cactus, and the state flower of Arizona. It grows very slowly, just over 2cm (1in) a year, and its massive column-like stems have a huge capacity for water storage. The oldest plants are estimated to be 200 years old. **BARK** Smooth, waxy, green.

creamy white petals

FLOWERING STEM downward-pointing spines

NECTAR-FILLED CACTUS

The Saguaro flowers every year even if there is no rainfall. The creamy-white petals surround a tube. Yellow stamens form a circle at the top of the tube. At the bottom of the tube is nectar. This, and the colour of the flowers, attract birds, bats, and insects that pollinate the flowers.

dense group of stamens

OPEN FLOWERS

LEAF Stout spines, 5cm (2in) long, in clusters on the stem's vertical ribs. **FLOWER** Bell-shaped, waxy, fragrant, about 10–12cm (4–4³⁄₄in) long and 9–12cm (3¹⁄₂–4³⁄₄in) wide, in clusters at the ends of stems and branches; numerous stamens surround a tube; only a few open at a time, and each one lasts only one night. **FRUIT** Greenish to reddish, oval, edible berry; contains red pulp and small, black seeds.

SAGUARO

Saguaro (*Carnegiea gigantea*) is supremely equipped for survival in the scorching deserts of the American West. In particular, its "pleated" trunk and branches expand to allow maximum uptake of water during rare periods of rainfall.

Phytolacca dioica

Bella Umbra

HEIGHT up to 18m (60ft)
TYPE Evergreen
OCCURRENCE Argentina, Brazil, Uruguay

Also known as Ombu or Belhambra, this fast-growing, herbaceous tree has a broad trunk with high water content. The only tree to live on the Pampas grasslands in South America, it is well adapted to grassland fires and scarcity of water due to its fire-resistant trunk that can store water. Its poisonous sap keeps browsing animals away. This tree is also valued for the shade it provides. **BARK** Pale brown, very spongy. **LEAF** Dark, glossy green, ovate or elliptic. **FLOWER** Small, greenish white, in clusters. **FRUIT** In clusters on stalks like a mass of curled up caterpillars, green turning crimson when ripe, up to 1cm (³⁄₈in) wide.

ovate leaf

LEAVES AND FLOWERS

flowers in long racemes

Nuytsia floribunda

Fire Tree

HEIGHT up to 10m (32ft)
TYPE Evergreen
OCCURRENCE Western Australia

Also known as the Western Australian Christmas Tree, this evergreen shrub or small tree is semi-parasitic, getting water and nutrients from the roots of grasses and other plants up to 150m (500ft) away. Its spectacular flowers bloom for several months around Christmas. Its thin, long leaves give the tree an untidy appearance. **BARK** Rough, grey-brown. **LEAF** Linear, dark green. **FLOWER** In clusters on branched inflorescences. **FRUIT** Dry nut with three broad, leathery wings.

FLOWERS   yellow-orange flowers

Santalum album

dark green,
glossy leaves

brownish
red flowers

**LEAVES AND
FLOWERS**

BARK

Sandalwood

HEIGHT up to 9m (30ft)
TYPE Evergreen
OCCURRENCE China, India, Indonesia,
Philippines

This tree is renowned for its oil and wood, which is used for making perfumes, herbal medicines, and fine furniture. It is a semi-parasitic tree, requiring roots of other plants to grow successfully. **BARK** Reddish brown. **LEAF** Elliptic-lanceolate, up to 3cm (1¼in) long, on thin stalks. **FLOWER** Small, in branched cymes. **FRUIT** Small, dark red, one-seeded drupe.

Cercidophyllum japonicum

Katsura

HEIGHT up to 18m (60ft)
TYPE Deciduous
OCCURRENCE China, Japan

Katsura is valued as a shade or specimen tree. In autumn, its leaves have a fragrance of burnt sugar or strawberries. **BARK** Initially smooth with many pores, becoming darker and splitting into thin, curling strips with age. **LEAF** Heart-shaped with bluntly-toothed margins, 5–8cm (2–3¼in) long, purple when emerging, turning scarlet to yellow in autumn. **FLOWER** Male and female flowers on separate trees, inconspicuous

LEAVES | autumn coloration

in reddish bracts, appearing before the leaves. **FRUIT** Small, to 2cm (¾in) long, curved seed pods in small clusters, initially red.

LEAVES

conical to
rounded habit

opposite
arrangement

Liquidambar orientalis

Levant Storax

HEIGHT up to 12m (40ft)
TYPE Deciduous
OCCURRENCE Turkey

This tree's resin has been used medicinally for over 700 years. **BARK** Purple-grey, corky. **LEAF** Alternate, palmate, cut into five three-lobed sections. **FLOWER** White, arranged in small, round solitary heads. **FRUIT** Spiny, globe-shaped capsule.

AUTUMN LEAVES / orange, scarlet, or purple coloration

Liquidambar styraciflua

Sweet Gum

HEIGHT up to 23m (75ft)
TYPE Deciduous
OCCURRENCE E. and S. USA

This tree has a pyramidal shape when young, becoming rounded with age. **BARK** Pale grey, later deeply fissured. **LEAF** Alternate, leathery, glossy green. **FLOWER** Solitary, yellow-green, rounded heads. **FRUIT** Spiny, spherical, brown.

LEAVES AND YOUNG FRUIT

fruit 2.3–3cm (1–1¼in) wide   palmate leaf

LABEL TO COME

Parrotia persica

Ironwood

HEIGHT up to 12m (40ft)
TYPE Deciduous
OCCURRENCE Iran

This is an ideal specimen tree with its pest-free nature, non-invasive roots, and superb autumn colours. **BARK** Silver, green, white, and brown when peeling. **LEAF** Alternate, oblong to oval, wavy to toothed margins, hairy, glossy green in summer, young leaves red-purple. **FLOWER** Petalless, many deep crimson stamens, emerge before leaves. **FRUIT** Dry, pale brown capsule 1cm (³⁄₈in) wide, contains seeds.

wavy margin

leaf 2–12.5cm (³⁄₄–5in) long   **LEAVES**

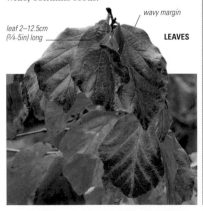

Staphylea pinnata

Bladdernut

HEIGHT up to 4.5m (15ft)
TYPE Deciduous
OCCURRENCE S.E. Europe and W. Asia

This tree is popular as an ornamental. **BARK** Greyish brown, smooth. **LEAF** Opposite; 3–7 leaflets, oblong to oval, toothed, dull green above, pale below. **FLOWER** White, stalked, about 1cm (³⁄₈in) long, in drooping panicles. **FRUIT** Inflated, papery capsule, with 2–3 lobes, containing yellowish brown, edible seeds.

leaf 5–12cm (2–4¾in) long

LEAVES, FLOWERS, AND FRUITS

Terminalia catappa

Indian Almond

HEIGHT up to 18m (60ft)
TYPE Deciduous
OCCURRENCE S. and S.E. Asia

The spreading, horizontal branches of this species make it an ideal shade tree, although it is invasive. Its fruit has many medicinal uses. **BARK** Smooth and grey. **LEAF** In clusters, oblong to oval, 30cm (12in) long, 15cm (6in) wide, shiny green.

FLOWER In long terminal clusters, 15cm (6in) long, males and females on same tree; females greenish white. **FRUIT** Oval drupe, with corky fibre covering a green to yellow husk that turns reddish when ripe; thin, green inner flesh encloses a nut that tastes of almonds.

FRUIT | drupe 5–7.5cm (2–3in) long

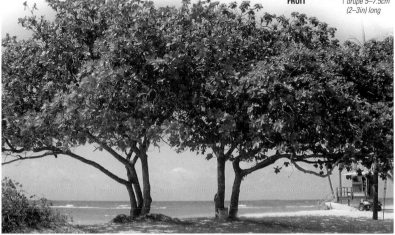

Lawsonia inermis

Henna

HEIGHT up to 6m (20ft)
TYPE Evergreen
OCCURRENCE N. Africa, S.W. Asia

The red-orange dye extracted from the leaves of the Henna tree is used for body art and as a hair colorant. **BARK** Greyish brown. **LEAF** Opposite pairs, 1–3cm (³⁄₈–1¹⁄₄in) wide. **FLOWER** Four-petalled, red, white, pink, or yellow, fragrant, in terminal clusters. **FRUIT** Berry, containing 40–45 small seeds.

leaf 1.2–5cm (³⁄₈–2in) long

greenish brown fruit

LEAVES

FRUIT

Corymbia ficifolia

Red-flowering Gum

HEIGHT up to 12m (40ft)
TYPE Evergreen
OCCURRENCE S.W. Australia

This tree is widely planted as an ornamental. **BARK** Fibrous, dark grey to brown. **LEAF** Oval, dull green. **FLOWER** Long, bright red stamens around yellow centres. **FRUIT** Urn-shaped capsule.

FLOWERS

leaf 7.5–22.5cm (3–9in) long

flowers in clusters

Eucalyptus brassiana

Cape York Red Gum

HEIGHT up to 30m (100ft)
TYPE Evergreen
OCCURRENCE Australia (Queensland), Papua New Guinea

Native to the Cape York peninsula, this is a popular shade tree. Its flowers are an important food source for bees. **BARK** Grey-white, smooth, peeling in narrow strips. **LEAF** Stalked, grey-green, yellowish or red midvein. **FLOWER** Umbels with 3–7 stalked, white flowers. **FRUIT** Semi-spherical, dry capsule, 6–10mm (1/4–4in) long.

Eucalyptus delegatensis

Alpine Ash

HEIGHT up to 80m (260ft)
TYPE Evergreen
OCCURRENCE S.E. Australia, Tasmania

The Alpine Ash is a high-altitude, sub-alpine tree that can tolerate extreme environmental conditions. It is a fast-growing timber tree and produces high-quality wood. **BARK** Rough, fibrous below, main branches smooth and stringy. **LEAF** Alternate; adults narrowly lanceolate, stalked, curved with uneven base, dull green with reddish tint; juveniles grey-green and broader. **FLOWER** Creamy white, in numerous axillary umbels of 7–11. **FRUIT** Goblet-shaped dry capsule, 1cm (3/8in) long, usually with four valves.

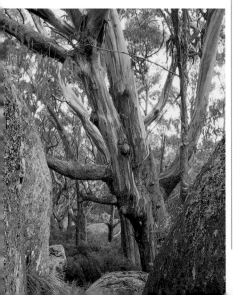

Eucalyptus camaldulensis

River Red Gum

HEIGHT up to 40m (130ft)
TYPE Evergreen
OCCURRENCE Australia

This tree, with its broadly columnar or spreading crown, is widespread in its native range. Its timber is hard, durable, and termite resistant. Its pollen and nectar make high quality honey. **BARK** Smooth, mottled white, grey, brown, or red. **LEAF** Alternate, grey-green, quite thick, turning oval to lanceolate with age. **FLOWER** In axillary clusters of 7–11, creamy white flowers. **FRUIT** Semi-spherical capsule, 7–8mm (7/32–5/16in) long, 5–6mm (3/16–1/4in) wide, yellow seeds.

long white stamens

leaves to 20cm (8in) long

LEAF AND FLOWER

Eucalyptus deglupta

Kamarere

HEIGHT up to 67m (225ft)
TYPE Evergreen
OCCURRENCE Papua New Guinea

Also known as the Rainbow Gum, the Kamarere tree is notable for its beautiful multicoloured bark. Its timber is used for pulp. **BARK** Shades of green, brown, and grey, prickly, peeling. **LEAF** Lanceolate, untoothed, darker green above, paler green beneath. **FLOWER** Creamy white, in numerous axillary umbels of 7–11. **FRUIT** Round, dry capsule.

peeling in vertical strips

BARK

faint lateral veins

LEAF

Eucalyptus diversicolor

Karri

HEIGHT up to 80m (260ft)
TYPE Evergreen
OCCURRENCE Western Australia

An extremely tall tree, Karri is a rich source of timber and provides shade. **BARK** Smooth, variously coloured, shedding in flakes. **LEAF** Opposite, broadly lanceolate, thick. **FLOWER** Creamy white, in axillary clusters. **FRUIT** Dry round to oval capsule, with a stalk.

BARK

dense crown

Eucalyptus gunnii

Cider Gum

HEIGHT up to 36m (120ft)
TYPE Evergreen
OCCURRENCE Tasmania

This tree is one of the hardiest species of *Eucalyptus*. **BARK** Reddish brown, grey, rough at base. **LEAF** Adults alternate, grey-green, sickle-shaped, aromatic; juveniles opposite, rounded, silvery blue. **FLOWER** Creamy white, with numerous stamens. **FRUIT** Dry, grey capsule.

BARK

peeling in flakes

LEAVES

Eucalyptus globulus

Blue Gum

HEIGHT up to 70m (230ft)
TYPE Evergreen
OCCURRENCE Australia

Found in Tasmania, southern Victoria, and New South Wales, this vigorous, large tree forms dense thickets. It is the Tasmanian floral emblem. Its four subspecies differ mainly in the flower arrangement and the shedding of bark. It has strong, durable wood, which is used as fuel and its oil is used in perfumes and soap-making. The Blue Gum tree is also a rich source of pollen and nectar for honey. **BARK** Rough, greyish blue, usually peeling in long ribbons on upper trunk and branches. **LEAF** Adults alternate, dark green, 10–30cm (4–12in) long, 2.5–5cm (1–2in) wide; juveniles silvery, blue-grey, broad, to 15cm (6in) long. **FLOWER** White, 5cm (2in) wide, with numerous long white stamens; borne singly, in pairs, or in threes in leaf axils. **FRUIT** Greyish, woody, prominently ridged capsule, 2.5cm (1in) wide.

LEAVES   sickle-shaped leaf

RIVER RED GUM
The most widely distributed of all Eucalyptus species, River Red Gum (*Eucalyptus camaldulensis*) is tolerant of a wide variety of conditions. It is typically found along watercourses, as here in a flooded area close to the Murribidgee River, South Australia.

Eucalyptus marginata

Jarrah

HEIGHT up to 50m (165ft)
TYPE Evergreen
OCCURRENCE Western Australia

This tree is well adapted to its dry habitat, which is prone to fire. It has long roots and develops large underground swellings called lignotubers that store carbohydrates, allowing young trees to grow back after a fire. One of Australia's most important hardwood trees, it is extensively harvested for its durable, dark red timber. As a result, untouched Jarrah forest has undergone a sharp decline. **BARK** Rough, greyish brown bark, shedding in long strips. **LEAF** Adults: alternate, shiny dark green above and lighter beneath, lanceolate, with a narrow, flattened or channelled stalk; juveniles: dull grey-green without stalks. **FLOWER** White, very fragrant, appearing at the top of the tree in umbels of 7–11. **FRUIT** Round capsules, 1–1.5cm (⅓–½ in) long, with a flat central disc.

FEAST FOR ALL

The Jarrah tree is a rich source of nectar and pollen for bees. Its scented flowers bloom once in two years, attracting bees to pollinate them, and the resulting dark coloured honey is nutritious and full of flavour. Research has also shown that Jarrah forest honey has anti-bacterial properties and can be used to heal wounds. Nectar from the tree is a food source for insects, birds, and marsupials as well.

HONEY

TRUNKS   vertical fissures

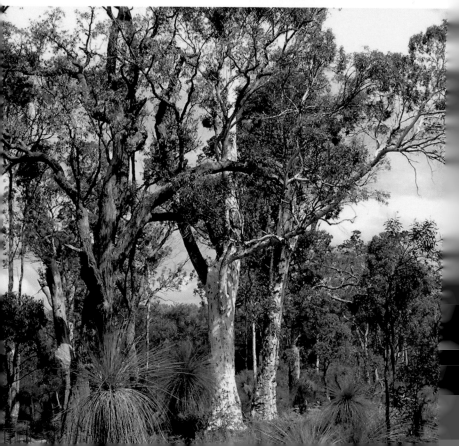

Eucalyptus microtheca

Coolibah

HEIGHT up to 20m (65ft)
TYPE Evergreen
OCCURRENCE Australia (except Victoria and Tasmania)

A fast-growing, single- or multi-trunked tree, the Coolibah grows well in arid and semi-arid areas and can be used to control erosion. Its timber is one of the strongest in the world. **BARK** Grey brownish, thick, fibrous, rough, does not peel off. **LEAF** Adults: narrowly lanceolate, 6–20cm (2¼–8in) long, dull green above and paler beneath, slightly thick and leathery; juveniles: broader, brighter green. **FLOWER** White, very small, short-stalked, in branched or compound umbels of 3–7. **FRUIT** Short-stalked capsule, 3–5cm (1¼–2in) long, with black seeds.

Eucalyptus microcorys

Tallowwood

HEIGHT up to 54m (180ft)
TYPE Evergreen
OCCURRENCE Australia (New South Wales, Queensland)

The Tallowwood's low-branching habit and dense, spreading crown makes it an effective windbreak. It is found in wet forests or rainforest margins, usually on slopes. This tall tree has strong, durable timber that takes a good polish. It is also used as an ornamental, for hedging, and as a shade tree. Koalas depend on it for food and shelter. **BARK** Soft, flaky, fibrous, brown to yellow-brown, with surface pores. **LEAF** Alternate, lanceolate, glossy dark green, stalked. **FLOWER** Small, creamy white, arranged in umbels in groups of five; hermaphrodite (have both male and female organs), pollinated by bees. **FRUIT** Narrow, funnel-shaped capsule.

Eucalyptus pilularis

Blackbutt

HEIGHT up to 70m (230ft)
TYPE Evergreen
OCCURRENCE New South Wales and Queensland (coastal plains)

This important commercial tree grows well in coppices, provides good fuel, and is also a source of food for the koala, insects, and other animals. **BARK** Rough, fibrous, shedding in strips. **LEAF** Dark green, narrowly lanceolate, curved. **FLOWER** White, small, in axillary clusters of 7–15. **FRUIT** Woody capsule.

Eucalyptus pauciflora

Snow Gum

HEIGHT up to 30m (100ft)
TYPE Evergreen
OCCURRENCE S.E. Australia

Long-lived and slow-growing, this tree has a crooked trunk and twisted branches. **BARK** Smooth, green, grey, or cream, sheds in ribbons. **LEAF** Adults: thick, glossy and waxy, linear-lanceolate; juveniles: more oval, dull grey-green. **FLOWER** White, scented, borne in clusters of 11 or more in leaf axils. **FRUIT** Semi-spherical or conical capsule.

adult leaf

flower clusters

LEAVES AND FLOWERS

SNOW GUM

Eucalyptus pauciflora is a highly adaptable tree that thrives in many different situations, including exposed ridge tops and snowy and wet conditions. It is found primarily in the Snowy Mountains of southeastern Australia.

Eucalyptus regnans

Mountain Ash

HEIGHT up to 90m (300ft)
TYPE Evergreen
OCCURRENCE Australia

This is the tallest hardwood tree in the world. **BARK** White or grey, smooth, rough base. **LEAF** Alternate, stalked, lanceolate. **FLOWER** White, small, in axillary clusters. **FRUIT** Pear-shaped, three-valved capsule.

TRUNK   *bark peels in strips*

Eugenia uniflora

Surinam Cherry

HEIGHT up to 8m (26ft)
TYPE Evergreen
OCCURRENCE South America

The Amazon rainforest is this tree's native habitat. **BARK** Pale brown, thin, and peeling. **LEAF** Opposite, oval to lanceolate. **FLOWER** White, with four curved petals. **FRUIT** Round berry, with orange-red pulp.

FRUIT-BEARING BRANCH   *dark red drupe*

glossy deep green foliage

Melaleuca quinquenervia

Broad-leaved Paperbark

HEIGHT up to 30m (100ft)
TYPE Evergreen
OCCURRENCE E. Australia, introduced in USA (Florida)

In Australia, this tree grows on the eastern coast and is planted in parks. However, in Florida, it can grow into immense forests and virtually eliminate all other vegetation. **BARK** Whitish, spongy. **LEAF** Alternate, short-stalked, narrowly elliptic, flat, leathery, with five parallel veins. **FLOWER** Small, white, with united stamens, borne at branch tips in brush-like spikes. **FRUIT** Cylindrical or squarish woody capsule with several seeds.

peeling in many layers

BARK

Metrosideros excelsa

Christmas-tree

HEIGHT up to 25m (80ft)
TYPE Evergreen
OCCURRENCE New Zealand

Known as the Christmas-tree because it flowers at Christmas, this coastal tree has long, hanging roots that enable it to cling to rocky cliffs. **BARK** Pale grey brown, plated. **LEAF** Leathery, hairy below, to 10cm (4in) long. **FLOWER** At branch tips in racemes, with small petals and several long stamens. **FRUIT** Papery capsule.

FLOWERS   *bright red stamens*

Psidium guajava

Guava

HEIGHT up to 8m (26ft)
TYPE Evergreen
OCCURRENCE American tropics,
cultivated in warm regions worldwide

Probably originating in southern Mexico,
this tree can be invasive and forms dense
thickets. In some countries, the fruit forms
the basis of an important industry. The
wood is used for carpentry, as fuelwood,
and charcoal. The bark and leaves contain
tannin, and are also used in traditional
medicine. **BARK** Pale reddish brown,
smooth, peeling in large flakes, green-
grey inner bark. **LEAF** Opposite,
brittle, oval to oblong-elliptic,
hairy beneath. **FLOWER** White,
2.5cm (1in) wide, with 4–5
petals, many white stamens;
in groups of 1–4 in leaf
axils. **FRUIT** White-yellow
or faintly pink berry, up
to 10cm (4in) long;
granular, sweet-
sour, juicy pulp.

PRESERVING PULP

The Guava fruit is high in
vitamin C. Uncooked guavas
are used in salads or desserts.
Commonly, the fruit is cooked to
eliminate its strong odour. The fruit
can be stewed, canned, jellied, or made
into paste and "cheese". Guava juice and
guava nectar are popular drinks, while guava
syrup can also be used to flavour desserts.

**GUAVA
CHEESE**

UNRIPE FRUIT

HALVED
RIPE
FRUIT

yellow
seeds

LEAVES

10–20 pairs of
prominent veins

Clove

HEIGHT up to 12m (40ft)
TYPE Evergreen
OCCURRENCE Indonesia (Molucca Islands), Philippines

The flower buds of the clove tree have been used as a spice for thousands of years. One of the earliest references to cloves says that people who visited the Chinese emperor had to place a few in their mouths to sweeten their breath. The tree has been

DENSE FOLIAGE

introduced throughout the tropics. Today, the main producers of cloves and clove oil are the islands of Zanzibar and Pemba, off the coast of East Africa. The tree once played an important part in world history. Wars were fought in Europe and with the native Moluccan islanders to secure rights to the lucrative clove trade. In 1816, the Dutch destroyed the trees in order to raise prices. This led to a bloody native insurrection, which proved to be a disaster for the Dutch. **BARK** Greyish and smooth. **LEAF** Oblong, up to 15cm (6in) long, fragrant. **FLOWER** Red and white, bell-shaped, in terminal clusters. **FRUIT** One-seeded berry.

pyramidal habit

glossy surface

LEAVES

yellow calyx

FLOWER BUDS

CLOVES AND CLOVE OIL

Cloves, the flower buds of the tree, are harvested and dried before they open, and are widely used as a spice. The oil extracted from cloves is used in cosmetics, confectionery, and herbal medicine. It also has a mild anaesthetic effect and is used externally to treat toothache.

CLOVES   **CLOVE OIL**

Syzygium cumini

Jambolan

HEIGHT up to 30m (100ft)
TYPE Evergreen
OCCURRENCE Indonesia, India

The Jambolan is a tropical and sub-tropical tree. Juice is extracted from its fruit, which is eaten both raw and cooked. In the Philippines and Surinam, it is used to make vinegar and liquor. All parts of the tree are used in traditional medicine. **BARK** Grey, smooth; the base is rough and flaking. **LEAF** Opposite, oblong; pink when young, dark green when mature. **FLOWER** Rose pink to white, in branched, fragrant clusters at stem tips; 4–5 fused petals, many stamens. **FRUIT** Purple-black, oval berry, up to 5cm (2in) long, whitish, juicy pulp with one seed.

Syzygium malaccense

Malay Apple

HEIGHT up to 18m (60ft)
TYPE Evergreen
OCCURRENCE S.E. Asia, Pacific Islands

This tropical tree is grown for its edible fruit, yielding more than 100kg (200lb) per tree. **BARK** Grey, smooth, and mottled. **LEAF** Opposite, leathery, dark green, soft. **FLOWER** Fragrant, in clusters of 2–8, with a funnel-like base, topped by five thick green sepals and four (usually pink to dark-red) petals; many stamens. **FRUIT** Pear-shaped, deep red, white, or pink berry.

TREE IN FLOWER

Tibouchina urvilleana

Lasiandra

HEIGHT up to 5m (16ft)
TYPE Evergreen
OCCURRENCE Brazil

Widely cultivated in warm regions for its showy flowers that bloom for most of the year and its velvety foliage, this tree is a popular ornamental. **BARK** Pale brown, thin. **LEAF** Opposite, lanceolate-ovate, dark green, often with red edges, and 3–5 prominent veins. **FLOWER** Purple blossoms, 12.5cm (5in) wide, with hooked stamens, held in terminal panicles above foliage. **FRUIT** Dry, hard brown capsule.

FLOWERS IN FULL BLOOM

Chrysobalanus icaco

Cocoplum

HEIGHT up to 6m (20ft)
TYPE Evergreen
OCCURRENCE USA (S. Florida) to N. South America, Africa

Usually shrubby, the Cocoplum grows in tropical coastal areas and is useful for stabilizing dunes and soil. **BARK** Grey-brown, with lenticels. **LEAF** Alternate, leathery, shiny dark green above, paler beneath, short-stalked. **FLOWER** Several, in cymes at ends of branches, with 4–5 white petals. **FRUIT** White to purple, plum-like drupe, with spongy, whitish, edible flesh.

rounded or elliptic leaves

fruit up to 3cm (1¼in) wide

LEAVES AND FRUIT

Parinari curatellifolia

Mobola

HEIGHT 8–12m (26–40ft)
TYPE Evergreen
OCCURRENCE Tropical Africa

The Mobola tree is a prized fruit tree in tropical Africa. **BARK** Rough, with deep fissures; emits a hissing sound when cut. **LEAF** Alternate, oblong to elliptic, with a rounded or tapering base. **FLOWER** Yellow-green, in drooping panicles, fragrant. **FRUIT** Plum-shaped, olive-green drupe.

Populus alba

White Poplar

HEIGHT up to 30m (100ft)
TYPE Deciduous
OCCURRENCE Europe, C. and W. Asia, N. Africa

This tree is useful for land stabilization, particularly in coastal areas, and makes an excellent park ornamental. **BARK** Whitish grey, smooth; base develops deep fissures with age. **LEAF** Alternate, 3–5 lobes, wavy margins, white when young, turning shiny dark green above and white beneath with age. **FLOWER** Males and females borne on separate trees, petalless, in catkins; males: grey, with crimson red anthers; females: greenish yellow. **FRUIT** Green capsule with fluffy seeds.

ADULT LEAVES

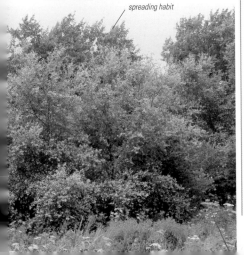

spreading habit

Pangium edule

Kepayang

HEIGHT up to 40m (130ft)
TYPE Evergreen
OCCURRENCE Malaysia, Indonesia, Philippines, Papua New Guinea

The Kepayang tree parts are highly toxic, but the seed is edible when thoroughly washed. **BARK** Reddish to dark brown, smooth or fissured. **LEAF** Alternate, spiral, ovate to cordate, dark green above. **FLOWER** Bright pale green, axillary; male in clusters; female solitary. **FRUIT** Brown, berry-like, soft when ripe.

oblong-ovoid fruit

FRUIT

LEAF

fissured bark

TRUNK

Populus grandidentata

Big-tooth Aspen

HEIGHT up to 20m (65ft)
TYPE Deciduous
OCCURRENCE N.E. and N.C. USA, S.E. Canada.

coarsely toothed margins

ovate to rounded leaves

This tree is a major source of wood pulp for paper and hardboard. It is also used as supplementary food for cattle. **BARK** Thin, pale greyish green, base irregularly fissured when old. **LEAF** Alternate, dark green above, hairy beneath, turning smooth with age. **FLOWER** Males and females on separate trees in cylindrical catkins; males with pale red anthers; females green. **FRUIT** Pear-shaped capsule, hairy seeds.

Populus x canadensis

Canada Poplar

HEIGHT 15–20m (50–65ft)
TYPE Deciduous
OCCURRENCE Garden origin

This tree is a hybrid between the American Cottonwood (*P. deltoides*) and the Black Poplar (*P. nigra*). **BARK** Pale grey-brown, deeply fissured. **LEAF** Alternate, dark green, broadly triangular, finely toothed margins. **FLOWER** Males and females separate, in drooping, cylindrical catkins; males with pale red anthers; females green. **FRUIT** Small capsule, with hairy seeds.

broadly columnar habit

Populus balsamifera

Balsam Poplar

HEIGHT up to 30m (100ft)
TYPE Deciduous
OCCURRENCE North America

This tree was used by Native Americans for its medicinal properties and to make glue and soap. Today, its soft wood is used for pulp and rough timber. **BARK** Pale grey to brown, smooth; grows darker and furrowed with age. **LEAF** Alternate, ovate, shiny dark green above, pale green below; resinous smell. **FLOWER** Green, small, petalless; males and females on separate trees, in cylindrical, pendent catkins. **FRUIT** Small, green capsule; seeds with fluffy hairs.

pointed tip

finely toothed margins

conspicuous veins

LEAF

Populus deltoides

Cottonwood

HEIGHT up to 30m (100ft)
TYPE Deciduous
OCCURRENCE E. USA

This tree is valued for pulp and paper production. **BARK** Greenish yellow; dark grey, furrowed with age. **LEAF** Alternate, triangular to ovate, with toothed margins. **FLOWER** Males and females in separate catkins; males with pale red anthers; females green. **FRUIT** Small capsule.

Populus maximowiczii

Doronoki

HEIGHT up to 30m (100ft)
TYPE Deciduous
OCCURRENCE N.E. Asia, Japan

Doronoki wood was used for making matchsticks, boxes, and pulp. Today, in Japan, it is used for stabilizing stream banks and sand. **BARK** Greenish white, turning grey, deeply fissured with age. **LEAF** Alternate, leathery, elliptic-ovate, toothed margins. **FLOWER** Males and females on separate trees; green, petalless, in hanging, cylindrical catkins. **FRUIT** Capsule, with fluffy seeds.

rounded crown

FRUIT WITH SEEDS

fluffy hairs

WHITE POPLAR
Populus alba, with its distinctive white trunk and dark markings, is an extremely vigorous tree that often outcompetes other species. This tendency can, however, be useful for pioneer planting in areas where other trees are less easily established.

Populus nigra

Black Poplar

HEIGHT up to 30m (100ft)
TYPE Deciduous
OCCURRENCE Europe, W. Asia

The "Mappa burl" veneer is made from the bossed trunk of this tree. **BARK** Dark grey-brown, deeply furrowed. **LEAF** Alternate, triangular to ovate, with finely toothed margins, shiny dark green above, pale green beneath. **FLOWER** In long catkins, males with red anthers; females green. **FRUIT** Small capsule, fluffy-haired seeds.

translucent margins

LEAVES

small, green capsules

Populus tremula

Aspen

HEIGHT up to 30m (100ft)
TYPE Deciduous
OCCURRENCE Europe, N. Africa, W. Asia

The flattened leaf stalks of this tree make the leaves quiver with a distinctive sound. **BARK** Smooth, pale grey, diamond-shaped lenticels, becoming darker, rough and ridged. **LEAF** Alternate, round, toothed, shiny dark green above, pale green below. **FLOWER** In long catkins, males with red anthers; females green. **FRUIT** Small capsule, with fluffy-haired seeds.

broadly ovate to rounded

LEAF

catkins bearing fluffy-haired seeds

Populus tremuloides

Canadian Aspen

HEIGHT up to 30m (100ft)
TYPE Deciduous
OCCURRENCE C. North America, W. North America (from Mexico to Alaska)

This aspen reproduces by means of vegetative suckers and forms stands of clones, the largest being a male clone in Utah that occupies 17.2 acres and has more than 47,000 stems. **BARK** Thin, smooth, whitish to pale yellow-brown. **LEAF** Alternate, broadly ovate, 2–7cm (1–3in) long. **FLOWER** Cylindrical catkins; males with pinkish red anthers; females green. **FRUIT** Small capsule.

LEAF   scalloped margin

Populus trichocarpa

Black Cottonwood

HEIGHT up to 60m (200ft)
TYPE Deciduous
OCCURRENCE W. North America

Like most poplars, the wood of this tree is light. It is used as pulp for high-grade book and magazine paper. It peels easily and is used in plywood and crate manufacture. **BARK** Ashy grey, deeply divided into broad, rounded ridges, breaks up in flakes. **LEAF** Alternate, ovate-lanceolate to triangular, shiny dark green above, whitish to rusty beneath. **FLOWER** Catkins, long, cylindrical; males with light purple anthers; females green. **FRUIT** Small capsule.

Salix alba
White Willow

HEIGHT up to 25m (80ft)
TYPE Deciduous
OCCURRENCE Europe, W. Asia, N. Africa

The bark of the willow tree has valuable medicinal properties. It is a natural source of salicin, which is the active ingredient of the analgesic drug aspirin. **BARK** Grey-brown, deeply fissured. **LEAF** Alternate, bluish green below with silky hairs. **FLOWER** In cylindrical catkins, petalless; males yellow; females green. **FRUIT** Small green capsule.

lanceolate leaf

LEAVES

Salix babylonica
Chinese Weeping Willow

HEIGHT up to 10m (33ft)
TYPE Deciduous
OCCURRENCE China

This willow was previously cultivated as a waterside tree. **BARK** Grey-brown, with irregular fissures. **LEAF** Alternate, lanceolate, toothed, greyish green beneath. **FLOWER** Cylindrical catkins; males yellow; females green. **FRUIT** Green capsule.

Salix purpurea
Purple Osier

HEIGHT up to 5m (17ft)
TYPE Deciduous
OCCURRENCE Europe, N. Asia

There are several commercial cultivars of this small, shrubby tree. **BARK** Olive-grey. **LEAF** Alternate or sub-opposite, oblanceolate, finely toothed near tip, green to bluish white below, sparsely hairy. **FLOWER** Cylindrical catkins, petalless; males yellow; females green. **FRUIT** Small green capsule.

ASPEN
Pictured here in the Targhee National Forest, Idaho, USA, the golden autumn foliage of the Aspen (*Populus tremula*) is one of the hallmark sights of the North American autumn. However, this species also grows widely in Europe and Asia.

Salix x sepulcralis

Golden Weeping Willow

HEIGHT 9–20m (30–65ft)
TYPE Deciduous
OCCURRENCE Garden origin

A hybrid between *S. alba* and *S. babylonica*, this tree has a rounded, spreading crown and drooping shoots. The largest "weeping" willow is 'Chrysocoma'. **BARK** Pale grey-brown. **LEAF** Alternate, margins finely toothed, smooth below or covered with silky hairs, ending in long tapered points. **FLOWER** Catkins; borne on separate trees, cylindrical, individual flowers small, petalless; males yellow; females green. **FRUIT** Small, green capsule, with fluffy white seeds.

SACRED WAY, BEIJING

Weeping Willows are used as ornamentals worldwide and are associated with death in many cultures. A symbol of sorrow and mourning, these trees are often planted near graveyards and tombs, as in this road leading to the Ming Tombs in Beijing. *S. babylonica* is also known as the tree of inspiration and enchantment.

LEAVES

shallow fissures

lanceolate leaf

BARK

Aleurites moluccana

Candlenut

HEIGHT up to 25m (80ft)
TYPE Evergreen
OCCURRENCE Thailand, Malaysia to
W. Polynesia and E. Australia

Also known as the Kukui nut or Kemiri, this tree has an irregular and whitish crown. **BARK** Rough, with lenticels. **LEAF** Alternate and spiral, ovate, dark green. **FLOWER** Greenish white, males and females on same plant in terminal panicles. **FRUIT** Bunches of 3–6 nuts, olive to yellowish green.

LEAF

3–5 lobes

slightly wavy margins

grey-brown to blackish

BARK

Euphorbia ingens

Tree Euphorbia

HEIGHT up to 10m (33ft)
TYPE Deciduous
OCCURRENCE Mozambique, Zimbabwe, South Africa

The latex of this densely branched tree is extremely toxic. **BARK** Grey, roughly fissured. **LEAF** Oblanceolate on seedlings and young plants, triangular on old growth. **FLOWER** Reddish. **FRUIT** Semispherical capsule, with 2–3 cavities.

fleshy terminal branches

Baccaurea ramiflora

Rambai

HEIGHT up to 15–25m (50–80ft)
TYPE Evergreen
OCCURRENCE India to S. China,
Thailand, Malay Peninsula, Andaman Islands

The crown of this tree is irregular and dense; the branches are pagoda-like. **BARK** Greyish brown, smooth or slightly flaky. **LEAF** Alternate, ovate to ovate-lanceolate, smooth to sparsely hairy below. **FLOWER** Yellowish green; males and females borne on separate plants in inflorescences on branches and trunk. **FRUIT** Drooping clusters of spherical nuts, red to orange-pink, turning purple when ripe; edible, sweet-sour taste.

Euphorbia candelabrum

Candelabra Tree

HEIGHT up to 12m (40ft)
TYPE Deciduous
OCCURRENCE E. Africa

The fleshy terminal branches of this succulent tree form a round crown. **BARK** Grey with rough fissures. **LEAF** Oblanceolate on seedlings and young plants, triangular on old growth. **FLOWER** Greenish yellow, on the topmost segment of every branch. **FRUIT** Semispherical capsule, with 2–3 cavities.

green stems

Hevea brasiliensis

Para Rubber

HEIGHT up to 30m (100ft)
TYPE Semi-deciduous
OCCURRENCE Tropical South America, introduced to S.E. Asia

Para Rubber trees were widely cultivated in Southeast Asian plantations for the abundance of white latex in their trunks, which was extracted and processed to make natural rubber. However, erratic supplies during the Second World War led to the development of synthetic rubber and a decline in the importance of natural rubber. **BARK** Greyish to pale brown, smooth, with rings. **LEAF** Alternate, trifoliate, with smooth, elliptic leaflets. **FLOWER** Greenish yellow, petalless, borne in axillary panicles; males and females on the same branch. **FRUIT** Oval capsule, with three lobes and furrowed seeds.

NATURAL RUBBER

The invention of the pneumatic tyre gave an impetus to the development of rubber. It was also used for waterproofing fabrics. At first, rubber was exported from Brazil but the seeds of the tree were smuggled to Britain and promoted across its colonies. Today, Thailand is one of the largest producers.

RUBBER TAPPING

untoothed margin

LEAFLETS

Mallotus philippensis

Kamala

HEIGHT up to 25m (80ft)
TYPE Evergreen
OCCURRENCE Tropical Asia, Australia

The Kamala tree has a short, often fluted trunk, and a dense crown. The red powder that covers the fruit was formerly collected and used as a natural dye, producing brilliant yellows and oranges. It is still used in small quantities by craft dyers. In India, the fruit is used in Ayurvedic medicine. **BARK** Grey-brown and smooth. **LEAF** Alternate, ovate to lanceolate, on reddish brown branchlets. **FLOWER** Greenish, small; males and females on separate trees; males solitary or in spikes; females in terminal and axillary spikes or racemes. **FRUIT** Three-lobed capsule that is covered with orange to reddish granules and contains black seeds.

RIPE FRUIT ON BRANCHES

Vernicia fordii

Tung

HEIGHT up to 20m (65ft)
TYPE Deciduous
OCCURRENCE S. China, Myanmar, N. Vietnam

This tree is cultivated for the oil in its seeds. Tung oil is used in paints, polishes, varnishes, and brake linings, and is the main ingredient in "teak oil". **BARK** Smooth. **LEAF** Alternate, ovate, with a heart-shaped base. **FLOWER** Pink, large; males and females on the same plant. **FRUIT** Oval to pear-shaped, green to purple capsule with 4–5 seeds.

shallow lobes

two red glands

LEAVES

LEAF BASE

Caryocar nuciferum

Swarri Nut

HEIGHT up to 40m (130ft)
TYPE Evergreen
OCCURRENCE South America

This tree usually flowers at night and is pollinated by bats. The fruit is coated by a fibrous husk and the fat from the kernels provides oil. Brazilians use the fruit to make liquor. The timber is very durable and is used to build boats. **BARK** Dull grey, develops deep, vertical cracks. **LEAF** Opposite, trifoliate, elliptic to elliptic-lanceolate leaflets, sometimes slightly toothed. **FLOWER** Large, powderpuff-like, 2–8, with blood red petals, several stamens, in racemes. **FRUIT** Soft, woody, kidney-shaped nuts with edible yellow pulp.

Calophyllum inophyllum

Alexandrian Laurel

HEIGHT up to 20m (65ft)
TYPE Evergreen
OCCURRENCE India, Indonesia, Philippines, Papua New Guinea, Malaysia, Pacific Islands

Found on sandy and rocky seashores, this tree is also known as the Indian Laurel. It has a broad crown, often with gnarled, horizontal branches, and is sometimes planted as a street tree in coastal areas.

BARK Grey-brown to blackish, deeply fissured, with yellow sap. **LEAF** Opposite, elliptic to obovate-elliptic. **FLOWER** Borne in axillary racemes, 4–8 white petals, with numerous yellow stamens. **FRUIT** Yellowish green, globose drupe.

untoothed margins

spherical fruit   **LEAVES WITH FRUIT**

Garcinia mangostana

Mangosteen

HEIGHT 6–25m (20–80ft)
TYPE Evergreen
OCCURRENCE Known only in cultivation

The mangosteen is probably the most highly praised tropical fruit and is usually eaten fresh. Cultivated trees of this species are always female, and they reproduce asexually, producing offspring that are identical to themselves. Together, they are thought to form a clone that has descended from a single parent plant. **BARK** Dark brown to black, flaking. **LEAF** Opposite, oblong to elliptic, smooth surface and margins. **FLOWER** Solitary or paired at the tips of the branchlets; large, fleshy petals, yellow-green with reddish edges. **FRUIT** Dark purple and globose berry, with the seed enveloped in an edible white structure (arillode).

RIPE FRUIT

edible layer

LEAVES WITH FRUIT   unripe fruit   glossy, deep green leaf

Rhizophora mangle

Red Mangrove

HEIGHT up to 25m (80ft)
TYPE Evergreen
OCCURRENCE USA (S. Florida), West Indies, coasts of tropical America, W. Africa

This species dominates mangrove swamps in the western hemisphere. Its bark has been a source of tannin, dyes, and medicines. **BARK** Grey to grey-brown, developing scaly ridges. **LEAF** Opposite, leathery, elliptic to obovate-elliptic. **FLOWER** Pale yellowish green; four sepals and four petals. **FRUIT** Leathery, initially conical berry, germinating on parent tree.

LEAVES WITH FRUIT

— untoothed leaf margin

embryonic root

Erythroxylum coca

Coca

HEIGHT 3–6m (12–20ft)
TYPE Evergreen
OCCURRENCE South America

The shrub-like Coca plant has many small branchlets, bearing leaves containing the alkaloid cocaine. It is one of the oldest domesticated shrubs, its cultivation dating as far back as 2,000–3,000 years. In the past, cocaine was used in tonics and patent medicines. It is now recognized as a highly addictive drug. **BARK** Greyish white. **LEAF** Alternate, oval to elliptical, 4–7cm (1 1/2–2 3/4in) long. **FLOWER** Solitary or in clusters in the leaf axils, small, yellowish green. **FRUIT** Red drupe.

COCA LEAVES

The tradition of chewing of Coca leaves is deeply entrenched among the Andean Indians, who use it to increase physical energy and to reduce the perception of pain, hunger, and thirst. The Coca leaf has great mythical and mystical significance in their culture and religion and is a symbol of Andean Indian identity.

RED MANGROVE
The Red Mangrove (*Rhizophora mangle*) is well adapted to aquatic conditions, such as those seen here on the coast of Boipeba Island, Brazil. Stilt roots support the plant above the water, while aerial roots extend to the surface to aid aeration.

Averrhoa bilimbi

Bilimbing

HEIGHT up to 15m (50ft)
TYPE Evergreen
OCCURRENCE India, S.E. Asia

Also called the Cucumber Tree, this tree has a short trunk and erect branches. The fruit is sour and usually not eaten raw. **BARK** Pinkish brown, smooth, sometimes slightly flaky. **LEAF** Alternate, pinnate, crowded at ends of branches, with a terminal leaflet; leaflets are ovate, in 7–19 pairs, sometimes hairy. **FLOWER** In small panicles, five petals, yellowish green or purplish, marked with dark purple, fragrant. **FRUIT** Oval to egg-shaped or nearly cylindrical berry, faintly five-sided, yellowish green to whitish.

Davidsonia pruriens

Davidson's Plum

HEIGHT up to 10m (33ft)
TYPE Evergreen
OCCURRENCE Australia (Queensland)

Ooray, as this tree is also known, is a popular garden plant. Despite being very acid, the fruit was prized by early European settlers. It is used to make jams and wines. **BARK** Brown, corky, and scaly. **LEAF** Alternate, pinnate, with a terminal leaflet; leaflets leathery, ovate-lanceolate, densely hairy, sharply and irregularly toothed. **FLOWER** Borne in panicles on trunk and leaf axils, reddish brown. **FRUIT** Dark purple, very similar in shape and size to a plum, grows in a large cluster.

Averrhoa carambola

Starfruit

HEIGHT up to 15m (50ft)
TYPE Evergreen
OCCURRENCE S.E. Asia, Florida

This many-branched, bushy tree has a broad crown, with drooping branches. **BARK** Pale brown, smooth. **LEAF** Alternate, pinnate, with a terminal leaflet, sometimes hairy. **FLOWER** In axillary panicles, light red with a purple heart. **FRUIT** Egg-shaped berry, orange-yellow when ripe.

5 prominent ribs

3–6 pairs of leaflets

FRUIT   FLOWERS AND LEAVES

Quillaja saponaria

Soapbark Tree

HEIGHT up to 20m (65ft)
TYPE Evergreen
OCCURRENCE Chile, Peru

First used by the Mapuche people of Chile, the bark extract of this tree is utilized as a foaming agent in beverages and a wetting agent in photography. **BARK** Grey-brown, finely pustular, turning darker and tough. **LEAF** Alternate, elliptic to ovate, margins smooth to toothed. **FLOWER** White, in terminal flat-topped clusters. **FRUIT** Follicle with winged seeds.

LEAVES simple, leathery leaves

Acacia aneura

Mulga

HEIGHT 5–10m (16–33ft)
TYPE Evergreen
OCCURRENCE Australia

This erect, spreading tree or shrub in rare cases reaches 18m (56ft) in height and is an exceedingly variable species with about ten varieties. It is long-lived and is such a prominent part of the Australian scrubland that areas in which it grows are referred to as "mulga country" or "mulga lands". The tree is of economic importance as fodder for grazing animals. **BARK** Dark grey, fissured. **LEAF** Straight or slightly curved, highly variable in shape, narrow, blue-green to grey-green, smooth or finely hairy. **FLOWER** Golden yellow, in stalked axillary, cylindrical spikes. **FRUIT** Flat, broad pod that is narrowly winged, ripening to brown.

Acacia dealbata

Silver Wattle

HEIGHT up to 20m (65ft)
TYPE Evergreen
OCCURRENCE S.E. Australia, Tasmania

TREE IN FLOWER

A broadly conical to spreading tree, the Silver Wattle is widely cultivated in the Mediterranean region. **BARK** Smooth, green or blue-green, turning almost black with age. **LEAF** Alternate, bipinnate, 12cm (4³/₄in) long, divided into numerous leaflets, about 5mm (³/₁₆in) long each, untoothed, blue-green, and finely hairy. **FLOWER** In panicles of small, rounded clusters; individual flowers are small, bright yellow, and have numerous stamens. **FRUIT** Flattened pod, ripening from green to blue-green to brown.

Acacia farnesiana

Opopanax

HEIGHT 1.5–8m (5–26ft)
TYPE Evergreen
OCCURRENCE Tropical America, parts of Africa, Australia

This small tree or thorny shrub is also called Golden Mimosa. Its flowers are used to produce "Cassie" perfume, which is an ingredient of many cosmetics and fine perfumes. **BARK** Dark brown, smooth. **LEAF** Alternate, bipinnate with linear to oblong leaflets in 10–25 pairs. **FLOWER** Mostly bisexual, in axillary, rounded flowerheads, with numerous stamens; sweetly scented. **FRUIT** Sausage-like, brownish black pod.

bright golden yellow flowerhead

LEAVES AND FLOWER

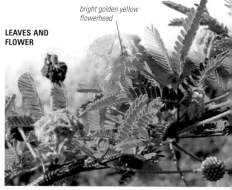

Acacia longifolia

Sydney Golden Wattle

HEIGHT up to 10m (33ft)
TYPE Evergreen
OCCURRENCE E. Australia

One of the hardiest acacias, this invasive tree was introduced into cultivation in 1792. It is fast-growing and excellent for screening purposes, but is short-lived. **BARK** Grey, fissured. **LEAF** Straight, linear to elliptic, with 2–4 prominent primary veins. **FLOWER** Golden to lemon yellow, arranged in cylindrical heads. **FRUIT** Rough brown pod.

leaf 5–15cm (2–6in) long

yellow flower spikes

FLOWERING BRANCHLET

Acacia mearnsii

Black Wattle

HEIGHT 5–30m (16–100ft)
TYPE Evergreen
OCCURRENCE S.E. Australia

Although this upright tree grows wild in woodland, it is also grown commercially for tannin from its bark. **BARK** Grey-brown, smooth. **LEAF** Alternate, bipinnate, with linear to oblong leaflets. **FLOWER** In panicles, creamy white to pale yellow, fragrant. **FRUIT** Grey, hairy or smooth pod with black seeds.

LEAVES AND FLOWERS

rounded flower-heads

16–70 pairs of leaflets

Acacia mangium

Mangium

HEIGHT 10–30m (33–100ft)
TYPE Evergreen
OCCURRENCE E. Australia, Aroe Islands, S. Moluccas, S.E. Asia

Planted as an exotic, this tree grows well on poor soil. It is grown for pulp and paper production. **BARK** Grey to dark brown, corrugated or cracked. **LEAF** Elliptic. **FLOWER** Greenish white to cream, in loose spikes. **FRUIT** Pod with black seeds.

Acacia melanoxylon

Blackwood

HEIGHT up to 25m (80ft)
TYPE Evergreen
OCCURRENCE E. and S. Australia

This erect or spreading tree is found in wet forests. Its wood is used for panelling. **BARK** Dark grey-black, deeply fissured, somewhat scaly. **LEAF** Alternate, narrowly elliptic to oblanceolate. **FLOWER** Cream, spherical flowerheads in short racemes. **FRUIT** Elongated, twisted pod with black seeds.

bipinnate juvenile leaves

undivided adult leaves

LEAVES

Acacia nilotica

Babul

HEIGHT up to 20m (65ft)
TYPE Deciduous
OCCURRENCE Introduced in Arabia and India

Also known as the Prickly Acacia, this thorny tree has a flat or rounded crown and spreading branches, with recurved spines. Since the time of the Pharaohs, large trees of this species have been exploited for their dark brown wood, which is strong and durable, and nearly twice as hard as teak. It makes an excellent fuel wood and good quality charcoal. Being termite resistant, the timber is especially suitable for railway sleepers. **BARK** Dark red-brown, thin, rough and fissured. **LEAF** Alternate, bipinnate, often with glands on stalk. **FLOWER** Globose, scented, in axillary flowerheads. **FRUIT** Dark brown pod that splits open when ripe, compressed over the seeds.

BRANCHES

long, light grey spines

7–25 pairs of leaflets

GUM ARABIC

Babul trees are a source of gum arabic. A piece of bark is removed and incisions are made in the surrounding bark with a mallet or hammer. The reddish gum is then extracted and is formed into rounded or oval "tears". Almost completely soluble and tasteless, it is resistant to insects and water because of its resins. Although inferior to other forms of gum arabic, it is used commercially in the manufacture of candles, inks, matches, and paints. The uses of gum arabic date back about 5,000 years to the ancient Egyptians.

GUM ARABIC "TEARS"

bright yellow flowerheads

LEAVES AND FLOWERHEADS

Acacia pycnantha

Golden Wattle

HEIGHT up to 8m (26ft)
TYPE Evergreen
OCCURRENCE S.E. Australia

The Golden Wattle is the official floral emblem of Australia and its bark is one of the richest sources of tannin in the world, although nowadays it is rarely used commercially. **BARK** Dark greyish brown, smooth or finely fissured. **LEAF** Sickle-shaped to oblanceolate, smooth, with prominent midrib. **FLOWER** In racemes, about five flowerheads. **FRUIT** Flat, linear pod.

golden yellow flowers

FLOWERS

deep green foliage

TREE IN FLOWER

Acacia seyal

Shittim

HEIGHT 6–15m (20–50ft)
TYPE Evergreen
OCCURRENCE N. Tropical Africa (Sahel zone)

This tree has an umbrella-shaped crown. Gum talha obtained from this species,

similar to gum arabic from *A. senegal*, is used as a thickener and emulsifier. **BARK** Rust-red or pale green, smooth, peeling, with a rusty, powdery coating. **LEAF** Alternate, bipinnate; 10–22 pairs of linear leaflets. **FLOWER** Bright yellow, in axillary, spherical flowerheads. **FRUIT** Slightly curved, pendent pod.

Acacia xanthophloea

Fever Tree

HEIGHT 15–25m (50–82ft)
TYPE Semi-deciduous
OCCURRENCE East Africa

With its spreading branches and open crown, this acacia grows mainly in depressions and shallow pans where underground water is present or surface water collects. Early European settlers mistakenly associated it with fever since people living near its swampy habitat contracted malarial fever. The young branches are covered with paired thorns. **BARK** Lime green to greenish yellow, luminous, slightly flaking, and coated with a yellow powdery substance. **LEAF** Alternate, bipinnate. **FLOWER** Borne in ball-like clusters on shortened side shoots at the nodes and towards the ends of branches, bright golden yellow, sweetly scented. **FRUIT** Yellow-brown pod.

Albizia julibrissin

Silk Tree

HEIGHT 4–12m (13–40ft)
TYPE Semi-deciduous
OCCURRENCE Asia, Mediterranean region, introduced in USA

A popular ornamental in warm climates, this short-lived tree has an umbrella-shaped crown. **BARK** Pale brown, smooth. **LEAF** Alternate, bipinnate. **FLOWER** In axillary clusters of about 20. **FRUIT** Flat, grey-brown pod.

fluffy, pinkish flowers

FLOWERS

40–60 leaflets

Amherstia nobilis

Pride of Burma

HEIGHT up to 12m (40ft)
TYPE Evergreen
OCCURRENCE Known only in cultivation

Widely cultivated in the tropics, this tree was found in the wild only once, in 1865. All the trees now in existence are progeny of a cultivated temple plant collected by the botanist Nathaniel Wallich in 1829. **BARK** Dark ash grey. **LEAF** Alternate, pinnate, with 6–8 pairs of leaflets, red to pink. **FLOWER** Five-petalled, bright red with yellow spots, in pendent racemes. **FRUIT** Flattened pod.

petal-like bracts

oblong leaves

LEAVES AND FLOWERS

Bauhinia variegata

Orchid Tree

HEIGHT up to 15m (50ft)
TYPE Semi-deciduous
OCCURRENCE E. Asia (India to China)

leaf 10–15cm (4–6in) wide

heart-shaped leaf base

flower 7.6–12.5cm (3–5in) wide

FLOWER AND LEAVES

Widely planted as an ornamental tree in warmer regions of the world, this tree is also called the Camel's Foot Tree. It blooms for several months. The bark has been used as a tannin, dye, and an astringent. The flowers can be eaten as a vegetable. **BARK** Grey-brown, smooth. **LEAF** Alternate, cleft in two lobes, up to one-third of surface, butterfly-shaped. **FLOWER** In a few clusters at the tips of branches, appearing when the tree is leafless; five petals, clawed, broad, in shades of lavender to purple or white, with a dark purple central petal. **FRUIT** Flat, oblong pod.

FEVER TREE
The species name of the graceful Fever Tree (*Acacia xanthophloea*) is derived from the Greek for yellow (*xanthos*) and bark (*phloios*). Its open crown is popular with nesting birds, and its leaves, flowers, and pods are a useful foodsource for animals.

Butea monosperma

Flame of the Forest

HEIGHT 10–15m (33–50ft)
TYPE Deciduous
OCCURRENCE India, S.E. Asia

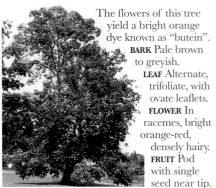

The flowers of this tree yield a bright orange dye known as "butein". **BARK** Pale brown to greyish. **LEAF** Alternate, trifoliate, with ovate leaflets. **FLOWER** In racemes, bright orange-red, densely hairy. **FRUIT** Pod with single seed near tip.

Cassia fistula

Golden Shower

HEIGHT 7–20m (23–65ft)
TYPE Deciduous
OCCURRENCE Mainland S.E. Asia, Sri Lanka

Widely cultivated in the tropics, this tree has a narrow crown and slender, drooping branches. **BARK** Pale brown, slightly cracked. **LEAF** Pinnate, alternate. **FLOWER** Large, in pendulous racemes. **FRUIT** Long, cylindrical pod.

flowers with yellow petals

ovate shape   **LEAFLET**

Cassia javanica

Rainbow Shower

HEIGHT up to 20m (65ft)
TYPE Deciduous
OCCURRENCE S.E. Asia

The Pink Shower, as this tree is also known, has a spreading crown. It is cultivated as an ornamental. **BARK** Grey-brown with black pustules. **LEAF** Pinnate, alternate, 10–20 pairs of broadly elliptic to ovate-oblong leaflets, shiny above, hairy beneath. **FLOWER** Pink, dark red, or pink and white, in racemes from short, leafless shoots. **FRUIT** Cylindrical black pod.

Castanospermum australe

Black Bean

HEIGHT up to 40m (130ft)
TYPE Evergreen
OCCURRENCE E. Australia, Fiji, New Caledonia

Commonly cultivated as an ornamental, this tree is valued for its wood, which is one of Australia's most prized cabinet timbers. **BARK** Grey to brown, rough with small pustules. **LEAF** Pinnate, with terminal leaflet, and alternate, 9–17 oblong-elliptic leaflets, glossy green above, paler beneath. **FLOWER** Orange-red and yellow, in axillary racemes. **FRUIT** Woody, spongy pod, with 3–5 bean-like brown seeds.

cylindrical pod   **FRUIT**

Ceratonia siliqua

Carob

HEIGHT up to 10m (33ft)
TYPE Evergreen
OCCURRENCE Uncertain, probably Arabian Peninsula

Unknown in the wild, this tree has been cultivated since ancient times, originally propagated by the Greeks. Its alternative names, Locust Tree and St. John's Bread, were derived from the Bible. St. John the Baptist is said to have sustained himself on the sweet, pulpy pods of this tree when wandering in the wilderness. The pods are used as fodder for livestock and also as a substitute for cocoa.

CARATS FROM CAROB

The Greek name of the Carob tree is "keration" from which the word "carat" is derived. Carob pod seeds have a uniform and consistent weight. In the ancient world, jewellers, seeking a standard weight measurement for gems, began to use the seeds to assess the value of individual stones.

CAROB PODS

to 31cm (12in) long

UNRIPE PODS

2.5–6cm (1–2¼in) long

LEAVES

BARK Brown, rough. **LEAF** Alternate, pinnate; 2–5 pairs of oval leaflets with rounded tips, shiny dark green above, paler beneath. **FLOWER** Green, tinted red, axillary or borne on the branches and trunk, in small clusters. **FRUIT** Oblong, leathery pod, containing soft, pale brown pulp and 5–15 flattened, hard seeds.

Cercis canadensis

Redbud

HEIGHT 12–15m (40–50ft)
TYPE Deciduous
OCCURRENCE N.E. and C. North America

This popular, small ornamental tree has several cultivars with white flowers, pendulous forms, and one with purple leaves called 'Forest Pansy'. Native Americans used extracts from the bark and roots as medicine. **BARK** Brown-grey, fissured and scaly plates, sometimes flaking in strips; cinnamon-orange inner bark revealed with age. **LEAF** Alternate, broadly ovate to rounded, with a heart-shaped base, palmately veined, smooth. **FLOWER** Pink, borne in clusters on old wood. **FRUIT** Pinkish red pod that ripens to brown.

pointed tip

untoothed margin

LEAF

Cercis siliquastrum

rose-purple flowers

irregular crown

Judas Tree

HEIGHT up to 10m (33ft)
TYPE Deciduous
OCCURRENCE S.E. Europe, W. Asia

According to legend, this is the tree on which Judas Iscariot hanged himself. The unopened buds are pickled or used as a caper substitute. **BARK** Grey-brown, finely fissured, cracking into small rectangular plates. **LEAF** Rounded, with a heart-shaped base, smooth on both sides, palmately veined. **FLOWER** In clusters on the branches and trunk, appearing before the leaves. **FRUIT** Flat pod, ripening to brown.

green when young

alternate leaf arrangement

YOUNG POD

LEAVES

Colophospermum mopane

Mopane

HEIGHT up to 30m (100ft)
TYPE Deciduous
OCCURRENCE Southern Africa

Mopane is an important tree for browsing mammals, including elephants, giraffe, and cattle, and its heavy termite-resistant timber is often used for furniture. **BARK** Greyish brown, deeply and vertically fissured. **LEAF** Alternate, deeply two-lobed, butterfly-like. **FLOWER** In small, green sprays. **FRUIT** Flat, crescent-shaped pod.

Colvillea racemosa

Colville's Glory Tree

HEIGHT 8–20m (26–65ft)
TYPE Deciduous
OCCURRENCE Madagascar

This plant is cultivated in the tropics as an ornamental. **BARK** Copper brown, with small, corky lenticels. **LEAF** Alternate, bipinnate, with 15–30 leaflets. **FLOWER** In grape-like cylindrical to conical clusters. **FRUIT** Two-valved, straight pod.

red and orange flowers

grey-green leaves

Cynometra cauliflora

Nam-nam

HEIGHT up to 15m (50ft)
TYPE Evergreen
OCCURRENCE Known only in cultivation

Small and many-branched, this tree has a knotty trunk. The tree is known for its edible fruit, which grows directly from the trunk, mostly at the base, instead of from the branches. The Nam-nam fruit has a pleasantly sweet-sour taste when ripe. In its unripe state it can be pickled or stewed with sugar. **BARK** Greyish brown, dappled, scaly. **LEAF** Alternate, pinnate, with 1–2 pairs of ovate to ovate-lanceolate, smooth leaflets, rarely covered with hairs. **FLOWER** Cauliflorous (growing directly from knots on the trunk), in compact clusters, with white petals, and pinkish white sepals curved back like petals. **FRUIT** Ovoid to kidney-shaped pod that is hard, rough, and knobbly, greenish yellow to brown.

Dalbergia decipularis

Brazilian Tulipwood

HEIGHT 8–12m (26–40ft)
TYPE Deciduous
OCCURRENCE Brazil (Bahia)

The Brazilian Tulipwood usually has multiple trunks and grows taller in the forest than in open areas. Its wood is greatly sought after for its colour and flower-like fragrance, and has been exported from Brazil for many decades.

The identity of the wood remained a mystery for years and its scientific description was available only in 1966, after a living tree was tracked down in Bahia. **BARK** Red-brown, peeling in narrow strips. **LEAF** Alternate, pinnate, with a terminal leaflet; 5–9 oblong-elliptic leaflets, with pointed tips, sometimes densely hairy beneath. **FLOWER** Terminal and lateral, white, pea-like, in corymb-like inflorescence. **FRUIT** Elliptical pod.

Dalbergia melanoxylon

African Blackwood

HEIGHT up to 9m (30ft)
TYPE Semi-deciduous
OCCURRENCE E. Africa

Found in deciduous woodland and dry savannah the African Blackwood usually has many branches, which bear thick spines at the nodes. Its wood produces a beautiful musical tone and is used for making complex musical instruments, especially woodwinds. It is also used to make chess pieces and ornamental boxes. **BARK** Pale grey, smooth and papery, sometimes peeling off in strips. **LEAF** Alternate, pinnate with a terminal leaflet; 7–13 leaflets. **FLOWER** White to pale pink, fragrant, pea-like, in axillary or terminal panicles. **FRUIT** Thin, narrow, papery pod.

BLACKWOOD MUSIC

Clarinets made of African Blackwood are known for their rich, mellow tone. The fine-grained, dense wood lends itself to the intricate machining needed for the manufacture of complex woodwind instruments. It can also withstand extreme temperatures.

CLARINET

Dalbergia nigra

Brazilian Rosewood

HEIGHT 15–20m (50–65ft)
TYPE Deciduous
OCCURRENCE Brazil (Bahia to São Paulo)

This tree yields a heavy, hard, dark-coloured wood that is streaked with black. It is highly prized as a cabinet timber and is used in the manufacture of guitars and pianos. The tree has been over-exploited to the verge of extinction and it is now illegal to trade in the species. However, some types of guitars are still made from the wood and people can log old stumps left in the forest. The strong odour of the heartwood is due to the presence of "nerolidol", an essential oil.

FINE FURNITURE

Prized for its exotic and beautifully figured appearance, Brazilian Rosewood was a favourite among cabinet-makers of the 18th and 19th centuries. Today, these pieces are highly sought after by collectors.

REGENCY BRAZILIAN ROSEWOOD CABINET

BARK Red-brown, thin, peeling in longitudinal plates. **LEAF** Alternate, pinnate with a terminal leaflet; 11–17 oblong leaflets that are softly hairy when young and become smooth with age. **FLOWER** Violet, fragrant and pea-like, borne in lateral flowering shoots. **FRUIT** Winged pod.

peeling plates

BARK

Delonix regia

Flamboyant

HEIGHT up to 15m (50ft)
TYPE Deciduous
OCCURRENCE Madagascar, widely planted

Considered one of the most colourful trees in the world for its scarlet-red blossoms, this fast-growing tree was introduced worldwide by Wenzel Bojer in 1828 from an isolated specimen in northeast Madagascar. The tree is found in conspicuous, spreading groups in forests, on karst limestone and escarpments. **BARK** Pale grey, smooth but crumbling surface. **LEAF** Alternate, pinnate or bipinnate; 10–25 pairs of primary leaflets, each with 15–30 pairs of secondary leaflets; elliptic to oblong, smooth or covered with short hairs. **FLOWER** In racemes, four spoon-shaped, spreading petals, fifth petal larger with yellowish white and scarlet markings, the rest scarlet-red. **FRUIT** Linear, leathery dark brown pod, up to 60cm (23½in) long.

large, showy flowers

petals to 7.5cm (3in)

FLOWERS

blue-grey seeds

POD AND SEEDS

AN ENDANGERED SPECIES

Although widely cultivated as a street tree the world over for its spreading branches, dense foliage, and striking flowers, this tree is endangered in the wild. The IUCN Red List classifies the native Madagascan population of the tree as globally vulnerable. It is threatened because it occurs in a charcoal production area.

URBAN PLANTING

Dipteryx odorata

Tonka Bean

HEIGHT 25–40m (80–130ft)
TYPE Evergreen
OCCURRENCE Orinoco region of Guyana and Venezuela, introduced in West Indies

oval fruit

This tree is tall, with a compact crown. Tonka bean seeds yield coumarin, used to give fragrance to pipe tobacco and soaps. Its bark is used in shipbuilding. **BARK** Grey, smooth and flaky, becoming furrowed and corky with age. **LEAF** Alternate, pinnate; leaflet oblong. **FLOWER** White, in axillary spikes. **FRUIT** Small, one-seeded pod.

black, wrinkled beans

SEEDS

FRUITING TREE

Erythrina caffra

Coast Coral Tree

HEIGHT 9–12m (30–40ft)
TYPE Deciduous
OCCURRENCE E. Africa, South Africa

Found in coastal forests, this tree has large flowers that produce vast amounts of nectar. Its coral-red seeds are used to make necklaces. **BARK** Grey-brown, sometimes with prickles. **LEAF** Alternate with three broadly ovate sharp-tipped leaflets up to 18cm (7in) long. **FLOWER** In clusters, pea-like. **FRUIT** Narrow pod; poisonous seeds.

scarlet-orange petals

FLOWER

spreading crown

Erythrina crista-galli

Coral Tree

HEIGHT up to 8m (26ft)
TYPE Deciduous
OCCURRENCE South America

The crimson flowers of this short-trunked tree are pollinated by carpenter bees and hummingbirds. The tree contains alkaloids and has been used for medicinal purposes. **BARK** Grey, smooth, sometimes with thorns. **LEAF** Alternate, with three leaflets, whitish beneath, often with spines. **FLOWER** Groups of 1–3 at ends of twigs, with five petals. **FRUIT** Large, long, thin brown pods.

pea-like crimson flowers

FLOWERS AND LEAVES

elliptic to ovate leaflets

Falcataria moluccana

Sau

HEIGHT up to 40m (130ft)
TYPE Deciduous
OCCURRENCE E. Malaysia, Indonesia (Molucca Islands), Papua New Guinea to Solomon Islands

This tree has been introduced into several Southeast Asian countries and other tropical regions. It has a flat, spreading, very wide crown and grows extremely rapidly, even on nutrient-poor soil. A one-year old tree may reach a height of more than 6m (20ft), while a ten-year old tree can reach a height of nearly

FLOWERS   *blackish seeds*

POD

yellowish brown mature pod

30m (100ft). The Sau is often planted as an ornamental and for reforestation. It is also used in coffee-growing areas as a shade tree. **BARK** Greenish white to grey, smooth, sometimes slightly warty. **LEAF** Alternate, bipinnate, with 15–25 pairs of elliptic, sickle-shaped, smooth leaflets. **FLOWER** Cream to greenish white, stalkless, numerous, borne in lateral panicles. **FRUIT** Flat, narrow, thin-walled pod.

TRUNK

LIGHT WOOD

The soft, light wood of the Sau tree is used to make matchsticks and to manufacture pulp and low density particleboard. It is a high quality core material for plywood, pallets and crating, and chopsticks. The wood is also used for light-weight construction, panelling, furniture components, toys, wooden shoes, and musical instruments.

MATCHSTICKS

Gleditsia triacanthos

Honey-locust

HEIGHT 22–45m (75–150ft)
TYPE Deciduous
OCCURRENCE N.E. and C. USA

The trunk of this tree has large, branched spines. The wood was formerly prized for bows, timber, and fence posts. Its pods are filled with a sticky pulp that is sweet and flavourful, but irritating to the throat. Native Americans used the pulp as a

bright green turns to yellow

AUTUMN LEAVES

sweetener and thickening agent, and as a medicine. **BARK** Dark grey-brown, deeply fissured. **LEAF** Alternate, first leaves from the spurs on the old wood pinnate, later leaves on the new shoots bipinnate; 18–28 elliptic to ovate, minutely toothed leaflets. **FLOWER** Pale yellow-green, in narrow racemes. **FRUIT** Dark reddish brown pod with seeds embedded in a succulent pulp.

leaflet to 4cm (1½in) long

BRANCHLET

twisted pod

FRUIT

Gymnocladus dioica

pointed tips

LEAFLETS

Kentucky Coffee Bean

HEIGHT 22–32m (72–105ft)
TYPE Deciduous
OCCURRENCE C. and E. USA

The wood of this tree is coarse-grained, heavy, and strong. It is used for fencing and construction. The raw seed is toxic. **BARK** Dark grey tinged with red, deeply fissured. **LEAF** Alternate, bipinnate; 6–14 ovate leaflets. **FLOWER** Whitish, fragrant, in conical panicles; females are three times the length of males, on separate plants. **FRUIT** Red-brown, leathery pod.

Koompassia excelsa

Tualang

HEIGHT up to 80m (260ft)
TYPE Evergreen
OCCURRENCE Malay Peninsula, Sumatra, Borneo

This tree mostly grows in river valleys and on hill slopes. It is rarely felled as its timber is hard, and is more valued for the honeycombs in its branches. **BARK** Grey with greenish tinge, smooth. **LEAF** Alternate, pinnate, elliptic, slightly hairy beneath. **FLOWER** In many-flowered panicles at the ends of shoots; fragrant, creamy white petals. **FRUIT** Winged pod.

7–12 leaflets

LEAVES

Koompassia malaccensis

Kempas

HEIGHT up to 45m (150ft)
TYPE Evergreen
OCCURRENCE Malay Peninsula, Sumatra, Borneo

The Kempas tree usually has steep buttresses up to 3m (9³⁄₄ft) long. Its wood makes an excellent heavy timber and is now increasingly used for parquet flooring. **BARK** Grey-brown, narrow, fine fissures, somewhat flaky. **LEAF** Alternate, pinnate; 5–9 ovate-elliptic to oblong leaflets with one terminal leaflet; slightly hairy beneath. **FLOWER** Small, faintly scented, borne in terminal panicles; round-tipped white petals greenish at the base. **FRUIT** Pod.

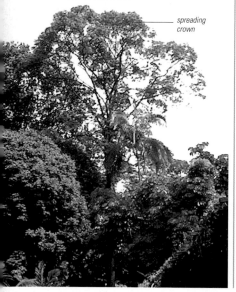
spreading crown

Laburnum anagyroides

Laburnum

HEIGHT up to 7m (23ft)
TYPE Deciduous
OCCURRENCE C. and S. Europe

Also known as Golden Rain, this tree has a narrow, irregular crown. It is rarely planted in public places because it is very poisonous. **BARK** Greenish brown, smooth, becoming shallowly fissured with age. **LEAF** Alternate, with three leaflets, dull green above, grey green beneath, silky. **FLOWER** In terminal drooping racemes, pea-like. **FRUIT** Linear brown pod.

elliptic leaflets

golden yellow flowers

TREE IN FLOWER

LEAVES AND FLOWERS

Leucaena leucocephala

Lead Tree

HEIGHT up to 9m (30ft)
TYPE Evergreen
OCCURRENCE S. Mexico,
N. Central America

Introduced throughout the tropics and
naturalized in many places, this tree is
used in reforestation, erosion control, and
soil improvement projects. It is a prolific
seed producer, and can regenerate and
spread rapidly. It has a wispy crown.
The green parts are used as a fodder and
green manure.
The wood is used
to make pulp or
small poles.
BARK Grey-brown,
with small,
pale brown
spots, smooth.
LEAF Alternate,
bipinnate, with

LEAVES AND FLOWERS

10–20 pairs of linear to oblong, dull
green leaflets that are smooth above,
hairy beneath, and fold up at night.
FLOWER Borne in solitary or paired,
spherical heads. **FRUIT** Strap-
shaped pod.

RIPE PODS

yellowish white
head

FLOWERS

Parkia biglobosa

Locust

HEIGHT up to 21m (69ft)
TYPE Semi-evergreen
OCCURRENCE W. Africa

The Locust tree has a wide crown and a short, crooked trunk. Its seeds are used to produce fermented thickening flour. **BARK** Grey, rough, with longitudinal fissures. **LEAF** Alternate, bipinnate; lanceolate leaflets. **FLOWER** Bright red, spherical, drooping heads of about 2,000 tightly-packed individual flowers; opens at night. **FRUIT** Long, pale brown pod, with black seeds in a sweet pulp.

FOLIAGE

14–30 pairs of leaflets

Parkia speciosa

Petai

HEIGHT up to 45m (150ft)
TYPE Evergreen
OCCURRENCE S.E. Asia

This steeply buttressed tree has an umbrella-shaped crown. **BARK** Reddish brown, becoming flaky. **LEAF** Alternate, bipinnate, glandular at base; 20–35 pairs of leaflets. **FLOWER** Creamy white, long-stalked. **FRUIT** Large green pod.

pendulous pods

FRUIT

Peltophorum pterocarpum

Yellow Flamboyant

HEIGHT 9–15m (30–50ft)
TYPE Deciduous
OCCURRENCE Tropical Asia, E. Australia

This tree bears flowers for a large part of the year and has a low, forked trunk. Usually found along the coast, it has been planted as a shade and street tree in areas with a monsoon climate. **BARK** Dark brown, vertically furrowed, red inner bark. **LEAF** Alternate, bipinnate; 8–20 pairs of elliptic-oblong leaflets. **FLOWER** Bright yellow, axillary racemes or terminal panicles; petals are wrinkled, with a reddish mark at the centre. **FRUIT** Flattened, oblong to elliptic pod.

yellow flowers

spreading crown

Afromosia

HEIGHT up to 36m (115ft)
TYPE Semi-deciduous
OCCURRENCE W. and C. Africa

The Afromosia tree has a flat-topped crown, with spreading branches. Its trunk is fluted and its buttressed base is bare of branches for up to 25–30m (82–98ft). It is found in drier areas of semi-deciduous forests. An important timber tree, the Afromosia yields a hard, heavy, and dark coloured wood that is streaked with black. The timber is considered an alternative for teak and is often used for boat-building, joinery, flooring, and decorative veneers. However, the species is now endangered in most of its range because of over-exploitation of its timber and minimal regeneration. **BARK** Creamy grey, smooth, peeling off in patches to expose the soft orange inner bark.
LEAF Alternate, pinnate with a terminal leaflet, usually with nine elliptic to ovate, smooth leaflets.
FLOWER Cream to greenish white, pea-like, in slender terminal panicles.
FRUIT Long, flat, winged pod.

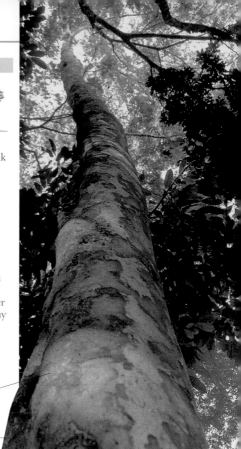

orange underbark

buttresses up to 3m (9¾ft) from base

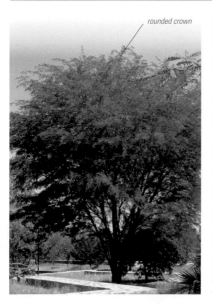

rounded crown

Algarroba

HEIGHT 3–10m (10–33ft)
TYPE Deciduous
OCCURRENCE Bolivia, Peru, Argentina, Chile

The Algarroba is an important tree in its native semi-desert habitat. It is valued for the shade, fuel, and concentrated forage it provides. The tree is a staple food for cattle in arid regions. The unripe green pods are bitter and of little value, but the ripe pods, which contain sugar, make excellent fodder. **BARK** Grey-brown, sometimes fissured. **LEAF** Alternate, bipinnate, with 10–30 linear leaflets.
FLOWER Greenish white to yellow, up to 5mm (³/₁₆in) long, arranged in axillary, cylindrical spikes or racemes that are 5–10cm (2–4in) long. **FRUIT** Broad, straight pod, 10–20cm (4–8in) long, flat and yellow when ripe, borne in drooping clusters; contains pale brown seeds, enclosed in a scaly seed coat.

Prosopis glandulosa

Mesquite

HEIGHT up to 15m (50ft)
TYPE Deciduous
OCCURRENCE S. USA, Mexico,
introduced in Australia, India, Saudi Arabia, S.W. Africa

The Aztec name for tree, "mesquite", gives this tree its common name. A small tree or shrub with zigzag branches and thorn-like spines, Mesquite often forms thickets in sandy, alluvial flats. Like other semi-desert species of the genus *Prosopis*, the Mesquite is used for shade, fuel, and concentrated forage. In addition, it was the most important gum-yielding species of North America in the past. The seeds of the pod were ground into flour and processed to make bread, which was a staple food for Native Americans in the deserts of southwestern USA.
BARK Reddish brown, fissured.
LEAF Alternate, bipinnate with 6–17 linear to oblong, smooth leaflets.
FLOWER In axillary spikes, small, greenish yellow, with inconspicuous, short-lobed petals. **FRUIT** Long, flat pod, with oblong seeds.

pod 10–30cm
(4–12in) long

FRUIT

USES OF MESQUITE

The dense hardwood of this tree is excellent for woodworking and is used for fencing. The bark has been used medicinally for the treatment of eye problems, skin ulcers, and sore throats, as well as a digestive aid. The clear sap is used to make candy and a black dye is extracted from the darker sap.

MESQUITE WOOD

greenish yellow
flowers

flower
spike

FLOWERS

Pterocarpus indicus

Angsana

HEIGHT 10–50m (33–165ft)
TYPE Deciduous
OCCURRENCE S.E. Asia, E. Asia, Pacific Islands

Also called Rosewood, this is the national tree of the Philippines. Its trunk is often twisted and gnarled, usually buttressed. **BARK** Yellowish to greenish brown, flaking in thin plates; inner bark yields red sap. **LEAF** Alternate, pinnate with 5–11 leaflets. **FLOWER** Borne in axillary racemes, yellow to orange-yellow, fragrant. **FRUIT** Circular pod.

smooth leaf surface

seed

ovate to oblong leaflets with wavy margins

LEAVES AND FRUIT

LEAVES

Pterocarpus santalinus

Red Sandalwood

HEIGHT up to 8m (26ft)
TYPE Deciduous
OCCURRENCE Asia, S. India

This tree is found in dry, tropical forests, often on dry, rocky soils. The timber, much sought after for furniture-making, is also used for producing dyes. In India, the felling of these trees is strictly monitored, and export is forbidden. **BARK** Blackish brown, flaking deeply. **LEAF** Alternate, trifoliate or rarely with five leaflets. **FLOWER** Few, in terminal racemes. **FRUIT** Spherical pod with thickened seed-bearing portion and wavy wings.

rectangular flakes

broadly elliptic leaflet

BARK

LEAF

Robinia pseudoacacia

Black Locust

HEIGHT up to 25m (80ft)
TYPE Deciduous
OCCURRENCE USA, Europe

Also known as False Acacia, this tree has a narrow crown and spiny branches. **BARK** Grey-brown, furrowed. **LEAF** Alternate, pinnate with elliptic to ovate leaflets. **FLOWER** White and pea-like, in pendent racemes. **FRUIT** Drooping pod with red-brown valve.

7–21 leaflets

reddish brown calyx

LEAVES AND FLOWERS

Samanea saman

Rain Tree

HEIGHT up to 20m (65ft)
TYPE Evergreen
OCCURRENCE Mexico, Guatemala, South America (Peru, Bolivia, Brazil)

Introduced into many tropical regions, such as the West Indies, Sri Lanka, India, and in 1876, to Singapore, this tree is widely cultivated. Its large, domed canopy provides plenty of shade, making it an important roadside and park tree. **BARK** Dark grey, rough, and deeply furrowed into thin plates or corky ridges. **LEAF** Alternate, bipinnate, with 6–16 squarish to elliptic leaflets, increasing in size from bottom to top of the tree; shiny above, with fine hairs below. **FLOWER** Spherical pink flowerheads in stalked clusters. **FRUIT** Straight or curved pod, with a sweet pulp; pods smell of honey when broken.

CICADA "RAIN"

The common name of this species, "Rain Tree", refers to the falling of "honeydew", a watery waste excreted by cicadas after they suck sap from the tree. While feeding, the cicadas squirt out this liquid. When large numbers of cicadas feed on the canopy, moisture drips from the tree, creating the effect of a rain shower.

CICADA

FLOWERHEADS

ring of pink petals

broad crown

Sophora japonica

Pagoda Tree

HEIGHT up to 25m (80ft)
TYPE Deciduous
OCCURRENCE China, Korea

As the name suggests, the Pagoda Tree was frequently planted in temple gardens. It is of historical significance as an agro-forestry tree recorded as far back as the 6th century. It was introduced into western horticulture in 1753 and is now planted in streets and parks. **BARK** Grey-brown, prominently ridged and fissured. **LEAF** Alternate, pinnate, with a terminal leaflet, dark green above, blue-green beneath, softly hairy. **FLOWER** White, pea-like, fragrant, in loose, hanging panicles at ends of shoots. **FRUIT** Pod, highly constricted between the seeds and resembling a string of beads.

spreading habit

round crown

bud enclosed at leaf base

LEAVES

sharp-pointed, ovate leaflets

Tamarindus indica

Tamarind

HEIGHT up to 25m (80ft)
TYPE Evergreen
OCCURRENCE E. Africa, India, widely cultivated in other tropical countries

This tree has a short trunk, drooping branches, and a rounded crown. The edible sweet and sour pulp in its pods is an important ingredient in many chutneys and sauces. **BARK** White-grey, rough, with irregular scales. **LEAF** Alternate, pinnate, without a terminal leaflet; 10–20 pairs of elliptic-oblong, usually smooth leaflets. **FLOWER** Red in bud opening yellow to cream, in racemes at the sides and ends of shoots. **FRUIT** Pod, with a dry outer shell, pulpy inside.

5 unequal lobes

FLOWER
flower up to 2.5cm (1in) long

Crataegus monogyna

Hawthorn

HEIGHT up to 10m (33ft)
TYPE Deciduous
OCCURRENCE Europe, N. Africa, W. Asia

Also known as the May Tree, this small tree has spiny branches; old trees often have fluted trunks. A herbal medicine for circulatory problems is extracted from its fruit and leaves. **BARK** Dark orange-brown or pink-brown; cracking into rectangles. **LEAF** Alternate, smooth, deeply cut into 3–7 lobes, glossy dark green above, paler beneath. **FLOWER** White, fragrant, in dense clusters on shoots. **FRUIT** Oval red pome, with one seed.

pink anthers

FLOWERS

leaves 5cm (2in) long

fruit 1.2cm (½in) wide

FRUIT

Cydonia oblonga

Quince

HEIGHT up to 8m (26ft)
TYPE Deciduous
OCCURRENCE Caucasus, N. Iran, South America, Mediterranean region

The fruit of this small tree is an important crop in South America and the Mediterranean. **BARK** Purplish grey-brown, flaking to orange-brown. **LEAF** Alternate, ovate to oblong, with untoothed margins. **FLOWER** Terminal, solitary, large with five whitish to pink petals. **FRUIT** Large, fragrant, pear-shaped pome, downy when young, yellow when ripe.

FRUIT

fruit 10cm (4in) long

LEAVES AND FLOWERS

flower 5cm (2in) wide

Eriobotrya japonica

Loquat

HEIGHT up to 6m (20ft)
TYPE Evergreen
OCCURRENCE China, Japan, India, Australia, South America, California, Mediterranean, South Africa

In the unusual flowering cycle of this tree, the flowers bloom with the onset of winter and the edible fruit ripens by spring. It has a dense, rounded, glossy dark green canopy. **BARK** Dark grey, smooth, and flaking. **LEAF** Alternate, smooth above, hairy beneath, toothed margins. **FLOWER** Large, white, fragrant, in terminal racemes. **FRUIT** Pear-shaped to oval pome.

oblong to obovate leaves

yellow fruit

FRUITING TREE

RIPE FRUIT

Malus trilobata

Turkish Crab Apple

HEIGHT up to 15m (50ft)
TYPE Deciduous
OCCURRENCE S.W. Asia, N.E. Greece

This narrowly conical tree grows in evergreen thickets in Asia and Greece. The flowers bloom in early summer. **BARK** Grey-brown, cracking into numerous small, square plates. **LEAF** Alternate, long-stalked, deeply cut into three lobes, smooth above, hairy beneath; glossy dark green turning yellow, red, and purple in autumn. **FLOWER** White, cup-shaped, with five petals and yellow anthers, appearing from woolly buds, borne in small clusters at the end of shoots. **FRUIT** Small, hard, green or red-green pome, up to 3cm (1¼in) wide.

flowers up to 4cm (1½in) wide

leaves up to 9cm (3½in) long

LEAVES AND FLOWERS

FRUIT

2–3cm (¾–1¼in) across

Malus sylvestris

Wild Apple

HEIGHT 8–12m (26–40ft)
TYPE Deciduous
OCCURRENCE Caucasus, N. Iran

This tree is an ancestor of most cultivated apples and is used as graft stock for many commercial varieties. It is found in hedgerows and at woodland edges. **BARK** Grey-brown to purple-brown, peeling in rectangular flakes. **LEAF** Alternate, elliptic to obovate, with toothed margins and a rounded leaf base. **FLOWER** Large, in clusters on short shoots. **FRUIT** Spherical, green to yellowish red pome.

pink to white flowers

FLOWERS

Prunus africana

Red Stinkwood

HEIGHT 3–40m (10–130ft)
TYPE Evergreen
OCCURRENCE Africa, Madagascar

In Africa the bark of this tree is used as a traditional medicine for chest pain, malaria, and fevers. An extract from the pulverized bark is also an ingredient of medications used in the treatment of

prostate gland enlargement, but methods of extraction, which involve excessive debarking and felling of trees, are threatening the species. **BARK** Dark brown to blackish, tough, resinous, peeling. **LEAF** Alternate, glossy dark green, elliptic to oblong, smooth surface, finely toothed margin. **FLOWER** Small, white to yellowish, in racemes on special shoots. **FRUIT** Oval drupe, red to black when ripe.

Prunus armeniaca

Apricot

HEIGHT up to 10m (33ft)
TYPE Deciduous
OCCURRENCE C. and W. Asia, N. China

The Apricot tree, with its rounded crown and open canopy, was originally cultivated in northeastern China over 3,000 years ago. The species is now widely cultivated for its sweet edible fruit. Historically, Apricots were grown from seedlings, and a few improved cultivars exist. **BARK** Red-brown, smooth,

LEAVES AND FRUIT

and glossy. **LEAF** Alternate, glossy dark green, broadly ovate to rounded with abruptly tapered tip, usually rounded base and finely toothed margin. **FLOWER** Large with five, white to pink petals, borne singly on old wood in spring before the leaves emerge. **FRUIT** Spherical, fleshy drupe, yellow-flushed orange-red, with a hard, smooth stone enclosing an edible white seed.

orange-red flesh

leaf to 10cm (4in) long

single stone

FRUIT

APRICOT PRODUCTS

Jam and preserves are made from the sweet cooked pulp of the apricot fruit. The Romans introduced apricots to Europe in 70–60BCE, and European settlers brought the tree to America. Turkey is the world's largest producer of apricots.   **JAM**

Prunus avium

Gean

HEIGHT up to 25m (80ft)
TYPE Deciduous
OCCURRENCE Europe, W. Asia, North America

Also known as Mazzard or Wild Sweet Cherry, Gean wood has been used for veneer, and also for furniture-making, particularly in France. The roots of this tree can cause problems for nearby buildings. The double-flowered cultivar 'Plena' is a popular ornamental tree. **BARK** Red-brown, peeling in horizontal bands. **LEAF** Alternate, elliptic to oblong or obovate, dull green above, covered with soft hairs below. **FLOWER** Large, white, borne in clusters on short shoots before the leaves emerge. **FRUIT** Spherical, bitter or sweet, edible red drupe.

FLOWERS

leaf to 15cm (6in) long

red berry

LEAVES AND FRUIT

Prunus cerasifera

Myrobalan

HEIGHT up to 10m (33ft)
TYPE Deciduous
OCCURRENCE Known only in cultivation

Also called Cherry Plum, this tree has a rounded crown. It is commonly used as a rootstock for grafting domestic plums and is often planted as an ornamental. 'Pissardii', its best known cultivar, has

FLOWERS

pink flowers and purple leaves; 'Nigra' is the selection from this cultivar which is usually grown today. **BARK** Purple-brown, thinly scaly, with horizontal orange-brown lenticels, becoming fissured with age. **LEAF** Alternate, ovate to elliptic or obovate with toothed margins, smooth above, covered with soft hairs below. **FLOWER** White, rarely pink, borne singly or in clusters, before the leaves. **FRUIT** Spherical, red or yellow, plum-like drupe.

APRICOT FLOWER
Stamens of the Apricot (*Prunus armeniaca*) flower as revealed by a scanning electron micrograph. Each stamen is made up of a green filament with a red anther at its tip, which releases pollen. The pollen is carried by insects to the female parts of the flower.

Prunus cerasus

Morello Cherry

HEIGHT up to 10m (33ft)
TYPE Deciduous
OCCURRENCE Garden origin

This tree was cultivated from wild populations growing around the Caspian and Black Seas. It has a broadly rounded crown. **BARK** Purple-brown, rough, scaly. **LEAF** Alternate, elliptic to ovate, with toothed margins. **FLOWER** In clusters of 3–5. **FRUIT** Spherical, sour-tasting drupe.

large white flowers

leaves 5–12cm (2–5in) long

red to black drupe

BRANCH WITH FLOWERS

FRUIT

Prunus laurocerasus

Cherry Laurel

HEIGHT up to 10m (33ft)
TYPE Evergreen
OCCURRENCE E. Europe, S.W. Asia

This large, common shrub is found in parks and woodland. **BARK** Dark grey-brown, smooth. **LEAF** Alternate, obovate. **FLOWER** Small, white and fragrant, borne in racemes. **FRUIT** Purple-black conical drupe.

dark green leaf

berry-like fruit

LEAVES AND FRUIT

wide, spreading habit

Prunus x domestica

Plum

HEIGHT up to 10m (33ft)
TYPE Deciduous
OCCURRENCE Garden origin

Many cultivars of this tree are grown for its culinary plum. Its crown is broad and spreading. **BARK** Grey-brown, fissured with age. **LEAF** Alternate, elliptic to obovate, toothed margins. **FLOWER** In clusters on short shoots, five white petals. **FRUIT** Ovoid drupe, yellow, red, or purple, sweet or sharp taste.

dull green surface

7.5cm (3in) long

LEAVES

FRUIT

Prunus mume

Mume

HEIGHT 6–10m (20–33ft)
TYPE Deciduous
OCCURRENCE China, Japan

Cultivated for over 1,500 years for its variously coloured blossoms, this Japanese apricot has more than 300 cultivars. It has a rounded crown. **BARK** Grey to greenish. **LEAF** Alternate, ovate, hairy, sharply toothed margins. **FLOWER** Large, white to pink to red, and fragrant; borne singly or in pairs on old wood. **FRUIT** Spherical to ovoid drupe, fleshy, yellow, barely edible.

Prunus dulcis

Almond

HEIGHT up to 8m (26ft)
TYPE Deciduous
OCCURRENCE C. and W. Asia,
North Africa

Widely cultivated since ancient times
for its green, edible fruit and as an
ornamental, the Almond thrived in the
USA, which today is by far the largest
producer of almonds in the world,
producing 75 per cent of the world's
crop. The tree has a
spreading crown and
smooth green or red-
flushed shoots.
BARK Dark grey, cracking
into small pieces.
LEAF Alternate, ovate-

flower to 5cm
(2in) wide

FLOWERS

HISTORY OF THE ALMOND

Explorers ate almonds while travelling on
the "Silk Road" between Asia and the
Mediterranean. Before long, almond
trees flourished in the Mediterranean,
especially in Spain and Italy. The
Almond tree was brought to California
from Spain in the mid-1700s by
Franciscan priests.

ALMONDS

---

lanceolate to narrowly elliptic, smooth,
finely toothed margin, dark green.
FLOWER Borne on lateral spurs before the
leaves, solitary or in pairs, large, pink to
whitish. **FRUIT** Oval,
compressed drupe, velvety
skin, dry and leathery flesh
enclosing a smooth,
pitted stone with an
edible kernel.

leaf to 12cm
(4¾in) long

LEAVES AND FRUIT

flesh splits
open as fruit
ripens

Prunus padus

Bird Cherry

HEIGHT up to 15m (50ft)
TYPE Deciduous
OCCURRENCE Europe, N. Asia to Korea, Japan

The conical crown of the Bird Cherry becomes rounded with age. **BARK** Grey-brown, smooth. **LEAF** Elliptic to obovate, dull green above, grey-green beneath, finely toothed. **FLOWER** White, small, fragrant. **FRUIT** Spherical, black drupe.

alternate leaves
drooping racemes

Prunus serrulata

Flowering Cherry

HEIGHT up to 20m (65ft)
TYPE Deciduous
OCCURRENCE China, Japan, Korea

This oriental cherry has several cultivars. In spring, many of them produce dazzling semi-double flowers. **BARK** Purple-brown or greyish. **LEAF** Alternate, ovate-oblong to obovate. **FLOWER** Pink to white, in clusters of 2–5. **FRUIT** Fleshy, purple-red to black drupe.

notched petals

FLOWERS

Prunus spinosa

Sloe

HEIGHT up to 5m (16ft)
TYPE Deciduous
OCCURRENCE Europe, N. Africa, N. Asia

Also known as Blackthorn, this many-branched, thicket-forming tree has spiny branches. **BARK** Dark blackish brown. **LEAF** Alternate, elliptic-ovate to obovate, toothed. **FLOWER** Single or in pairs, white, small. **FRUIT** Spherical, smooth drupe.

4cm (1½ in) long

blue-black berry

LEAF   **RIPE FRUIT**

Prunus subhirtella

Winter-flowering Cherry

HEIGHT up to 10m (33ft)
TYPE Deciduous
OCCURRENCE Japan

sharply toothed margin

bronze green young leaf

deep green mature leaf

LEAVES

This tree has a rounded crown and upright branches. One popular cultivar, 'Autumnalis', flowers throughout mild winters, when its branches are bare of leaves. **BARK** Grey-brown, smooth, with horizontal lenticels. **LEAF** Alternate, elliptic to ovate. **FLOWER** Pale pink to white, notched petals, in clusters of 2–4 on short shoots. **FRUIT** Spherical, fleshy black drupe.

Prunus persica

Peach

HEIGHT up to 8m (26 ft)
TYPE Deciduous
OCCURRENCE China

Cultivated since ancient times, this tree has many different varieties, with differing shapes, flowers, and fruit. The tree's shape can be bushy or weeping, and its flowers single- or double-petalled. Peaches typically have downy-skinned fruit, with yellow or white flesh. However, in nectarines, the fruit's skin is smooth – a difference controlled by a single gene. **BARK** Dark grey, becoming fissured with age. **LEAF** Alternate, narrowly elliptic to lanceolate, with finely toothed margins. **FLOWER** Borne singly or in pairs, pink, sometimes white. **FRUIT** Large, spherical drupe, with velvety or smooth skin; sweet, fleshy, white or orange-yellow pulp, with a deeply pitted stone and a white seed.

4 cm (1½ in) wide

pitted stone

FRUIT AND SEED

FLOWERS

ORIGINS OF THE PEACH

Peaches were probably the first fruit crop domesticated in China about 4,000 years ago. The tree was introduced to Persia (Iran) by way of the ancient silk trading routes. Greeks and Romans spread the peach throughout Europe and England in 300–400BCE. Peaches then came to North America with the explorers of the 16th and 17th centuries.

PEACH TREE IN BLOOM

red-flushed skin

8cm (3¼ in) wide

FLOWERING CHERRY
In Japan, which is famous for its Flowering Cherry trees (*Prunus serrulata*), the brief blossom season in March–April is a time of celebration, marked by parties, or "hanami", held in the shade of the trees. This tree is popular worldwide as an ornamental.

Prunus x yedoensis

Yoshino Cherry

HEIGHT up to 16m (52ft)
TYPE Deciduous
OCCURRENCE Japan, of garden origin

Also known as the Flowering Cherry, this fast-growing Japanese hybrid is one of the favourite cultivated cherry trees of Japan. With its broadly spreading crown, arching branches, and spectacular display of early spring flowers, it is now a very popular ornamental tree throughout the world, especially as an avenue tree. It was planted on United States soil for the first time in 1912, when the people of Japan presented the tree as a gift of friendship. **BARK** Purple-grey, with thick bands of corky lenticels. **LEAF** Alternate, elliptic to obovate, 6cm (2½in) wide, with tapered tips and sharply toothed margins; they are pale green and downy when young, particularly on the underside,

notched petal tips

reddish brown twig

FLOWERING BRANCH

flower to 4cm (1½ in) wide

the surface becoming smooth and glossy with age. **FLOWER** Pale pink, fading to nearly white, with five large petals, numerous, borne in small clusters on side spurs in early spring, before the young leaves emerge. **FRUIT** Fleshy, spherical drupe, red at first, ripening to black.

leaf to 11cm (4½in) long

LEAVES AND UNRIPE FRUIT

fruit to 1.2cm (½in) wide

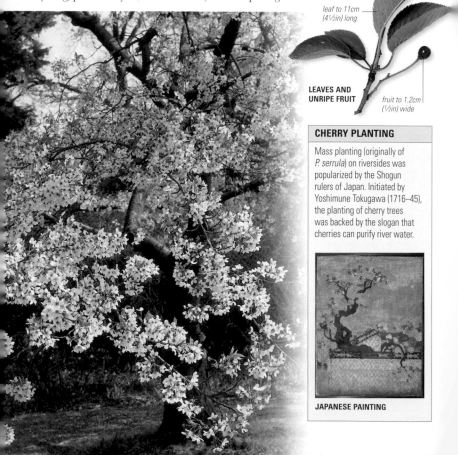

CHERRY PLANTING

Mass planting (originally of *P. serrula*) on riversides was popularized by the Shogun rulers of Japan. Initiated by Yoshimune Tokugawa (1716–45), the planting of cherry trees was backed by the slogan that cherries can purify river water.

JAPANESE PAINTING

Pyrus communis

Pear

HEIGHT up to 20m (65ft)
TYPE Deciduous
OCCURRENCE Known only in cultivation (grown in gardens and orchards); occasionally naturalized in Europe

A broadly conical to columnar tree, the Pear is a hybrid of several European species. Along with its cultivars, it is widely grown for its edible fruit. In its wild form, it has a spiny habit when young. It is usually found in woodland and scrub. **BARK** Dark grey, cracking into rectangular plates. **LEAF** Alternate, ovate to elliptic, glossy deep green. **FLOWER** Five white petals with deep pink anthers, in clusters on short shoots. **FRUIT** Fleshy, yellowish green pome.

toothed margins

LEAVES

FRUIT-BEARING BRANCHES

to 10cm (4in) long

RIPE FRUIT

CULTIVATED PEARS

The original pear fruit were small, hard, gritty, sour, and astringent, and may have resembled the stewing pears that survive today. There are over 5,000 cultivated varieties of pears of which 10–25 are commercially grown. In the USA, 75 per cent of the pears cultivated are "Bartletts", which is the same as the British "Williams" pear, and of which there are greenish yellow and red varieties.

RED PEAR

WILLIAMS PEAR

Pyrus pyrifolia

Nashi

HEIGHT up to 12m (40ft)
TYPE Deciduous
OCCURRENCE C. and W. China

This tree was brought into cultivation in China 3,000 years ago. **BARK** Dark grey to purplish brown. **LEAF** Alternate, ovate to ovate-oblong, bristle-toothed margins. **FLOWER** White, borne in clusters of 6–9. **FRUIT** Brown to yellow, rounded pome.

FLOWERS AND LEAVES

five petals

reddish new leaves

Pyrus salicifolia

Willow Pear

HEIGHT up to 10m (33ft)
TYPE Deciduous
OCCURRENCE W. Asia

This spreading tree has slender, pendent shoots and willow-like leaves. It is considered one of the best cultivated ornamental pears. **BARK** Pale grey-brown. **LEAF** Alternate, lanceolate. **FLOWER** Large, white, on short shoots. **FRUIT** Yellow-brown pome, hairy; later smooth.

tapering tips

UNRIPE FRUIT

in clusters

FLOWERS   **LEAVES**

Sorbus aria

Whitebeam

HEIGHT up to 25m (80ft)
TYPE Deciduous
OCCURRENCE Europe

This tree is found on well-drained chalk and limestone. **BARK** Grey, cracking with age. **LEAF** Alternate, ovate to elliptic-oblong, covered with hairs when young, pale green above, whitish hairs beneath. **FLOWER** In flattened terminal clusters, with five white petals. **FRUIT** Red-orange, spherical to egg-shaped pome.

Sorbus aucuparia

Rowan

HEIGHT up to 15m (50ft)
TYPE Deciduous
OCCURRENCE N. Africa, W. Asia

The dried berries of this tree are used mainly in the food and beverage industries. **BARK** Grey, smooth and shiny. **LEAF** Alternate, pinnate, with a terminal leaflet; 9–15 elliptic to lanceolate leaflets, dark green above, blue-green beneath. **FLOWER** White, in large flat clusters. **FRUIT** Orange-red, round pome.

LEAVES AND FLOWERS

pointed tips

RIPE FRUIT

Sorbus domestica
Whitty Pear

HEIGHT up to 20m (65ft)
TYPE Deciduous
OCCURRENCE S. Europe, N. Africa, S.W. Asia

This broadly columnar tree, once grown for its fruit, is now becoming rare. **BARK** Dark brown, scaly. **LEAF** Alternate, pinnate; oblong to lanceolate leaflets, smooth above, hairy beneath. **FLOWER** White, in large clusters. **FRUIT** Yellow-green pome.

pyramidal clusters

berry-like pome

FRUIT WITH LEAVES

FLOWERS

Sorbus torminalis
Wild Service Tree

HEIGHT up to 25m (80ft)
TYPE Deciduous
OCCURRENCE Europe, N. Africa, S.W. Asia

The wood, used in carpentry, of this broadly columnar tree is quite dense due to its slow-growing nature. **BARK** Dark brown, scaly. **LEAF** Alternate, deeply lobed at base. **FLOWER** White, in flattened clusters. **FRUIT** Small, brown, rounded pome.

open flower clusters

cracking in scaly plates

LEAVES AND FLOWERS triangular-ovate lobes

BARK

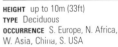

Hovenia dulcis
Raisin Tree

HEIGHT up to 10m (33ft)
TYPE Deciduous
OCCURRENCE China, Japan, Korea

The fruit stalks of this tree are edible while the fruit itself is not. **BARK** Smooth, grey when young, paler and furrowing with age. **LEAF** Alternate, toothed, long-stalked. **FLOWER** Cream to greenish white, small. **FRUIT** Purple-black, fleshy drupe.

oval crown

Ziziphus jujuba
Chinese Date

HEIGHT up to 10m (33ft)
TYPE Deciduous
OCCURRENCE S. Europe, N. Africa, W. Asia, China, S. USA

This tree has been cultivated in China for more than 4,000 years. It has a broad crown and drooping branches. The sweet fruit can be dried or candied. **BARK** Grey to dull black, rough. **LEAF** Alternate, smooth or slightly hairy on the veins below. **FLOWER** Yellowish green, small, in axillary cymes. **FRUIT** Purple-red, egg-shaped, fleshy drupe.

irregularly cracked

BARK

finely toothed margins

3 main veins

LEAVES

Ziziphus lotus

Lotus

HEIGHT up to 2m (7ft)
TYPE Deciduous
OCCURRENCE S. Europe, N. Africa

A sprawling shrubby tree, the Lotus has zig-zag branches that are armed with spines. It is well adapted to drought and hot climates. It is thought to be the source of the famous sweet fruit from which the ancient lotus-eaters of North Africa took their name. It was believed that once the fruit was eaten or liqueur made from it was consumed, travellers gave up all desire to return to their native lands. The fruit, which is rich in vitamins and in sugar, is eaten fresh, pickled or dried, or made into confectionery. Its mealy flesh can also be made into a fermented drink. In the Arabian Peninsula, a kind of bread is made from the fruit, which is dried and then pounded in a wooden mortar to separate the stones. The meal is mixed with water and formed into cakes which resemble sweet gingerbread. The common name of this tree should not be confused with different types of water lilies. **BARK** Pale ash grey. **LEAF** Alternate, ovate to oblong, smooth, with slightly toothed margins and three lateral veins. **FLOWER** Small, with yellow petals, in axillary clusters. **FRUIT** Yellow to reddish brown, rounded drupe, with sweet, edible flesh.

stalkless leaves

LEAVES

Trema micrantha

Guacimilla

HEIGHT 2.5–10m (8–33ft)
TYPE Evergreen
OCCURRENCE USA (Florida), Mexico, West Indies, Central and South America

This fast-growing species produces soft wood used to make tea-chests and matchsticks. **BARK** Dark or grey-brown, shallowly furrowed. **LEAF** In flat sprays, ovate, toothed, pale green above, white-hairy beneath. **FLOWER** Petalless, greenish white calyx, in clusters. **FRUIT** Spherical orange drupe.

alternate leaves

FOLIAGE

Ulmus americana

White Elm

HEIGHT 30–36m (100–120ft)
TYPE Deciduous
OCCURRENCE E. USA, S.E. Canada

This tree's wood, as with other elms, is hard to split and was used for wheel hubs. Native Americans used a decoction of the bark medicinally. **BARK** Ash grey, deeply fissured, with scaly ridges.

LEAF

doubly toothed margins

LEAF Alternate, ovate-oblong to elliptic, downy beneath.
FLOWER Reddish, tiny, petalless, in axillary clusters on long, drooping stalks.
FRUIT Nutlet, notched at top, with hairy margin.

slender zig-zag twigs

red anthers

FLOWERING SHOOT

Ulmus glabra

Wych Elm

HEIGHT up to 40m (130ft)
TYPE Deciduous
OCCURRENCE N. and C. Europe, W. Asia

The Wych Elm has a broad crown and short trunk. Its wood is very durable in wet conditions and was popular for troughs, cribs, and coffins. It is still used for the construction of breakwaters for coastal defences and harbours. **BARK** Grey, smooth. **LEAF** Alternate, elliptic to oblong-obovate, coarse and uneven at bases, double-toothed margins, dark green and roughly hairy above, usually downy beneath.
FLOWER Tiny, with reddish anthers, petalless, in dense, axillary clusters. **FRUIT** Smooth nutlet surrounded by a membranous wing.

prominent veins **LEAF**

FLOWER CLUSTERS

Ulmus procera

English Elm

HEIGHT up to 30m (100ft)
TYPE Deciduous
OCCURRENCE W. Europe

Regarded by some as a variety of *Ulmus minor* – *Ulmus minor* var. *vulgaris* – the English Elm was probably introduced into Britain by the Romans, who used this tree to train grapevines. It has a broad, columnar habit, strong branches, and shoots that can become corky when the tree is a few years old. This elm reproduces by means of suckers that grow extensively around its base.

DUTCH ELM DISEASE

Dutch elm disease, which was first identified in the Netherlands, is a yeast-like fungus that is spread by elm bark beetles. It was first recorded in Britain in 1927, but the devastating infection that killed 12 million English Elm trees in the 1970s was the result of an aggressive form of the disease that came from America.

ELM BARK BEETLE

flowers open on bare shoots   **FLOWER CLUSTERS**

LEAVES

double-toothed margin

BARK Grey-brown, smooth when young, becoming fissured with age.
LEAF Alternate, very variable in shape, elliptic to obovate, with an unequal base; dark green and rough to the touch above, hairy beneath.
FLOWER Reddish, petalless, in dense clusters. **FRUIT** Nutlet, slightly notched, smooth, surrounded by a narrow membranous wing. Nearly all the seeds are infertile.

Ulmus pumila
Siberian Elm

HEIGHT up to 25m (80ft)
TYPE Deciduous
OCCURRENCE N. China, E. Siberia, Korea

Broadly columnar in shape, this fast-growing tree is sometimes planted as a windbreak in North America.
BARK Greyish brown, deeply furrowed.
LEAF Alternate, elliptic to elliptic-lanceolate.
FLOWER Red, very small, petalless, in dense clusters. **FRUIT** Winged, slightly notched nutlet.

LEAVES

sharply toothed margins

Celtis australis
Nettle Tree

HEIGHT up to 25m (80ft)
TYPE Deciduous
OCCURRENCE S. Europe, W. Asia, N Africa

This tree has a broadly columnar to spreading crown. **BARK** Grey, smooth.
LEAF Alternate, narrowly oval, sharply toothed, dark green and scaly above, grey-green and softly hairy beneath.
FLOWER Greenish, tiny, petalless, long-stalked, open singly or in small clusters. **FRUIT** Ovoid purple-brown to blackish drupe.

*to 15cm
(6in) long*

LEAVES

Zelkova serrata
Keaki

HEIGHT up to 30m (100ft)
TYPE Deciduous
OCCURRENCE China, Korea, Japan

The wood of this tree is valued in Japan, and is used to make furniture, lacquer-ware, and trays. A broadly spreading tree, it grows on moist soil near streams.
BARK Smooth, grey, flaking with age.
LEAF Alternate, ovate to ovate-oblong or elliptic, dark green with scattered hairs above, smooth or slightly hairy on the veins beneath, sharply toothed margin.
FLOWER Green, small, petalless; males and females in separate clusters on the same plant. **FRUIT** Small spherical drupe.

*to 12cm
(4¾in) long*

LEAVES

Celtis occidentalis
Beaverwood

HEIGHT up to 40m (130ft)
TYPE Deciduous
OCCURRENCE N.E. and N.C. USA

Although the fruit of this tree is not very fleshy, it was used by Native Americans to flavour food. **BARK** Smooth, dark brown, scaly with age. **LEAF** Alternate, ovate to ovate-oblong, oblique at the base, with three veins, margin sharply toothed near the tip. **FLOWER** Greenish, small, petalless, singly or in small clusters. **FRUIT** Berry-like, orange-red to purple, edible drupe.

*broadly columnar
crown*

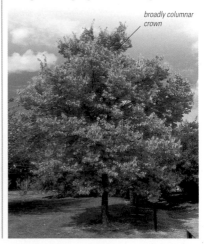

Artocarpus altilis

Breadfruit

HEIGHT up to 30m (100ft)
TYPE Evergreen/Deciduous
OCCURRENCE New Guinea, Pacific Islands

Widely cultivated for its edible fruit, the Breadfruit tree has a straight trunk and a wide crown with large, spreading branches. **BARK** Grey, smooth; exudes sticky white latex. **LEAF** Alternate, large, with 5–11 lobes, pointed tips, glossy bright green above, stiff hairs beneath, with prominent yellowish nerves; stipules are large and conical, leaving scars encircling the stem at the nodes when they fall off. **FLOWER** Males and females borne on the same tree, inconspicuous, grouped in fleshy inflorescences; males: yellowish brown, densely set on a drooping, cylindrical to club-shaped spike; females: upright, in a rounded to oval prickly head which develops into a compound fruit.

warty surface

FRUIT

yellow-green fruit

FOLIAGE leaves in spirals

FRUIT Spherical to oblong syncarp, often with a warty or spiny surface, 10–30cm (4–12in) wide, borne singly or in clusters of two or three at the ends of branches; white, starchy when unripe, usually fragrant when ripe, few seeds, sometimes seedless.

MALE FLOWER cylindrical spike

STARCH STAPLE

This food pounder from Tahiti, known as a *poi,* was used to grind breadfruit pulp. Captain James Cook wrote of this process in his journal: "Of breadfruit they make two or three dishes by beating it with a stone pestle till it makes a paste, mixing water or cocoa nut liquor or both with it, adding ripe plantains..."

POUNDER

Artocarpus heterophyllus

Jak

HEIGHT 10–20m (33–65ft)
TYPE Evergreen
OCCURRENCE S.E. Asia, known only in cultivation

waxy surface

unripe fruit

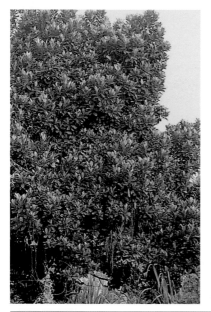

LEAVES AND FRUIT

The fruit of this tree is the largest tree-borne fruit in the world. It can be eaten fresh, dried as confectionery, or canned. The pulp is used to flavour beverages and ice cream. The seeds can be roasted and used as table nuts. **BARK** Blackish brown, thick; exudes white latex. **LEAF** Alternate, elliptic to obovate. **FLOWER** Males and females borne on the same tree; males: on new wood among the leaves, small, ellipsoidal, and covered with pollen when mature; females: larger than the males, borne on short stalks on the stem and branches. **FRUIT** Yellowish brown syncarp, up to 50kg (110lb) in weight, covered with conical warts, waxy, golden yellow, aromatic pulp; 30–500 oval seeds, surrounded by a thick, gelatinous jacket.

green coloration

YOUNG BARK

Antiaris toxicaria

Upas Tree

HEIGHT up to 45m (150ft)
TYPE Evergreen
OCCURRENCE India to S. China, Malaysia, Africa

The Upas Tree has a conical crown and its trunk is sometimes buttressed. The latex is toxic and contains cardiac glycosides, which can cause heart failure. It has been widely used by some tribal peoples in north India and Borneo to poison arrowheads. **BARK** Yellowish to greyish white, smooth, usually with lenticels; exudes creamy white, watery latex; it has a fibrous inner bark. **LEAF** Alternate, oblong-elliptic to obovate, hairy, sometimes toothed. **FLOWER** Males and females on the same tree; males: fleshy, green, with rounded heads; females: solitary in a pear-shaped receptacle. **FRUIT** Purple-red pear-shaped drupe, ripening to black, immersed in a fleshy receptacle.

BARK

Broussonetia papyrifera

Paper Mulberry

HEIGHT 10–20m (33–65ft)
TYPE Deciduous
OCCURRENCE S.E. Asia

FRUIT

red ripening
fruit

The name "Paper Mulberry" comes from the fine fibre that this tree yields from its inner bark, which is used to make paper and Polynesian tapa cloth (used for ceremonial purposes, clothing, and bedding). The tree has a broadly spreading habit and bristly shoots.
BARK Dark grey-brown, smooth; exudes white latex. **LEAF** Alternate, ovate to elliptic-ovate, purplish at first, turning matt green; hairy and scaly above, densely hairy beneath, unlobed or with 3–5 lobes on young trees, with scalloped to toothed margins. **FLOWER** Males and females on separate trees; males: white, in drooping, cylindrical catkins; females: green, in dense, spherical heads. **FRUIT** Spherical syncarp in clusters, the fleshy part turning orange-red.

WASHI AND TAPA

In China, bark fibres of the Paper Mulberry were used to make paper and bark cloth from 105CE, and continues to be used in the making of some lampshades. By the 6th century, classic washi paper-making had reached Japan. Early Polynesian voyagers took the tree and the skills of making bark-cloth with them to the Pacific, and it is here that tapa cloth-making reached its highest art.

PAPER-MAKING

LEAVES AND FLOWERS

leaf to 20cm
(8in) long

female flowers
with purple
stigmas

LEAVES

Ficus benghalensis

Banyan

HEIGHT up to 25m (80ft)
TYPE Evergreen
OCCURRENCE India

This spreading tree is a strangling fig, with massive pillar roots that have grown downward from another tree. In this species, the branches root themselves (a process known as layering), over a large area. It is because of this characteristic and its longevity that the Banyan is a symbol of immortality and an integral part of the myths and legends of India. It is also the national tree of India. The English name comes from "banians", the Hindu merchants who often set up markets in the shade of the tree.
BARK Pale brown to grey, smooth; exudes white latex. **LEAF** Alternate, ovate, with heart-shaped base, smooth and leathery, untoothed. **FLOWER** Males and females on the same tree; tiny, enclosed in a fig receptacle.
FRUIT Fig-like; small, round, rose-red.

*fruit to 1.5cm
(½in) wide*

RIPE FRUIT

TRUNK

LEAVES

*leaf 12.5–25cm
(5–10in) long*

THE LARGEST BANYAN TREE

Beginning life as a seedling in the crown of a date palm in 1782, this Banyan tree in the Indian Botanical Gardens at Howrah, Kolkata (Calcutta), is now reputed to be the world's largest, covering some 1.6 hectares (4 acres), appearing like a small forest in itself.

Ficus benjamina

Weeping Fig

HEIGHT up to 20m (65ft)
TYPE Evergreen
OCCURRENCE India to S. China,
S.E. Asia, N. Australia, Pacific Islands

A strangling fig that often grows into a large spreading tree, the Weeping Fig usually has many hanging aerial roots, some of which develop into independent trunks. While it remains small as a houseplant, in the wild it develops a dense, spreading crown. There are several ornamental cultivars and it is popular for bonsai. **BARK** Pale brown to greyish white; exudes white latex. **LEAF** Alternate, ovate to elliptic, smooth and leathery. **FLOWER** Tiny, enclosed in a fig receptacle; males near the opening, females beneath. **FRUIT** Round, stalkless fig, red with white dots.

leaf to 13cm (5in) long

red fruit

LEAF AND FRUIT

Ficus carica

Common Fig

HEIGHT up to 10m (33ft)
TYPE Deciduous
OCCURRENCE W. Asia, introduced in Mediterranean region

This tree has been cultivated for thousands of years for its edible fruit. Its remnants have been found at Neolithic sites dating back to 5000BCE. The Arab expansion in the 6th–8th centuries brought new and better cultivars to the Mediterranean region. Today, there are about 700 known cultivars. **BARK** Greyish brown, smooth and porous. **LEAF** Alternate, ovate to round with heart-shaped base, 3–5 deep lobes, toothed or wavy margins, rough above, softly hairy beneath. **FLOWER** Tiny, fleshy, numerous, enclosed in a hollow fig receptacle; males on the inner walls near the small opening at the top, females beneath. **FRUIT** Reddish purple, pear-shaped to globose fig.

divided into deep lobes

long stalk

LEAF

Ficus elastica

Indian Rubber Tree

HEIGHT 20–30m (65–100ft)
TYPE Evergreen
OCCURRENCE S. and S.E. Asia

Often grown as a houseplant, this strangling fig can attain an impressive size in the wild. It has numerous, slender aerial roots on its trunk and main branches. It is widely planted as an ornamental and street tree. There are several cultivars, including ones with variegated leaves. **BARK** Pale grey, smooth. **LEAF** Alternate, smooth and leathery, glossy dark green, with pink to purplish stipules. **FLOWER** Tiny, enclosed in a fig receptacle; males near the opening, females beneath. **FRUIT** Oblong, stalkless fig, turning yellow when ripe.

variegated leaves

HOUSEPLANT FOLIAGE

Ficus macrophylla

Moreton Bay Fig

HEIGHT 15–55m (50–180ft)
TYPE Evergreen
OCCURRENCE E. Australia

One of Australia's largest figs, this massive strangler has a deeply buttressed trunk. When mature, its crown can be up to 50m (165ft) wide, sometimes supported by prop roots. **BARK** Grey-brown, smooth; exudes white latex. **LEAF** Alternate, dark green above, golden brown beneath. **FLOWER** Tiny, enclosed in a fig receptacle; males near the opening, females beneath. **FRUIT** Globose fig, purple when ripe.

ovate to elliptic leaves

white dots on ripe fig

LEAVES AND FIGS

MORETON BAY FIG
The enormous buttress roots of this fig species (*Ficus macrophylla*) make it suitable only for parks and large open spaces. The scale of the root system is matched by the width of its spreading crown. The examples seen here are located in Hawaii.

Ficus religiosa

Bo-tree

HEIGHT 15–35m (50–115ft)
TYPE Deciduous
OCCURRENCE C. and E. India

Also known as Bodhi Tree or Pipal, this tree has a broad crown and a fluted or ribbed trunk. It is said to be the tree under which the Buddha meditated for six years and achieved enlightenment. The daughter of the Indian king Ashoka, *long, pointed tip* took a shoot of the Buddha's tree to Sri Lanka in the 3rd century BCE. It was planted at the Mahavihara monastery where it still flourishes today. **BARK** Grey, smooth, or with shallow longitudinal fissures. **LEAF** Alternate, ovate, with slightly wavy margins. **FLOWER** Red, minute; males and females on the same tree, enclosed in a fig receptacle. **FRUIT** Fig; greenish yellow, turning red, rounded and flat-topped, stalkless, in pairs.

LEAVES

broad crown

Ficus sycomorus

Sycomore Fig

HEIGHT 8–30m (26–100ft)
TYPE Evergreen
OCCURRENCE Tropical Africa, Arabian Peninsula

In its native habitat, the Sycomore Fig is found primarily in savanna areas along riverbanks, where the soil remains humid even during the hot and dry summer. Cultivated today in Egypt, Israel, and Syria, it was introduced to Egypt during the First Dynasty (3000BCE). In the absence of its pollinators, tiny insects called the chalcidoid wasps, the Egyptians worked out a way to cause the fruit to develop without fertilization. The wood of the tree was frequently used for the construction of coffins (sarcophagi). **BARK** Greenish yellow to creamy brown, smooth. **LEAF** Alternate, ovate to elliptic, rough to the touch, heart-shaped base, slightly wavy margin. **FLOWER** Males and females borne on the same tree, enclosed in a fig receptacle, minute; males near the opening of the fig, females below. **FRUIT** Green fig, turning yellowish to reddish when ripe.

spreading crown

TRUNK | short and buttressed

Ficus sumatrana

Strangler Fig

HEIGHT up to 40m (130ft)
TYPE Evergreen
OCCURRENCE S.E. Asia

Like its many relatives, this rainforest fig is a parasite that uses other trees for support. It begins life high in the forest canopy, as a seed dispersed by birds. Initially, the young fig takes root among mosses and dead leaves, but as it grows, it sends out long roots which snake their way to the ground. Over a period of years, these roots surround the host tree's trunk, preventing further growth. Eventually, the host tree dies and rots away, leaving the fig standing in its place. **BARK** Pale brown to greyish white. **LEAF** Alternate, elliptic to ovate-oblong. **FLOWER** Males and females in a fig receptacle; males near the opening, females beneath. **FRUIT** Yellowish to orange-red fig, with minute hairs.

aerial root

smooth texture

STRANGLER CLASPING HOST

Maclura pomifera

Osage Orange

HEIGHT up to 20m (65ft)
TYPE Deciduous
OCCURRENCE S. and C. USA

Often used as a hedge plant outside its native habitat, this tree was cultivated extensively by Native Americans for its roots and durable wood, which was used for making weapons and a yellow dye. It has a short trunk and an irregular to rounded crown. **BARK** Orange-brown, scaly ridges with irregular furrows, with milky sap. **LEAF** Alternate, ovate to oblong-lanceolate, smooth surface, glossy dark green above, turning yellow in autumn. **FLOWER** Males and females on separate trees, both small and inconspicuous; males: in short, terminal racemes; females: in flowerheads. **FRUIT** Cluster of green to orange syncarps.

untoothed margins

clusters up to 1cm (³/₈in) long

yellow-green flowers

to 10cm (4in) wide

pointed tip

LEAVES   **FRUIT**   **FLOWERS**

Milicia excelsa

Iroko

HEIGHT up to 50m (165ft)
TYPE Deciduous
OCCURRENCE Tropical Africa

Also known as the African Teak, the Iroko has a straight and cylindrical trunk, usually with short buttresses. It is one of the most important timber trees of Africa, often used as a teak substitute. East Africa once was a major source but the tree has been logged out in the region. West Africa, despite its over-exploitation, remains an important supplier. The timber is used mainly for construction. **BARK** Grey to brown-black, rough; exudes white latex. **LEAF** Alternate, elliptic, 10–20cm (4–8in) long. **FLOWER** Males and females on separate trees; males: white, borne on slender, pendent, catkin-like spikes; females: greenish, in short cylindrical spikes. **FRUIT** Wrinkled, fleshy, caterpillar-like syncarp, green, 5–7.5cm (2–3in) long, 2.5cm (1in) thick.

brown to dark-brown wood

IROKO WOOD

Morus alba

White Mulberry

HEIGHT up to 14m (45ft)
TYPE Deciduous
OCCURRENCE Native to C. and N. China, cultivated in Asia, Europe, USA

In about 550CE two monks smuggled eggs and seeds of the White Mulberry, the food-plant of silkworms, out of China. This led to the start of the European silk industry, breaking the monopoly of the "Silk Road" trade from Asia. Usually the tree has a spreading round crown, but there are cultivars with pyramidal and pendulous forms, large or cut-leaved forms, and several non-fruiting varieties used for landscaping. **BARK** Pale brown to grey, smooth; later develops scaly ridges.

LEAF Alternate, toothed, ovate to rounded, smooth above, hairy below. **FLOWER** Small, green; males: in pendent, spike-like inflorescences; females: in compact clusters. **FRUIT** In clusters, stalked, fleshy, edible syncarps, purple-red when ripe.

leaf to 20cm (8in) long

fruit to 2.5cm (1in) long

LEAVES AND FRUIT

Morus nigra

Black Mulberry

HEIGHT up to 10m (33ft)
TYPE Deciduous
OCCURRENCE Native to W. Iran, cultivated in China, W. Asia, Europe

Since antiquity, this tree has been popular in southern Europe for its edible fruit. **BARK** Orange-brown, ridged, fissured. **LEAF** Alternate, broadly ovate, roughly hairy above, smooth beneath. **FLOWER** Small, green; males in pendent racemes; females in clusters. **FRUIT** Fleshy syncarps in clusters, purple-red when ripe.

spreading crown

fruit to 2.5 cm (1in) long

toothed leaf margin

LEAVES AND FRUIT

Cecropia peltata

Trumpet Tree

HEIGHT up to 20m (65ft)
TYPE Evergreen/Deciduous
OCCURRENCE C. and N. South America, West Indies, naturalized in parts of Africa

In the rainforests, Aztec ants inhabit the hollow stems of this tree. **BARK** Grey-brown, smooth, ringed. **LEAF** Alternate, rounded, dark green, rough above, dense white hairs beneath. **FLOWER** Yellowish green, small, in drooping catkin-like spikes. **FRUIT** Long, thin, pencil-like pod, fleshy.

lobed leaves   **BRANCHES**

Musanga cecropioides

Umbrella Tree

HEIGHT up to 20m (65ft)
TYPE Semi-evergreen
OCCURRENCE Africa (Guinea to Zaire, Angola, and eastwards to Uganda)

Fast-growing and invasive, the Umbrella Tree has a straight trunk, conspicuous roots, and a spreading crown. Its light wood is used to make floats and rafts. **BARK** Grey to brownish green, smooth with large lenticels. **LEAF** Alternate, 12–15 oblanceolate leaflets radiating from stalk tip, greyish white felt-like hair below. **FLOWER** Axillary, males in branched clusters; females in compact heads on long stalks. **FRUIT** Yellowish green, oval, succulent.

LEAVES

Dendrocnide excelsa

Gympie Stinger

HEIGHT 10–40m (33–130ft)
TYPE Deciduous
OCCURRENCE E. Australia (New South Wales and Queensland)

The stinging hairs on the leaves of this tree contain a virulent poison. **BARK** Yellowish grey, ringed. **LEAF** Alternate, with toothed margins. **FLOWER** Yellowish green, small. **FRUIT** Small achene, on a fleshy stalk.

LEAVES

heart-shaped base

Dendrosicyos socotranus

Cucumber Tree

HEIGHT up to 6m (20ft)
TYPE Deciduous
OCCURRENCE Yemen (Socotra Island)

Sometimes cultivated as a succulent, this tree is found among coastal vegetation. **BARK** Pallid dirty white. **LEAF** Alternate, ovate to round, five-lobed, tendrils absent. **FLOWER** Yellow, borne on the same plant in axillary clusters. **FRUIT** Orange, cylindrical berry with a beaked tip.

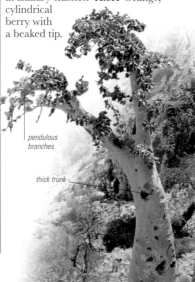

pendulous branches

thick trunk

Nothofagus cunninghamii
Myrtle Beech

HEIGHT up to 30m (100ft)
TYPE Evergreen
OCCURRENCE Australia (Victoria, Tasmania)

A large rainforest tree, this species can also grow as a shrub at high altitudes. **BARK** Dark, scaly. **LEAF** Alternate, small, ovate, bluntly toothed margin, base tapered to blunt. **FLOWER** Males and females in groups of 1–4. **FRUIT** Husk (cupule), usually containing three nuts.

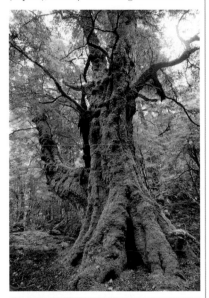

Nothofagus antarctica
Antarctic Beech

HEIGHT up to 35m (115ft)
TYPE Deciduous
OCCURRENCE South America (Chile)

The Antarctic Beech was introduced into cultivation in 1830. **BARK** Grey, scaly. **LEAF** Alternate, ovate, often heart-shaped, sometimes shallowly lobed. **FLOWER** Males and females in groups of 1–4. **FRUIT** Husk (cupule) with three nuts.

fruit husk

wavy leaf margin

BRANCHLET WITH FRUIT

Nothofagus solanderi
Black Beech

HEIGHT up to 25m (80ft)
TYPE Evergreen
OCCURRENCE New Zealand

The timber of this tree is used for general construction. **BARK** Black, rough, and furrowed. **LEAF** Alternate, elliptic-oblong, dark green, smooth above, greyish white hairs below. **FLOWER** Males and females in groups of 1–4. **FRUIT** Husk (cupule), containing 2–3 nuts.

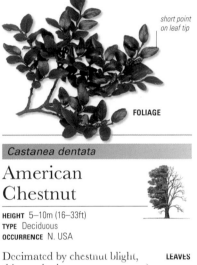

short point on leaf tip

FOLIAGE

Castanea dentata
American Chestnut

HEIGHT 5–10m (16–33ft)
TYPE Deciduous
OCCURRENCE N. USA

Decimated by chestnut blight, this species is now rare in the wild. **BARK** Dark greyish brown, scaly. **LEAF** Alternate. **FLOWER** Males in long spikes; females on spikes or at the base. **FRUIT** Spiny husk, with 2–3 nuts.

LEAVES

lanceolate-oblong

FRUIT

LEAVES

coarse, bristly teeth

Castanea sativa

Sweet Chestnut

HEIGHT up to 30m (100ft)
TYPE Deciduous
OCCURRENCE S.E. Europe,
naturalized elsewhere

The Sweet Chestnut has been cultivated for 3,000 years. In some parts of Europe, the fruit formed an important food source and item of exchange as it could be ground into flour. The expansion of the tanning industry, which uses its bark, coincided with the "ink disease" that infected European trees in the late 19th century. This led to a rapid reduction of the chestnut forests. Alcohol can be made from the fruit – chestnut beer is still produced in Corsica. Today, China and Korea supply 55 per cent of the annual production of chestnuts. **BARK** Grey, smooth, becoming longitudinally fissured and spirally twisted. **LEAF** Alternate, oblong-lanceolate, dull dark green above, paler and hairy below. **FLOWER** Small, creamy yellow, in long pendulous spike-like catkins. **FRUIT** Spiny husk, enclosing 2–3 nuts.

green husks

FRUIT

male and female flowers
clustered on same spike

FLOWERS

FAVOURED NUTS

Before potatoes were introduced, chestnuts were the basic food of the poor in much of southern Europe. Today, throughout most of Europe, cultivated chestnuts are a delicacy. Roasted chestnuts are a wintertime favourite on both sides of the Atlantic.

Castanea pumila

Chinquapin

HEIGHT up to 15m (50ft)
TYPE Deciduous
OCCURRENCE S.E. USA

The Chinquapin is often shrubby and forms dense thickets. **BARK** Reddish brown, plate-like scales. **LEAF** Alternate, elliptic-oblong, sharply toothed, grey hairs below. **FLOWER** Yellowish; males in erect spikes; females solitary, short-stalked. **FRUIT** Nut surrounded by a spiny husk.

FLOWERING SHOOT

yellow-green leaf

flowers in catkins

Chrysolepis chrysophylla

Golden Chestnut

HEIGHT 15–30m (50–100ft)
TYPE Evergreen
OCCURRENCE S.W. USA

This broadly conical tree is often used as an ornamental. **BARK** Dark red-brown, with scales and ridges. **LEAF** Alternate, leathery, lanceolate, dark green above, golden yellow below. **FLOWER** Creamy white; male catkins on erect spikes; female stalkless. **FRUIT** Nutlets, about 1–3, surrounded by a spiny husk, which ripens in two years.

male flower

LEAVES, FLOWERS, AND FRUIT

Fagus crenata

Japanese Beech

HEIGHT up to 30m (100ft)
TYPE Deciduous
OCCURRENCE Japan

The Japanese Beech is considered to be the finest Beech species for bonsai because of its small, neat foliage and thin, delicate twigs. Like the European Beech, the bark turns white with age. **BARK** Grey, smooth. **LEAF** Alternate, ovate to elliptic, with wavy margins. **FLOWER** Males in catkins; females inconspicuous in leaf axils. **FRUIT** Husk with long bristles, splitting into four to reveal the nut.

FOLIAGE

glossy green leaves

Fagus grandifolia

American Beech

HEIGHT 20–24m (70–80ft)
TYPE Deciduous
OCCURRENCE N.E. USA

The American Beech produces abundant fruit every 3–5 years. **BARK** Blue-grey, smooth. **LEAF** Alternate, ovate-oblong, 9–14 lateral veins, dark green, with coarsely toothed margin. **FLOWER** Males in drooping clusters; tiny females in the leaf axils. **FRUIT** Nut, enclosed by husk.

AUTUMN FOLIAGE

female flower

Fagus sylvatica

Common Beech

HEIGHT up to 30m (100ft)
TYPE Deciduous
OCCURRENCE Europe, excluding the north

A slow-growing tree with a majestic, spreading crown, the Common Beech casts a deep shade when it is in full leaf. Its fine-grained timber is used for furniture and parquet floors. There are many cultivars – pendulous, columnar, and cut-leaved – which may have green, purple, or variegated leaves. **BARK** Smooth, blue-grey. **LEAF** Alternate, ovate to elliptic, with silky hairs, margins with rounded teeth, 5–9 lateral veins.

FRUIT

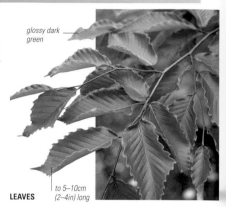

glossy dark green

LEAVES to 5–10cm (2–4in) long

FLOWER Yellow males in pendulous clusters; green females, inconspicuous, in leaf axils. **FRUIT** Woody husk that has long, straight bristles and splits into four to reveal one or two edible nuts.

Quercus alba

White Oak

HEIGHT 25–30m (80–100ft)
TYPE Deciduous
OCCURRENCE N.E. North America

The wood of the White Oak is used for furniture, flooring, and veneers. **BARK** Pale grey, divided into narrow, flat scales. **LEAF** Alternate, oblong to ovate lobes, hairy when young. **FLOWER** Yellow-green males in catkins; bright red, unstalked females. **FRUIT** Rounded acorn that matures in the first season.

untoothed lobes

scaly cup

ACORN **LEAVES**

Quercus coccinea

Scarlet Oak

HEIGHT up to 25m (80ft)
TYPE Deciduous
OCCURRENCE E. North America

This widespread American oak gets its name from its spectacular autumn colours. **BARK** Pale grey-brown with irregular ridges. **LEAF** Alternate, elliptic, dark green above, triangular-toothed lobes. **FLOWER** Males in slender catkins; females on short hairy stalks. **FRUIT** Acorn enclosed up to one-half in a glossy cup.

AUTUMN LEAVES

Quercus cerris

Turkey Oak

HEIGHT up to 35m (115ft)
TYPE Deciduous
OCCURRENCE C. and S. Europe

Long, frilly, thread-like stipules, which surround the buds, characterize this ornamental oak. **BARK** Dark brown, furrowed. **LEAF** Alternate, oval or oblong, with 4–9 pairs of lobes. **FLOWER** Males in numerous, yellow-green catkins; females unstalked. **FRUIT** Acorn, half enclosed in a cup.

variable leaf lobing

LEAVES

Quercus ilex

Holm Oak

HEIGHT 20–27m (65–90ft)
TYPE Evergreen
OCCURRENCE S. Europe

This spreading, extremely hardy tree is considered an excellent species for cultivation. **BARK** Grey to blackish, scaly, divided into small squares. **LEAF** Alternate, ovate to lanceolate, glossy dark green above, whitish down beneath that turns grey with age. **FLOWER** Males in catkins; females on short, downy stalks. **FRUIT** Acorn enclosed in a scaly cup.

rounded crown

BEECH

The graceful Beech (*Fagus sylvatica*) is sometimes named "the Lady of the Woods". Beech woods are a rich habitat for many animals who feed on beech nuts, including squirrels and wild boar. This beech forest is located in Hertfordshire, England.

Quercus imbricaria

Shingle Oak

HEIGHT 20–30m (65–100ft)
TYPE Deciduous
OCCURRENCE W. to N.E. USA

Early settlers in North America used the wood of this tree to make shingles, which explains its common name. **BARK** Grey-brown, ridged, with brownish red scales. **LEAF** Alternate, oblong-lanceolate to obovate, glossy green above, with brown hairs beneath. **FLOWER** Males in golden yellow catkins; females on short, stout stalks. **FRUIT** Acorn, one-third to one-half covered by cup.

ACORN

overlapping red brown scales

LEAVES

Quercus macrolepis

Valonia Oak

HEIGHT up to 15m (50ft)
TYPE Semi-deciduous
OCCURRENCE S. Europe to W. Asia

The acorn cups of this tree have a high content of tannin and were formerly in high demand, with Turkey being the leading exporter. **BARK** Dark, fissured. **LEAF** Alternate, elliptic to oblong, with 3–7 pairs of triangular, bristle-tipped lobes; smooth above, densely woolly beneath. **FLOWER** Males in catkins; females on short stalks. **FRUIT** Acorns, up to 5cm (2in) wide, with elongated scales.

Quercus pubescens

Downy Oak

HEIGHT 15–20m (50–65ft)
TYPE Deciduous
OCCURRENCE S. Europe, W. Asia

up to 10cm (4in) long

shallow lobes

This oak has a broadly spreading crown and hairy young shoots. **BARK** Grey-brown, deeply furrowed. **LEAF** Alternate, obovate, deeply cut into 4–8 pairs of lobes, dark grey-green above, paler grey-green, with velvety hairs beneath. **FLOWER** Males in drooping catkins; females inconspicuous, on short stalks. **FRUIT** Ovoid acorn, up to 4cm (1½in) long, one-third to one-half enclosed in a cup covered with dense, overlapping, downy scales; ripens in the tree's first year.

LEAVES

Quercus petraea

Sessile Oak

HEIGHT 25–40m (80–130ft)
TYPE Deciduous
OCCURRENCE Europe, W. Asia

Also called Durmast Oak, this tree is often found on light, poor soils. **BARK** Fissured, grey-brown. **LEAF** Alternate, obovate, smooth beneath, with an acute base, distinctly stalked. **FLOWER** Males in catkins; females on short stalks. **FRUIT** Ovoid acorns, in stalkless clusters.

rounded lobes

LEAVES

Quercus robur

English Oak

HEIGHT 25–40m (80–130ft)
TYPE Deciduous
OCCURRENCE Europe, W. Asia, N. Africa

Also known as Pedunculate Oak, this tree has a spreading habit and smooth shoots. Oak forests were once a valuable resource for industrial and naval activities. Its bark is also used in the tanning industry. A famous heritage tree in Britain is "The Major" in Sherwood Forest, which is estimated to be 800 years old; legend has it that Robin Hood hid in this tree. **BARK** Greyish brown, vertically ridged. **LEAF** Alternate, obovate, with 5 9 lobes, dark green above, blue-green beneath. **FLOWER** Males in drooping catkins; females inconspicuous, on short stalks. **FRUIT** Ovoid, long-stalked acorns, one-third to one-half enclosed in a cup, initially green, ripening to brown in first year.

lobed leaves

young acorn

UNRIPE ACORNS

fissured surface

overlapping scales on cup

BARK

MATURE ACORN

SHIP-BUILDING

From Viking longboats to Lord Nelson's flagship, HMS Victory, oak has a long history in ship-building. Some 6,000 oak trees were used to build the HMS Victory. Trees planted in 1802 are now being used to repair the same ship.

LONGBOAT

SESSILE OAK
Quercus petraea is the species from which French oak wine barrels are usually made. These trees can grow up to 40 metres (130ft) tall and may live for up to 1,000 years, although in a woodland setting such as this they may not reach such great stature or age.

Quercus rubra

Red Oak

HEIGHT 18–25m (60–80ft)
TYPE Deciduous
OCCURRENCE E. North America

Often planted as a shade tree, this oak is also grown in avenues for its reddish to yellow-brown autumn foliage. **BARK** Dark brown tinged with red, divided into plates. **LEAF** Alternate, elliptic, matt green. **FLOWER** Males in catkins; females on short stalks. **FRUIT** Large acorns.

bristle-tipped lobes

in shallow cup

LEAF

ACORNS

Quercus velutina

Quercitron

HEIGHT 20–25m (70–80ft)
TYPE Deciduous
OCCURRENCE C. and
N.E. North America

Also known as Black Oak, this tree has a broadly spreading habit. Its bark was formerly used in the tanning industry and to prepare a yellow dye. **BARK** Dark brown to black, with a scaly surface. **LEAF** Alternate, ovate to oblong, 3–4 pairs of triangular-toothed lobes, glossy above, slightly hairy below with tufts of rusty hairs in the vein axils. **FLOWER** Males in slender catkins; females on short, hairy stalks. **FRUIT** Ovoid acorns, enclosed halfway in the cup, maturing in the second year.

large terminal tooth

ridged and furrowed

MATURE BARK

LEAVES

Quercus macrocarpa

Burr Oak

HEIGHT up to 40m (130ft)
TYPE Deciduous
OCCURRENCE E. North America

The acorns of this broadly spreading tree are larger than those of any other North American oak. **BARK** Grey, rough, deeply furrowed. **LEAF** Obovate, deeply cut into round-ended lobes, broader towards the base, glossy green and smooth above, paler and hairy beneath. **FLOWER** Males in yellow, drooping catkins; females inconspicuous, borne separately on the same plant. **FRUIT** Acorn, enclosed in a cup that is rimmed with a fringe of scales.

widely spaced lobes

LEAVES

Quercus suber

Cork Oak

HEIGHT up to 20m (65ft)
TYPE Evergreen
OCCURRENCE W. Mediterranean, especially Portugal

Cork forests form an environmentally friendly ecosystem, rich in wildlife. These broadly spreading trees grow on hills in open woodland. The cork is harvested every 9–12 years. Bottle corks account for 15 per cent of production by weight but 65 per cent of value of a $3 billion industry. Stripping the bark, from which cork is produced, does not damage the living tissue of the plant, which grows a new outer layer within a few years. **BARK** Thick, furrowed, and corky, with prominent ridges. **LEAF** Alternate, ovate to oblong, toothed margins, covered with minute grey felt beneath. **FLOWER** Males: borne in slender catkins; females: inconspicuous, on short downy stalks, borne separately on the same plant. **FRUIT** Acorn, enclosed halfway in the cup, covered by elongated grey-brown scales, matures in the first season.

CORKY OLD WHISTLER

The oldest Cork Oak is the "Whistler" (so called because of the numerous songbirds nesting in its canopy), which was planted in 1783 and last harvested in 2000. Located in the Alentejo region of Portugal, it has been producing cork every nine years since 1820. The average Cork Oak produces enough for 4,000 corks per harvest; the Whistler produces about 100,000 corks.

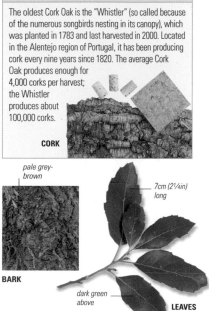

CORK

pale grey-brown

BARK

7cm (2¼in) long

dark green above

LEAVES

Morella cerifera

yellow-green leaves

LEAVES

Wax Myrtle

HEIGHT 6–12m (20–40ft)
TYPE Evergreen
OCCURRENCE S.E. USA

The leaves of this tree are aromatic when crushed. Early European settlers would boil the fruit and skim off the wax, which could then be used to make candles. **BARK** Smooth, pale grey. **LEAF** Alternate, oblanceolate, usually coarsely toothed above centre; dark glands above, bright orange glands beneath. **FLOWER** Males and females on separate trees, both in short, spike-like catkins. **FRUIT** Spherical, pale green drupe.

fruit coated with pale bluish wax

BRANCH WITH FRUIT

Morella faya

Faya

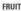

HEIGHT up to 8m (26ft)
TYPE Evergreen
OCCURRENCE Azores, Canary Islands, Madeira Islands, naturalized in Hawaii

Introduced into Hawaii by Portuguese labourers who made wine from the fruit, this tree has since become a serious invasive weed, although it is not invasive in its native habitat. **BARK** Smooth, brownish grey. **LEAF** Alternate, oblanceolate, smooth surface but dotted with tiny glands, margins untoothed or irregularly and bluntly toothed towards the tip. **FLOWER** Males and females on separate trees in short, spike-like catkins. **FRUIT** Fleshy, glistening drupe.

LEAVES AND FRUIT

4–11cm (1½–4¼ in) long

dark red to black drupe

Alnus crispa

Green Alder

HEIGHT 3–8m (10–26ft)
TYPE Deciduous
OCCURRENCE E. North America

The bark of the Green Alder has some astringent qualities and has been used medicinally by Native Americans. The aromatic young leaves are slightly sticky to the touch. **BARK** Reddish to greyish brown, smooth or slightly grooved. **LEAF** Alternate, ovate to broadly elliptic, toothed margins, smooth or slightly hairy beneath. **FLOWER** Males: pale yellowish green, in pendulous catkins; females: red, solitary, and small. **FRUIT** Woody, winged, cone-like.

FRUIT

long stalks

Alnus glutinosa

Alder

HEIGHT up to 25m (80ft)
TYPE Deciduous
OCCURRENCE Europe, W. Asia, N. Africa

Also known as the Black Alder, this water-loving tree is commonly seen along watersides and riverbanks, where it provides both erosion control and ornamental appeal. It has a straight trunk and a narrow crown. Its wood has been used extensively in constructing buildings near water because it does not rot when wet. It was also popular with clog-makers in Britain. Since the Alder grows on relatively infertile soils, it is also used for site reclamation. **BARK** Smooth on young trees, becoming dark greyish black, fissured, and scaly. **LEAF** Alternate, usually obovate, green beneath, with coarsely double-toothed margins; smooth or with tufts of hairs in the vein axils; 5–10 pairs of lateral veins; young leaves and twigs sticky. **FLOWER** Males and females on same tree; males: reddish brown, in drooping catkins; females: red, solitary. **FRUIT** Woody, oval, cone-like.

VENICE ON PILINGS

Built on islands in a lagoon of the Adriatic Sea between the 9th and 16th centuries, most of Venice is supported on pilings. These slender, sharpened poles were made from Alder wood, which is ideal for the job because of its durability in water. The foundations of buildings in Venice consisted of oak wood planks and layers of marble placed over pilings.

LEAVES AND FRUIT

leaf 4–9cm (1½–3½in) long

unripe fruit

male catkins in clusters

FLOWERS

Alnus incana

Grey Alder

HEIGHT up to 20m (65ft)
TYPE Deciduous
OCCURRENCE N. and N.E. Europe, North America, W. Asia

Also called Black Alder, this tree is found on flood plains and in mountain valleys. **BARK** Yellowish grey, smooth. **LEAF** Ovate, alternate, slightly lobed, double-toothed margins. **FLOWER** Borne separately on the same plant; males: reddish, in catkins, females: solitary, red, upright. **FRUIT** Woody, cone-like.

fruit

male catkins

LEAVES, FLOWERS, AND FRUIT

Betula alleghaniensis

Yellow Birch

HEIGHT 25–30m (80–100ft)
TYPE Deciduous
OCCURRENCE C. and E. North America

About 75 per cent of birch lumber comes from the Yellow Birch. **BARK** Silvery yellow-brown, peeling into ribbon-like strips. **LEAF** Alternate, ovate to oblong, double-toothed margins. **FLOWER** Borne on the same tree in catkins; males: yellow, drooping, females: reddish green, upright, cone-like. **FRUIT** Winged nutlets.

peels horizontally

large catkins

BARK

MALE FLOWERS

Betula lenta

American Black Birch

HEIGHT 20–25m (70–80ft)
TYPE Deciduous
OCCURRENCE E. North America

This broadly spreading tree can be found in moist woods or on mountains. **BARK** Fissured into large plates, does not peel. **LEAF** Alternate, sharply toothed margins, smooth or slightly hairy below. **FLOWER** Borne on the same tree, in catkins; males: yellow, drooping, females: green, upright, ovoid. **FRUIT** Winged nutlets borne in an oval, upright, cone-like structure.

pointed tip

LEAVES

reddish brown

BARK

Betula utilis

Himalayan Birch

The word "birch" is thought to have been derived from the Sanskrit word *bhurga*, "tree whose bark is used to write upon". The oldest surviving manuscripts, from Buddhist monasteries, date back 2,000 years. **BARK** Yellowish red-brown, peeling. **LEAF** Alternate, ovate to broadly elliptic, double-toothed margins. **FLOWER** Males and females borne on the same tree in catkins; males: yellow, drooping, females: green, upright. **FRUIT** Winged nutlets borne in an oval, upright, cone-like structure.

HEIGHT 17–35m (55–115ft)
TYPE Deciduous
OCCURRENCE Himalayas

conical to columnar crown

Betulus papyrifera

Paper Birch

HEIGHT up to 30m (100ft)
TYPE Deciduous
OCCURRENCE E. to W. North America

A fast-growing conical tree, the Paper Birch has resinous bark that is impervious to water and was used to make canoes and roofing for wigwams. **BARK** Creamy-white, peeling in thin layers to expose a pinkish orange layer beneath.
LEAF Alternate, margins coarsely double-toothed, dark green above, often hairy on veins beneath. **FLOWER** Borne separately on the same tree, in drooping catkins; males: yellow, females: green. **FRUIT** Winged nutlets.

ovate leaves

numerous horizontal lenticels

green, drooping catkins

LEAVES AND FEMALE CATKINS   **BARK**

Betula pendula

Silver Birch

HEIGHT up to 20m (65ft)
TYPE Deciduous
OCCURRENCE Europe, W. and N. Asia

A short-lived pioneer species, the Silver Birch has a distinctive pendulous habit. The twigs were, and still are, used to make traditional besoms. **BARK** Smooth, pale yellow-brown, becoming white with age and developing dark, rough cracks.
LEAF Alternate, ovate to triangular with coarsely double-toothed margins.
FLOWER Borne in catkins on the same tree; males: yellow, drooping females: green, upright, later pendulous, cylindrical.
FRUIT Winged nutlets borne in catkins.

female catkin

double-toothed margins

LEAVES AND FLOWER

Carpinus betulus

Hornbeam

HEIGHT up to 25m (80ft)
TYPE Deciduous
OCCURRENCE Europe, S.W. Asia

This tree has a fluted trunk and a broadly spreading habit. Often planted as hedging, it is also commonly used as a street tree. Its cultivars are the columnar 'Fastigiata', the pendulous 'Pendula', and 'Purpurea' and 'Variegata', which have purple or variegated leaves. **BARK** Smooth, grey, becoming slightly fissured with age. **LEAF** Alternate, ovate to oblong, double-toothed, 7–15 pairs of lateral veins, dark green above, downy beneath, usually turning yellow in autumn.

FLOWER In pendulous catkins on the same plant; males axillary, females at tips of shoots. **FRUIT** Nutlet at the base of a green, three-lobed bract, which is usually untoothed, with 3–5 veins.

yellow-brown
male catkins

green female
catkins

FLOWERING SHOOT

Carpinus caroliniana

American Hornbeam

HEIGHT up to 12m (40ft)
TYPE Deciduous
OCCURRENCE E. North America, Mexico

Also called the Blue Beech, this tree has a fluted trunk. **BARK** Smooth, pale grey-brown, sometimes with dark horizontal bands. **LEAF** Alternate, ovate to oblong, 7–15 pairs of lateral veins, dark green above, downy on veins below, usually turning orange-red in autumn. **FLOWER** In pendulous catkins on the same plant; males: yellowish, axillary, females: green, at tips of shoots. **FRUIT** Nutlet at the base of a green, three-lobed bract, usually toothed, with 5–7 veins.

double-toothed margin

LEAF

Corylus avellana

Hazel

HEIGHT up to 6m (20ft)
TYPE Deciduous
OCCURRENCE Europe

This shrubby, spreading tree often forms thickets. It has multiple stems and is known for its edible nuts. It has many cultivars, such as 'Contorta', the interesting horticultural corkscrew hazel cultivar, which has markedly twisted branches. There are also three rare cultivars – 'Aurea', a yellow-leaved form, the cut-leaved 'Heterophylla', and the pendulous 'Pendula'. **BARK** Smooth, copper brown, sometimes peeling in thin strips. **LEAF** Alternate, dark green, rounded to broadly obovate, double-toothed. **FLOWER** Males and females on the same plant; males: in long catkins, females: small, bud-like, with red stigmas. **FRUIT** Nut surrounded by a bract-like husk only slightly longer than the nut.

HAZEL COPPICES

The shoots of the Hazel are often coppiced or cut back to encourage thick growth of its branches. They were once used to make hoops for barrels; they are still used to make fencing hurdles, thatching spars, and hedges. The remains were bundled as "faggots" for fuel.

COPPICING

deeply lobed husk

NUTS

to 10cm (4in) long
pale yellow catkins

LEAVES

MALE FLOWERS

Corylus maxima

Filbert

HEIGHT up to 10m (33ft)
TYPE Deciduous
OCCURRENCE S.E. Europe, W. Asia

This often shrub-like tree, usually has several main stems and a spreading habit. It is often grown in orchards (sometimes known as "plats") for its edible cobnuts. **BARK** Grey-brown, smooth, with horizontal lenticels. **LEAF** Alternate, broadly ovate to obovate, double-toothed, dark green, usually turning yellow in autumn. **FLOWER** Males: in long, drooping yellow catkins; females: small, bud-like, with red stigmas. **FRUIT** Softly hairy nut with a notched tip, in a husk.

LEAF

pale brown shell
to 12cm (4¾in) long

RIPE FRUIT

bract-like husk

male catkin to 8cm (3¼in) long

FLOWERS   **UNRIPE FRUIT**

Corylus colurna

Turkish Hazel

HEIGHT up to 25m (80ft)
TYPE Deciduous
OCCURRENCE S.E. Europe, W. Asia

Widely planted as an ornamental in parks and gardens, this hazel is also useful as a street tree. It has a compact and conical head. It rarely sets fruit in northern Europe. **BARK** Dark grey, corky, deeply furrowed. **LEAF** Alternate, ovate to broadly ovate, rarely obovate, double-toothed margins, dark green, usually turning yellow in autumn. **FLOWER** Males and females on the same plant, appearing before the leaves; males: in long, drooping, pale yellow catkins; females: small, bud-like, with red stigmas. **FRUIT** Edible nut surrounded by a bract-like husk, divided almost to the base into linear segments.

FLOWERS

to 15cm (6in) long

male catkin to 10cm (4in) long

LEAVES

Ostrya carpinifolia

Hop Hornbeam

HEIGHT up to 20m (65ft)
TYPE Deciduous
OCCURRENCE S. Europe, W. Asia

The wood of this tree is very hard and tough and has been used for handles, levers, and mallets. **BARK** Grey-brown, smooth when young, becoming vertically fissured and scaly. **LEAF** Alternate, ovate, with double-toothed margins, sparsely hairy on both sides, 12–15 pairs of lateral veins, usually turning yellow in autumn. **FLOWER** Males and females on the same plant in pendulous catkins; males: yellow, axillary; females: green, at tips of shoots, tiny. **FRUIT** Drooping, cone-like structure consisting of a nut within a creamy, bladder-like husk.

FRUIT AND LEAVES

Casuarina equisetifolia

Beefwood

HEIGHT 6–35m (20–115ft)
TYPE Evergreen
OCCURRENCE Myanmar, Malaysia, Indonesia, Philippines, Papua New Guinea, Polynesia, N. and N.E. Australia

STABILIZED SAND DUNES

Beefwood roots contain nitrogen-fixing bacteria, which enable it to flourish in soils that are too poor for other trees. As a result, it can be used to stabilize dunes and to control soil erosion. In exposed areas, it can also be used as windbreaks to protect crops.

Found on coastlines, this tree is sometimes invasive. Its stems resemble horsetails and the wood is an excellent source of fuel and charcoal. **BARK** Grey-brown to black, scaly, becoming fissured. **LEAF** Scale-like, tiny, 4–10 in each whorl, borne on green stems. **FLOWER** Males and females on the same tree; males: in cylindrical spikes at tips of twigs; females: in red-brown heads along branches. **FRUIT** Small, round, cone-like nutlet, with winged seeds.

female flowers

male flowers

FLOWERS

LEAVES

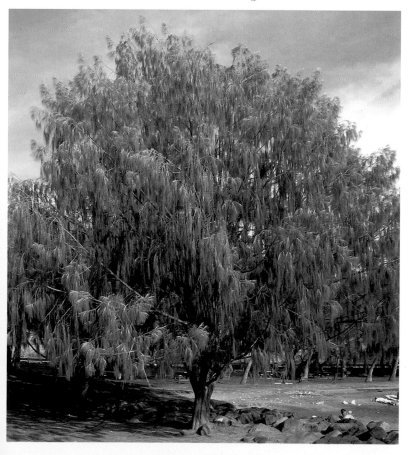

Carya illinoinensis

Pecan

HEIGHT 30–55m (100–180ft)
TYPE Deciduous
OCCURRENCE S. North America

Commercial cultivation of the Pecan tree began by the end of the 19th century. It is now widely grown on plantations in the USA, especially Texas, which has chosen it as its State tree. There are over 500 cultivars. **BARK** Pale grey-brown tinged with red, furrowed and deeply ridged, scaly surface.

slightly curved at tips

green husk

LEAF

FRUIT

FLOWERS | yellow-green male catkins

LEAF Alternate, pinnate; 9–17 lanceolate, coarsely toothed leaflets. **FLOWER** Small and petalless; males in axillary pendulous catkins; females stalkless, in terminal spikes. **FRUIT** Reddish brown, ovoid-oblong, thin-shelled nut containing grooved, edible seeds.

CENTENNIAL NUTS

In 1846, an African-American slave gardener from Louisiana successfully grafted a superior wild Pecan to seedling Pecan stocks. This increased the tree's productivity significantly and led to the development of the variety called "Centennial" from which the 500 current varieties originate.

PECANS

Juglans cinerea

Butternut

HEIGHT up to 30m (100ft)
TYPE Deciduous
OCCURRENCE E. and C. North America

Formerly used for panelling, Butternut is seldom planted as an ornamental. In the wild, it is highly prone to butternut canker, a virulent fungal disease. **BARK** Grey, deeply fissured, with small scales on the ridges. **LEAF** Alternate, pinnate, with 11–17 oblong-lanceolate, coarsely toothed leaflets, hairy on both sides. **FLOWER** Small, petalless; males in axillary hanging catkins; females stalkless, in few-flowered spikes. **FRUIT** Egg-shaped nuts in clusters of 3–5, with sweet, oily seeds.

pointed green husk

unequal rounded base

LEAVES

FRUIT

Juglans nigra

Black Walnut

HEIGHT up to 50m (165ft)
TYPE Deciduous
OCCURRENCE North America

This shade-intolerant tree secretes a substance that prevents vegetation from growing around it. Its timber is used for cabinets and veneers. **BARK** Dark grey-brown to blackish, with deep, scaly ridges. **LEAF** Alternate, pinnate, with 11–19 ovate-lanceolate, coarsely toothed leaflets. **FLOWER** Small, petalless; males in axillary catkins; females stalkless, in few-flowered spikes. **FRUIT** Spherical ribbed nut, solitary or in pairs.

FRUIT

green husk

pointed tips

LEAVES WITH CATKINS

yellow-green male catkins

Juglans regia

Walnut

HEIGHT up to 30m (100ft)
TYPE Deciduous
OCCURRENCE S.E. Europe, Himalayas to China

The cultivation of the walnut dates back to 7000BCE. It was introduced to Europe from Persia by the Romans. The first plantations in the USA were established in 1867, and the main area of cultivation is now California. All parts of the fruit are utilized: the cracked shells are ground to form an industrial abrasive, and walnut oil extracted from the kernel is used as a salad oil. **BARK** Pale silvery grey, smooth, eventually becoming deeply fissured with age. **LEAF** Alternate, pinnate; 5–9 ovate to elliptic or obovate leaflets, with unequal, rounded bases. **FLOWER** Males and females on the same plant, both small and petalless; males: in axillary pendulous catkins, females: stalkless, on few-flowered spikes. **FRUIT** Round nut borne singly or in pairs, up to 5cm (2in) long, with an edible, sweet kernel.

MALE FLOWERS   catkins to 10cm (4in) long

FRUIT AND LEAFLETS

green husk of unripe fruit

leaflet to 45 cm (18in) long

smooth, hard husk

MATURE FRUIT

Pterocarya fraxinifolia

Wingnut

HEIGHT 20–30m (65–100ft)
TYPE Deciduous
OCCURRENCE W. Asia, Caucasus

The Wingnut has a very wide crown and grows best in moist soil near water. **BARK** Pale grey, smooth, becoming deeply furrowed with age. **LEAF** Alternate, pinnate; ovate to oblong-lanceolate, unstalked leaflets; sharply toothed.

FLOWER Males and females on the same plant, both small and petalless; males in axillary pendulous catkins, females in very long, pendulous catkins. **FRUIT** Nut with two wings.

LEAVES AND FRUIT

11–25 leaflets

BARK

deep, interlacing ridges

winged fruit in hanging catkin

Carica papaya

Papaya

HEIGHT 2–10m (6–33ft)
TYPE Evergreen
OCCURRENCE West Indies, N. South America

A fast-growing tree with hollow stems, the Papaya is widely cultivated throughout the tropics for its fruit. The unripe fruit, stems, and leaves produce a latex that contains the enzyme papain. This is used as a dietary supplement to aid digestion and as a meat tenderizer. **BARK** Greenish to grey-brown, smooth, with prominent leaf scars, and thin milky sap. **LEAF** Alternate, clustered at the stem tip, palmately divided into 7–11 lobes. **FLOWER** Males and females on separate trees, with pale

LUSCIOUS FRUIT

The papaya fruit has orange, yellow, or pink, creamy sweet flesh surrounding soft edible black seeds. In its native range, much of the delicate, perishable fruit is grown in home gardens and sold in local markets for fresh consumption, with little entering international trade. The fruit needs to be harvested with care as scratching its skin releases latex, which stains the fruit.

DRIED FRUIT

FRESH PAPAYA

yellow or pink petals; males in pendent panicles, females solitary or in few-flowered clusters. **FRUIT** Large ovoid-oblong, fleshy berry, with yellowish orange pulp and black seeds.

fruit weighs to 10kg (22lb)

UNRIPE FRUIT

7–13 veins

deeply divided lobes

LEAF

FLOWERS

stalkless male flowers

Vasconcellea x heilbornii

Babaco

HEIGHT 1–2m (3–7ft)
TYPE Semi-evergreen
OCCURRENCE Ecuador, known only in cultivation

Also known as Mountain Papaya, this fast-growing tree-like giant herb is thought to be a hybrid between two Andean papayas, *V. pubescens* and *V. stipulata*. **BARK** Greenish to grey-brown, smooth, with prominent leaf scars. **LEAF** Alternate, clustered at the stem tip, rounded, palmate, deeply divided and toothed, with 5–7 lobes, 1–7 veins and a long stalk. **FLOWER** Solitary, each on a pendulous stalk, with yellowish green petals, forming on the trunk during its growth phase. **FRUIT** Large torpedo-shaped green berry, yellow when ripe, borne on the stem; thin, edible skin, creamy flesh.

Moringa oleifera

Horse-radish Tree

HEIGHT up to 10m (33ft)
TYPE Deciduous
OCCURRENCE N.W. India

European colonists in India used the root of this slender tree as a substitute for horse-radish (not advisable as it contains toxic alkaloids), hence the common name. Widely cultivated in the tropics, its leaves, rich in vitamins and minerals, are used as a vegetable supplement. However, the immature green fruit is the most valued part of the

in 4–6 pairs

LEAFLETS

drooping branches

plant and is prepared in a similar fashion to green beans. Oil derived from the seeds has been used for cooking, for lubrication, and in cosmetics. **BARK** Pale, smooth to slightly corky. **LEAF** Alternate, three-pinnate, with a terminal leaflet; leaflets ovate to elliptic or oblong, untoothed, finely hairy when young, turning smooth later. **FLOWER** White to cream, borne in large axillary, spreading panicles. **FRUIT** Long, pendulous capsule.

FRUIT

bean-like capsules

Bixa orellana

Anatto

HEIGHT 3–10m (13–33ft)
TYPE Evergreen
OCCURRENCE Tropical South America, S.E. Asia

Historically used for making body paint and fabric dye, this bushy tree is now used mainly as a food colorant for dairy products. **BARK** Pale to dark brown, later fissured. **LEAF** Alternate, in spirals, ovate, with a heart-shaped to blunt base. **FLOWER** Large terminal panicles, 5–7 obovate petals, usually pinkish. **FRUIT** Flattened, ellipsoidal capsule, with bristles, bright red when mature.

seeds in red-orange pulp
FRUIT

FLOWERS AND FRUIT

Cochlospermum religiosum

Silk-cotton Tree

HEIGHT up to 10m (33ft)
TYPE Deciduous
OCCURRENCE India, Myanmar, Thailand

Mostly found in dry monsoon areas, this small tree is also known as the Buttercup Tree. It is cultivated within its region for its abundant single yellow flowers, but it is uncommon outside its natural habitat. **BARK** Creamy grey and smooth. **LEAF** Alternate, palmate, with 3–5 divided lobes, softly hairy below, wavy margins. **FLOWER** Large, borne in terminal inflorescences on bare branches, with numerous stamens. **FRUIT** Large open capsule, with woolly seeds.

orange-red stamens

yellow petals

Bombax ceiba

Simul

HEIGHT up to 25m (80 ft)
TYPE Deciduous
OCCURRENCE Sri Lanka, China, Malaysia, Australia

Often planted as a street tree, the Simul is a blaze of colour when in flower. **BARK** Greyish white. **LEAF** Alternate, palmate; 5–7 oblong-lanceolate, smooth leaflets. **FLOWER** Solitary, terminal, large, brilliant scarlet, with numerous stamens. **FRUIT** Woody capsule; seeds surrounded by fluffy hairs.

Adansonia digitata

Baobab

HEIGHT 10–25m (33–80ft)
TYPE Deciduous
OCCURRENCE Tropical Africa

The Baobab, which can live for over 1,000 years, is a focus for myth: it is said that a devil uprooted the tree and replanted it upside down; spirits are linked with its night-opening flowers (the tree is pollinated by bats). The Baobab has edible leaves, seeds, and pulp, and the inner bark is used to make rope. The massive trunk stores water, which can be tapped for drinking. **BARK** Greyish brown, tinged mauve, smooth. **LEAF** Alternate, digitate, with 5–7 elliptic-oblong to ovate leaflets that are hairy below when young. **FLOWER** Axillary, solitary, large, sweet-scented, with waxy and crinkled white to cream petals, numerous stamens. **FRUIT** Ovoid brown capsule, velvety hairy outside; black seeds.

Adansonia gregorii

Boab

HEIGHT 5–15m (16–50ft)
TYPE Deciduous
OCCURRENCE N.E. Australia (Kimberley region)

The short trunk of this tree is enlarged and bottle-shaped, enabling it to store water. **BARK** Greyish brown, smooth. **LEAF** Alternate, with 3–7 elliptic to ovate or obovate leaflets. **FLOWER** Axillary, solitary, large, with oblong to spoon-shaped petals, white to cream, numerous stamens. **FRUIT** Brown capsule, velvety hairy surface, with kidney-shaped seeds.

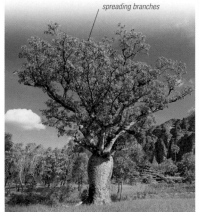

spreading branches

Brachychiton acerifolius

Flame-tree

HEIGHT 35m (115ft)
TYPE Deciduous
OCCURRENCE E. Australia

Considered one of the most spectacular trees of Australia, this tree has bright coral red flowers. **BARK** Grey, fissured or wrinkled. **LEAF** Alternate or whorled, ovate to lanceolate, sometimes with 3–5 lobes, especially in juvenile foliage. **FLOWER** Petalless, in large terminal panicles on leafless branches. **FRUIT** Dry, boat-shaped, woody follicle.

Ceiba speciosa

Floss Silk Tree

HEIGHT 15–22m (50–75ft)
TYPE Deciduous
OCCURRENCE South America (Brazil, N.E. Argentina), planted elsewhere in the tropics

Locally cultivated in South America before the arrival of the Europeans, this tree is characterized by a spiny, swollen trunk that can store water, and its green avocado-like fruit, which releases cotton-like fibres when ripe. This tree is often planted in southern USA as a street tree for its display of spectacular deep pink flowers. **BARK** Yellowish green, spiny, particularly when young. **LEAF** Alternate, digitate, with 5–7 narrowly elliptic leaflets.

FLOWER

purple streaks on flower base

FLOWER Deep pink, 7–11cm (2¾–4¼ in) long, with a streaked white to yellow base and oblong to spoon-shaped petals. **FRUIT** Large, woody, pear-shaped capsule; seeds in a mass of silky hairs.

LEAVES

large, glossy seeds

elliptic to lanceolate leaf

RIPE FRUIT

pyramidal spines

Durio zibethinus

Durian

HEIGHT 30–40m (100–130ft)
TYPE Evergreen
OCCURRENCE Sumatra, Borneo, cultivated elsewhere in S.E. Asia

The Durian is famous – or notorious – for its fruit: though a delicacy, they are banned in hotels and public transport because of their overpowering smell. **BARK** Grey to reddish brown, flaking irregularly. **LEAF** Alternate, smooth above, covered with hairs and silvery scales beneath. **FLOWER** In axillary clusters, with five yellowish white petals and five pale golden sepals. **FRUIT** Green to yellow, spherical capsule; seeds covered with creamy sweet flesh.

BAOBAB
Baobabs rise above the Madagascan forest canopy.
These majestic trees are a characteristic feature of
this island's landscape. Several Baobab species have
been identified, of which *Adansonia grandidieri* is
perhaps the best known.

Ceiba pentandra

Kapok

HEIGHT 18–70m (60–230ft)
TYPE Deciduous
OCCURRENCE South America, Africa

One of the tallest trees of the Amazon forests, Kapok was held sacred by the ancient Mayas and many other Native American tribes, probably because of its stature. Its base has pronounced exposed roots and is sometimes buttressed. The broad, pagoda-shaped crown is formed by superimposed branches arranged in groups of three. Kapok flowers, which bloom in the dry season from December to January, have a foetid, milky smell that attracts bats. The seeds, leaves, bark, and resin are used for various medicinal purposes. The tree is now cultivated in Southeast Asia and Africa. **BARK** Pale grey; with conical spines when young. **LEAF** Alternate, long-stalked, palmate, with 5–11 oblong-lanceolate leaflets. **FLOWER** Pink or off-white, in axillary clusters of 2–15. **FRUIT** Capsule; seeds embedded in a mass of woolly hairs (floss).

bell-shaped flowers

FLOWERS

KAPOK FLOSS

The Kapok was formerly cultivated for the floss of its fruit, mainly in Sri Lanka, Java, and the Philippines. The harvested fruit was opened and the seeds separated from the kapok floss, which was dried and then baled. This fibre has been used to stuff mattresses and as buoyancy material in life-jackets. The oil from the seeds was used for soap-making.

FRUIT POD

Guazuma ulmifolia

Bastard Cedar

HEIGHT up to 20m (65ft)
TYPE Evergreen
OCCURRENCE South America

This tree has widely spreading, horizontal branches and is common in secondary forests. **BARK** Grey to grey-brown, rough. **LEAF** Alternate, in flattened rows, ovate to lanceolate, toothed. **FLOWER** In axillary panicles, with five greenish yellow petals. **FRUIT** Globose green capsule; black and honey-scented when ripe.

forked styles

curving petals

FLOWER

Lagunaria patersonia

Norfolk Island Hibiscus

HEIGHT up to 20m (65ft)
TYPE Evergreen
OCCURRENCE Australia

orange or golden anthers

LEAVES AND FLOWERS

5 petals

leaf to 10cm (4in) long

Usually pyramidal in shape, this tree is cultivated as an ornamental street or park tree in many warm, temperate, or sub-tropical climates. The hairs of the fruit can cause itching. **BARK** Greyish, fissured lengthwise. **LEAF** Alternate, ovate to elliptic, densely scaly below. **FLOWER** Pink to rose-lilac, axillary, solitary. **FRUIT** Capsule lined with hairs.

Ochroma pyramidale

Balsa

HEIGHT up to 30m (100ft)
TYPE Evergreen
OCCURRENCE Tropical South America, West Indies

This tree has a straight trunk and a sparsely branched, spreading crown. It produces the lightest commercial wood in the world. Its flowers are pollinated by bats. **BARK** Greyish brown, smooth, porous. **LEAF** Alternate, rough, shallowly lobed and covered with reddish hairs. **FLOWER** Axillary, solitary; white to yellowish petals, numerous stamens. **FRUIT** Capsule that looks like a rabbit's foot.

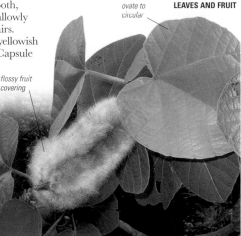

ovate to circular

LEAVES AND FRUIT

FLOWER

flossy fruit covering

KAPOK
The spreading roots of a Kapok tree (*Ceiba pentandra*) invade temple ruins at Angkor, Cambodia. Originally a native of South America, the Kapok was sacred to the Mayans, who believed that the souls of the dead ascended to heaven via its branches.

Pachira aquatica

Shaving-brush Tree

HEIGHT up to 20m (65ft)
TYPE Semi-evergreen
OCCURRENCE Tropical Mexico, Central and South America

Also known as the Guyana Chestnut, this tree has branches in whorls, particularly when young. It is found along estuaries and lakesides and can be used as a hedge or for general planting. Its seeds, which resemble the Sweet Chestnut in flavour, can be toasted and ground to prepare a hot chocolate-like beverage. **BARK** Grey, slightly cracked lengthwise. **LEAF** Alternate, palmate, with 4–7 smooth, elliptic to oblong-lanceolate leaflets. **FLOWER** Axillary, solitary, yellow to creamy white petals, turning back to reveal numerous stamens, clustered in groups of about 15. **FRUIT** Large, egg-shaped capsule, with edible seeds.

spreading habit

yellowish brown capsule

FRUIT

FLOWERS pink-tipped stamens petals 20–30cm (8–12in) long

Tilia americana

Whitewood

HEIGHT 25–40m (80–130ft)
TYPE Deciduous
OCCURRENCE E. North America

Often the dominant tree in the moist woodland where it grows, Whitewood has a broadly columnar to rounded crown. It is sometimes planted as a street tree. Its bark was widely used by the Native Americans for making rope and baskets. **BARK** Brownish grey, deeply fissured with scaly ridges. **LEAF** Alternate, broadly ovate, coarsely toothed, with a heart-shaped base. **FLOWER** Pale yellow-green, in axillary or terminal, stalked clusters of up to ten flowers, fragrant. **FRUIT** Woody, rounded drupe, four-ribbed, covered with grey-brown hairs.

LEAF

Tilia cordata

Small-leaved Lime

HEIGHT up to 30m (100ft)
TYPE Deciduous
OCCURRENCE Europe, W. Asia

This tall tree has a somewhat pyramidal crown. Its wood is soft and can be worked with ease. **BARK** Grey-brown, smooth when young; dark grey, ridged at maturity. **LEAF** Alternate, ovate to rounded, glossy green above, waxy beneath, with sharply toothed margins. **FLOWER** Axillary or terminal, stalked clusters of up to ten flowers, pale green bracts at base, fragrant. **FRUIT** Woody, spherical nut-like drupe, smooth.

pale yellow-green
flowers

LEAVES AND FLOWERS

broadly columnar
habit

Tilia x europaea

Common Lime

HEIGHT up to 40m (130ft)
TYPE Deciduous
OCCURRENCE Europe

The Common Lime is rare as a natural hybrid and is usually cultivated. Its trunk often has burrs, usually with numerous suckers at the base. This is the commonly planted lime tree in Europe in parks and streets. **BARK** Grey-brown, smooth when young; dark grey, ridged at maturity. **LEAF** Alternate, broadly ovate, glossy green above, tufts of hairs beneath. **FLOWER** Pale yellow-green, with pale green bracts at base, fragrant, in axillary or terminal, stalked clusters of up to ten. **FRUIT** Woody, rounded nut-like drupe, faintly ribbed, covered with grey-brown hairs.

LEAVES WITH FRUIT

toothed leaf
edges

nutlets

Tilia tomentosa

Silver Lime

HEIGHT up to 30m (100ft)
TYPE Deciduous
OCCURRENCE S.E. Europe, S.W. Asia

The flowers of this tree are inconspicuous but exceptionally fragrant. They are used to make linden tea (tisane), which helps to induce sweating and to counter colds and fevers. The flowers are picked when fully fragrant and then dried. This and other *Tilia* species are popular with beekeepers for honey production. **BARK** Grey, with a network of shallow ridges and furrows. **LEAF** Alternate, broadly ovate to rounded, slightly lobed, green and slightly hairy above, covered with silvery hairs beneath. **FLOWER** Pale yellow-green, with a pale green bract beneath, in axillary or terminal, stalked clusters of up to ten. **FRUIT** Egg-shaped, warty nut-like drupe.

silvery underside of leaf

pendulous fruit

sharply toothed leaf margins

broadly columnar crown

Triplochiton scleroxylon

Obeche

HEIGHT up to 65m (215ft)
TYPE Deciduous
OCCURRENCE Tropical W. Africa (from Guinea to Cameroon)

This species accounts for almost half the timber produced in West Africa. Its trunk is straight, but sometimes fluted in old trees. **BARK** Grey to orange-brown, becoming scaly. **LEAF** Alternate, broadly ovate to triangular, lobed to about one-third of the length, with 5–7 lobes. **FLOWER** In short panicles, somewhat saucer-shaped, with white petals that are red-purple at the base. **FRUIT** Up to five winged carpels.

Theobroma cacao

Cocoa

HEIGHT up to 10m (33ft)
TYPE Evergreen to semi-deciduous
OCCURRENCE S. Mexico, Central America, cultivated in W. Africa

Cultivated in tropical regions for its seeds – the cocoa "beans" used to make cocoa and chocolate – this tree has a low, spreading crown. The seeds of the fruit pod are scooped out, fermented, and dried, and then shipped to chocolate producing countries for shelling, roasting, and processing. **BARK** Dark brown, rough, fissured. **LEAF** Alternate, large, elliptic to oblong, pendulous. **FLOWER** Pink to white, with petals that are hood-shaped at the base and spreading sepals; borne singly or in groups on the trunk and branches at the same time as the fruit. **FRUIT** Ovoid-oblong, yellow to reddish purple pod, five-celled, furrowed, with numerous reddish brown seeds embedded in a whitish, sweetish, buttery pulp.

"BITTER WATER"

The word "chocolate" derives from the Mayan "xocolatl", which means "bitter water". Christopher Columbus brought cocoa beans to Europe from America, but it was only in 1875 that milk chocolate was invented by Swiss chemist Henri Nestlé.

COCOA POD

CHOCOLATE

TRUNK

small white flowers on trunk

untoothed margin

UNRIPE FRUIT

wrinkled pod

LEAVES

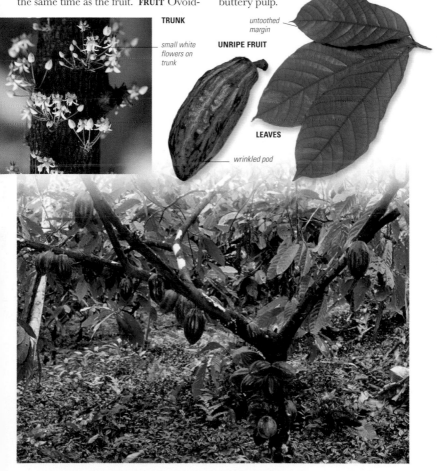

Muntingia calabura

Jam-tree

HEIGHT up to 12m (40ft)
TYPE Evergreen
OCCURRENCE Mexico, Caribbean, South America, introduced in S.E. Asia

prominent yellow stamens

5 petals

SOLITARY FLOWER

Also known as the Jamaican Cherry, this tree was introduced into Asia during the time of the Spanish Empire and was transported on the Acapulco–Manila galleon route. It has an umbrella-shaped crown and widespreading horizontal, drooping branches. Its twigs are covered with sticky, glandular red hairs. The sweet berries can be eaten fresh or made into jam. The bark can be made into ropes and the flowers are used in traditional medicine. **BARK** Pale brownish grey, smooth, fibrous. **LEAF** Alternate, ovate-lanceolate, dark green above, covered with sticky hairs beneath that radiate from the centre; asymmetrical base, three veins. **FLOWER** White, borne in axillary groups of 1–5. **FRUIT** Dull red fleshy berry, with numerous tiny seeds.

toothed margin

LEAVES

1–1.25cm (⅜–½in) wide

UNRIPE FRUIT

Hopea odorata

Thingwa

HEIGHT up to 45m (150ft)
TYPE Evergreen
OCCURRENCE S.E. Asia

Mainly grown for its strong timber, this tree is also planted as an ornamental and shade tree. **BARK** Dark brown or black, cracks into small pieces. **LEAF** Alternate, 10–20cm (4–8in) long, tapering at the tip. **FLOWER** Small, with five pinkish to white petals, hairy on both sides, in branched terminal or axillary panicles. **FRUIT** Single-seeded, round nut.

Neobalanocarpus heimii

Chengal

HEIGHT up to 33m (110ft)
TYPE Evergreen
OCCURRENCE Thailand, Malaysia

The heavy, durable timber of this tree used to be the best-known in Malaysia. **BARK** Greyish, flaky. **LEAF** Leathery, lanceolate to crescent-shaped, with an unequal base, tip tapers to a long, blunt point. **FLOWER** Pale greenish yellow with 15 stamens, borne in terminal or axillary panicles. **FRUIT** Oblong to cylindrical, shiny nut, with a short point at the tip.

Shorea robusta

Sal

HEIGHT up to 35m (115ft)
TYPE Evergreen
OCCURRENCE Myanmar, India, Nepal

This tree has a straight, cylindrical trunk. Younger trees have a pointed habit, which becomes more rounded with age. Although an evergreen, the tree sheds nearly all its leaves in dry areas, between February and April. Sal provides very good quality, durable timber, which is much sought after for construction, especially for purposes that require strength with flexibility such as railway sleepers, house- and bridge-building. The tree is revered by Buddhists as it is said that the Buddha meditated in a grove of Sal trees. **BARK** Dark brown, with deep longitudinal furrows in mature trees. **LEAF** Tough, shiny leaves, 10–25cm (4–10in) long with a rounded base, oval-oblong in shape, ending in a blunt point, 10–12 pairs of secondary veins. **FLOWER** Yellowish, inner petals orange, calyx and petals are covered with white down on the outside; borne in large axillary or terminal, racemose panicles. **FRUIT** Winged nut; seeds may germinate on the tree.

MORE THAN TIMBER

Like many tropical tree species, the Sal is used for far more than timber. The seeds of the tree are used for oil and the oilcake is used to feed livestock. The leaves can also be used for cattle feed. The tree yields a white, aromatic resin when tapped, which is burnt as incense during religious ceremonies. It is also used for caulking boats and ships and in paints and varnishes. The resin has medicinal uses.

LEAF HARVEST

glossy foliage

FLOWERING BRANCHES conspicuous flowers

Shorea albida

Alan

HEIGHT 40m (130ft)
TYPE Evergreen
OCCURRENCE N.W. Borneo

This tree occurs on peat swamps, the largest trees growing at the edges and the smallest in the centre. The intermediate trees are an important source of red meranti timber. **BARK** Greyish, deeply fissured. **LEAF** Oblong-elliptic, tip tapers to a long point, leathery; 16–20 pairs of slender, secondary veins. **FLOWER** Borne in terminal or axillary, doubly branched panicles up to 18cm (7in) long; branchlets carry up to three flowers, with cream petals and 20–25 stamens. **FRUIT** Egg-shaped nuts, 1.2cm (³⁄₈in) long, covered in greyish-buff hairs.

Shorea javanica

Damar

HEIGHT up to 33m (110ft)
TYPE Semi-evergreen
OCCURRENCE Sumatra

This tree is grown in plantations in southern Sumatra. The timber is valued for plywood production, which is its most important use. The tree is also used for its high-quality, clear resin – known as "damar". The Damar trees begin their production of resin after 20 years, yielding it for about 30 years before dying some time between 50 and 60 years of age. On average, a tree will yield some 48kg (105lb) per year. In dry areas, it sheds nearly all its leaves between February and April. Its branchlets are covered with a tawny down. **BARK** Reddish, rough. **LEAF** Oblong-elliptic to ovate, tip tapers to a long blunt point, leathery; 19–25 pairs of very slender, secondary veins, midrib slender above. **FLOWER** In terminal or axillary, single-branched panicles up to 14cm (5¹⁄₂in) long, about three flowers, each with white petals and 15 stamens, on a branchlet. **FRUIT** Egg-shaped nut up to 1.4cm (¹⁄₂in) long and 1cm (³⁄₈in) wide, covered in tawny-brown down, with a prominent point at tip.

Dryobalanops aromatica

Kapur

HEIGHT up to 33m (110ft)
TYPE Evergreen
OCCURRENCE Malaya, Borneo, Sumatra

A gigantic tree, often with a trunk over 2m (6¹⁄₂ft) wide, Kapur is an important source of timber and camphor. **BARK** Reddish, flaky. **LEAF** Dark green, leathery, waxy, triangular to heart-shaped. **FLOWER** In panicles, white petals in a rosette, about 30 yellow stamens. **FRUIT** Smooth nut.

glossy green foliage

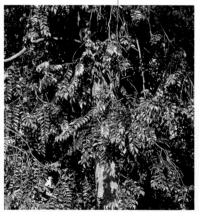

Aquilaria malaccensis

Agarwood

HEIGHT up to 45m (150ft)
TYPE Evergreen
OCCURRENCE S. and S.E. Asia

This tree yields the world's most valuable incense. Its bark produces strong fibres that are used for making rope and cloth. **BARK** Whitish, smooth, cracking irregularly. **LEAF** Elliptic-oblong to oblong-lanceolate, with pointed tip. **FLOWER** Green to yellow, in groups of 1–3 umbels, each with about ten flowers. **FRUIT** Hairy, spherical capsule.

Gonystylus bancanus

Ramin

HEIGHT up to 50m (165ft)
TYPE Evergreen
OCCURRENCE Malaysia, Indonesia

The Ramin grows in freshwater swamps and seasonally flooding forests. It is highly valued for its timber. **BARK** Dark brown, shallowly fissured. **LEAF** Alternate, often folded, leathery, elliptic, oblong, or rounded. **FLOWER** In clusters, covered with yellowish down, with 13–20 petals. **FRUIT** Rough, spherical capsule.

Acer campestre

Field Maple

HEIGHT 6–10m (20–33ft)
TYPE Deciduous
OCCURRENCE Europe, N. Africa, W. Asia

The Field Maple occurs in broad-leaved woodlands and is common in hedgerows. In rare cases, it can grow up to 28m (92ft). In Europe, it is sometimes planted as a shade or street tree. **BARK** Grey-brown, scaly or fissured. **LEAF** Opposite, palmate, 3–5 lobes; the stalk yields sap. **FLOWER** Green, in small, erect clusters. **FRUIT** Winged keys, arranged in pairs.

winged fruit

LEAVES AND FRUIT

leaves divided halfway

Acer negundo

Box Elder

HEIGHT 15–20m (50–65ft)
TYPE Deciduous
OCCURRENCE S.E. Canada, E. USA

Also called the Manitoba Maple, this tree grows along the banks of streams and lakes and on swampy ground. Its wood is soft and weak and has been used as an inferior timber. In Europe, it is often used for windbreak and street planting. **BARK** Pale to light brown, scaly, furrowed with age. **LEAF** Opposite, pinnate with 3–7 ovate leaflets. **FLOWER** Males and females on separate trees; yellow-green, in drooping clusters. **FRUIT** Winged keys, arranged in pairs.

winged keys

FRUIT

Acer palmatum

Japanese Maple

HEIGHT 8–12m (26–40ft)
TYPE Deciduous
OCCURRENCE Japan, China, Korea

Long cultivated in Japan, the Japanese Maple was introduced into Europe in 1820. This tree has a graceful and spreading habit and slender shoots that end in small, paired buds. It is commonly planted in gardens for its autumn colours. **BARK** Grey-brown, with pale and longitudinal stripes, which are variable in some cultivars. **LEAF** Opposite, palmate, with 5–9, deep, taper-pointed lobes. **FLOWER** Small, purple, arranged in small and upright clusters. **FRUIT** Winged keys, arranged in pairs.

LEAVES AND FRUIT

finely pointed leaf lobes

red winged fruit

MEDLEY OF COLOURS

The Japanese Maple has more than 500 cultivars. They differ in the depth of division of the leaf lobes – these are themselves dissected sometimes, or narrowly linear – and in the leaf colour, which ranges from green to purple to golden or variegated. There is also a dwarf group, which is popular for bonsai.

Acer pseudoplatanus

Sycamore

HEIGHT 20–30m (65–100ft)
TYPE Deciduous
OCCURRENCE Europe, N. Africa, W. Asia

The Sycamore is an invasive maple with a broad, spreading crown, colonizing open areas. Control of invasive populations is possible by selecting only male trees. **BARK** Grey-brown, smooth, flaking into irregular plates in older trees. **LEAF** Opposite, palmate, with five deep, coarsely toothed lobes, heart-shaped at the base, dark green above, paler beneath. **FLOWER** Green, arranged in small pendulous clusters from the slender shoots. **FRUIT** Winged keys, arranged in pairs, up to 2.5cm (1in) long.

LEAVES AND FLOWERS

leaf to 7.5–15cm (3–6in) wide

clustered winged fruit

FRUIT

pendulous flowers

Acer rubrum

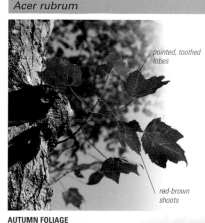

pointed, toothed lobes

red-brown shoots

AUTUMN FOLIAGE

Red Maple

HEIGHT up to 25m (80ft)
TYPE Deciduous
OCCURRENCE North America (N.E. USA, S.E. Canada)

Growing in diverse habitats and climates, the Red Maple is one of the species that account for the striking red autumn colours of North American forests. **BARK** Pale grey and smooth, with plate-like scales on mature trees. **LEAF** Opposite, with three shallow, sharply toothed lobes. **FLOWER** Dull yellowish red to bright yellow, on long-stalked clusters, appearing before the leaves. **FRUIT** Winged keys, in pairs.

Acer saccharum

Sugar Maple

HEIGHT 30–36m (100–120ft)
TYPE Deciduous
OCCURRENCE N.E. USA, S.E. Canada

This large, fast-growing tree provides abundant shade and beautiful autumn foliage, and is an excellent tree for larger parks and estates. It is an important timber tree, as well as the source of maple syrup and sugar. It takes about 40 gallons of sap to make one gallon of syrup. **BARK** Grey-brown, smooth or slightly fissured, becoming darker, deeply furrowed, and scaly on older trees. **LEAF** Opposite, with 3–5 shallow lobes and conspicuous veins, deep matt green, turning yellow to orange or red in autumn. **FLOWER** Small, greenish yellow, in unstalked clusters hanging from long stems, appearing with or slightly before the leaves; males and females on the same tree or separate trees. **FRUIT** Winged keys arranged in pairs, 2.5cm (1in) long, in clusters, turning brown when mature in autumn.

FRUIT

fruit to 2.5cm (1in) long

flower to 5mm (³⁄₁₆in) long

FLOWER CLUSTERS

leaf to 13cm (5in) long

LEAF

deep fissures

BARK

SWEET SYRUP

In the past, gashes were made in the bark of the tree and the sap collected in birch buckets, poured into hollowed out tree stumps, and then evaporated by adding hot stones, to make maple syrup. Today, the sap is tapped directly through plastic tubing which runs into a central storage tank.

PANCAKES WITH SYRUP

Aesculus hippocastanum

Horse Chestnut

HEIGHT up to 40m (130ft)
TYPE Deciduous
OCCURRENCE Native to the Balkans, naturalized throughout Europe

The common name of this tree is derived from the horseshoe-shaped leaf scars that can be seen below the sticky terminal buds. The large seeds (sometimes known as conkers) are inedible. **BARK** Dark brown, flaking into plates. **LEAF** Opposite, digitate, with 5–7 obovate leaflets, each with a narrow triangular base, sparsely hairy

below, with toothed margins. **FLOWER** In columnar, upright panicles, with 4–5 creamy white petals veined pink to red at the base. **FRUIT** Green, spherical capsule, with glossy brown seeds.

smooth seed

spiny husk

unstalked leaflets

FRUIT **LEAF**

LEAVES AND FLOWERS

Blighia sapida

Akee

HEIGHT up to 10m (33ft)
TYPE Evergreen
OCCURRENCE W. Africa

If not prepared correctly, the fruit of the Akee is highly poisonous. The national fruit of Jamaica, it is named after Captain Bligh who collected samples in Jamaica and sent them to the Kew Gardens. **BARK** Grey, smooth to slightly rough. **LEAF** Alternate, pinnate with 3–5 pairs of elliptic leaflets, no terminal leaflet, smooth above, hairy below.

FLOWER White, fragrant, borne in racemes. **FRUIT** Leathery to fleshy three-valved capsule, opening to reveal three dark brown, poisonous seeds; large white, fleshy, edible aril, which is attached to the fruit by a red or pink membrane.

dense spreading branches

RIPE FRUIT red tinged with yellow

JAPANESE MAPLE

A favourite among horticulturalists and garden designers, the Japanese Maple (*Acer palmatum*) is valued for its delicate foliage and brilliant autumn colours. The subspecies shown here, *A. palmatum dissectum*, is a variety with deeply divided leaves.

Longan

HEIGHT up to 40m (130ft)
TYPE Evergreen
OCCURRENCE S. China, S.E. Asia

Although the Longan is a tropical fruit that is best eaten fresh, there is a considerable canning industry for the fruit as they retain their flavour better than the lychee or rambutan. The fruit can be dried, either whole, or after removal of the outer skin, and is used to prepare a refreshing drink. The seeds are high in saponin (a soap-like compound) and can be used for shampoos. **BARK** Smooth, becoming slightly flaky. **LEAF** Alternate, pinnate, without a terminal leaflet; 4–10 elliptic to ovate-oblong, untoothed leaflets, glossy green above, grey-green beneath, minutely hairy. **FLOWER** Yellow-brown, smooth to densely woolly, borne in a terminal inflorescence. **FRUIT** Smooth to warty, spherical to oval fleshy drupe, with a sticky, translucent white aril.

dense, dark green foliage

drooping clusters of yellow-brown fruit

FRUIT

UNRIPE FRUIT

triangular, 3-sided capsule

Golden Rain

HEIGHT up to 12m (40ft)
TYPE Deciduous
OCCURRENCE China

Planted as an ornamental for its yellow flowers, bladder-like fruit, and yellow autumn colour, this tree has a broadly spreading crown. In China, the flowers have been used as a yellow dye and are a component in a traditional medicine. **BARK** Grey-brown, fissured into scaly ridges. **LEAF** Alternate, ovate to ovate-oblong, smooth above, with irregularly toothed margins. **FLOWER** Numerous, small, yellow with red centre, in terminal panicles. **FRUIT** Bladder-like capsule, green, tinged red, ripening to brown.

conical panicle

7–14 leaflets

LEAVES AND FLOWERS

Litchi chinensis

Lychee

HEIGHT up to 30m (100ft)
TYPE Evergreen
OCCURRENCE S. China to N. Vietnam, cultivated in N. Thailand, Australia, India, Madagascar, Mauritius, Réunion, South Africa

The Lychee tree was cultivated as early as 1500BCE. The crop has spread very slowly to new areas due to its exacting

to 5cm (2in) long

FRUIT

climatic requirements. It can be grown in many areas but fails to set fruit unless the conditions are ideal. Today, fresh lychees are available in European markets; the canned product has long been exported. **BARK** Grey, smooth. **LEAF** Alternate, pinnate without a terminal leaflet; leaflets in 2–4 pairs, elliptic- to ovate-lanceolate, glossy deep green above, waxy beneath. **FLOWER** Borne in large branched, terminal clusters, numerous, petalless, with golden, hairy calyx. **FRUIT** Showy, spherical to ovate, fleshy capsule in loose, pendent clusters; usually reddish when mature; seeds covered with a fleshy, edible aril.

TRUNK AND BRANCHES

Nephelium lappaceum

Rambutan

HEIGHT 10–25m (33–80ft)
TYPE Evergreen
OCCURRENCE Cultivated in S.E. Asia from Sri Lanka to Papua New Guinea

The Rambutan thrives in the humid tropics and its fruit is usually eaten fresh locally. Thailand is one of the major producers of the fruit, followed by Malaysia, Indonesia, and the Philippines. Young shoots are used to make green dye for silk already dyed yellow. **BARK** Grey to brown, smooth, with white flecks. **LEAF** Alternate, pinnate; 2–4 pairs of ovate to obovate, untoothed leaflets. **FLOWER** Yellowish green to white, small, petalless, in clusters; males and females on separate trees. **FRUIT** Oval to spherical, strawberry red, rose pink, or yellowish capsule; translucent white to pinkish, fleshy edible aril.

glossy, deep green leaflets

loose, pendent clusters of fruit

FRUIT AND LEAVES

Boswellia sacra

Frankincense

HEIGHT up to 5m (16ft)
TYPE Deciduous
OCCURRENCE Arabian Peninsula

A small tree with a trunk that is often branched at the base, the Frankincense tree is known for its aromatic resin, which is used as incense. Historically, it was worth its weight in gold, and most famously it was one of the gifts offered to Christ by the three Magi, who carried it, along with gold and myrrh, to Bethlehem. In ancient Egypt, the first female Pharaoh, Queen Hatshepsut, found living Frankincense trees in the Land of Punt (now Somalia) and planted them in the grounds of the Temple of Karnak. **BARK** Papery, peeling. **LEAF** Alternate, pinnate, with a terminal leaflet; 6–8 pairs of obovate-oblong leaflets, hairy above and below, margins with small rounded teeth. **FLOWER** Small, white to pink, borne in axillary racemes at the ends of branches. **FRUIT** Small green drupe.

egg-shaped drupe

FRUIT

flowers in racemes

leaf clusters at ends of branches

FLOWERING BRANCHES

white to reddish bark

SACRED FRAGRANCE

Frankincense was burnt in religious rites in ancient Egypt and Rome and in Jewish tabernacles; it is still used in Catholic and Coptic churches. At the height of trade, some 3,000 tons were used annually. Today, world production is about 500 tons.

FRANKINCENSE RESIN

Bursera simaruba

Gumbo Limbo

HEIGHT 5–20m (16–65ft)
TYPE Deciduous
OCCURRENCE USA (S. Florida),
West Indies, Mexico to Venezuela

Found in coastal mangroves, this tree,
also known as the Tourist Tree, has a
thick trunk and massive, spreading
branches. Commonly used as a living
fence, it has been planted as a street tree
in coastal towns and as an ornamental.
The trunk yields resin and the bark,
formerly used as a medicine for gout,
is used to make glue, varnish, and incense.
BARK Reddish brown to copper coloured,
smooth. **LEAF** Alternate, pinnate, with
a terminal leaflet; 3–7 ovate-oblong
leaflets, dark green above, paler below.
FLOWER Cream, males and females borne
on separate trees in terminal and lateral
narrow clusters; males about twice as
long as the females.
FRUIT Red, three-
sided, angular drupe-
like capsule, splitting
into three valves to
release the bony seeds.

peeling in papery flakes
MATURE BARK

Commiphora myrrha

Myrrh

HEIGHT 2–4m (6–12ft)
TYPE Deciduous
OCCURRENCE Arabian
  Peninsula, Horn of Africa

These small trees or shrubs have knotted
and spiny branches. Myrrh resin came
from Arabia along the "incense road" in
long camel trains to Egypt, Rome, and
further west. About 10,000 camel
loads were transported annually on
this trade route. Myrrh was used as an
incense, for embalming, and as a
medicine. It is still used in Chinese
traditional medicine. **BARK** Green to pale
brown, peeling, papery; exudes a greyish
resin. **LEAF** Alternate, trifoliate, with a
well-developed, obovate to elliptic terminal
leaflet; small, poorly developed lateral
leaflets. **FLOWER** Yellow-green to white,
borne at the ends of short lateral
branches. **FRUIT** Smooth drupe,
containing a hard stone.

*spiny
branches*

Anacardium occidentale

Cashew

HEIGHT 4–12m (15–40ft)
TYPE Evergreen
OCCURRENCE N.E. Brazil, introduced
in India, S.E. Asia, Africa

kidney-shaped
nuts

prominent veins

FLOWER Borne in a
terminal panicle, with
yellow-green to pinkish
petals. **FRUIT** Nut at the end
of a fleshy, fruit-like stalk.

The Cashew tree is widely cultivated in
the tropics for its nut. The Portuguese
brought the cashew nut to India from
Brazil in the 16th century, from where it
was introduced to Africa. Vietnam has
emerged as its leading producer today.
BARK Grey to brown, smooth, fissured
with age; exudes sap that turns black
on exposure. **LEAF** Alternate, obovate
to obovate-oblong,
untoothed margin.

LEAVES

recurved petals

elongated
style

pink streaks

FLOWERS

Gluta renghas

Renghas

HEIGHT up to 50m (165ft)
TYPE Evergreen
OCCURRENCE Malaysia, Indonesia, Philippines,
Papua New Guinea

Found in swamp forests, this tree has a
dense crown and its trunk is sometimes
buttressed. It yields a reddish timber with
a beautiful grain, but this is rarely utilized
because felling and processing of the
wood can cause allergic reactions. The
seeds can be eaten after being roasted.
BARK Pale brown, becoming greyish with
age; exudes black, resinous, irritant sap.
LEAF Alternate, leathery, elliptic to oblong
or oblanceolate. **FLOWER** White, fragrant,
in axillary panicles.
FRUIT Spherical,
pinkish brown,
fleshy drupe.

scaly surface

BARK

Harpephyllum caffrum

Kaffir Plum

HEIGHT 6–15m (20–50ft)
TYPE Evergreen
OCCURRENCE S. and E. Africa

The name of this tree is derived from its place of origin, Kaffraria, now part of Eastern Cape, South Africa. It has a small, compact, and roundish crown. An ornamental shade tree, it is planted as a street tree in South African towns and cities. Its fruit is used to make jams and jellies, and can also be fermented into a wine. **BARK** Silvery white to brown, with raised ridges or cracked segments. **LEAF** Alternate, pinnate; 4–8 pairs of sickle-shaped leaflets, with wavy or untoothed margins. **FLOWER** Whitish green, males and females on separate trees, borne in panicles near ends of branches. **FRUIT** Plum-like drupe, red when ripe, edible, with a sour taste.

LEAVES

Mangifera indica

Mango

HEIGHT 10–45m (33–150ft)
TYPE Evergreen
OCCURRENCE Known only in cultivation

Mangoes have been in cultivation for over a thousand years. There are over 1,000 cultivars with some 500 of these in India alone. They are divided into two types: the Indian type with a single embryo per seed, and those with multiple embryos, mostly from Southeast Asia. In India, the unripe fruit is made into pickles and chutney. It is also dried and powdered to be used as a spice or as a meat tenderizer. **BARK** Greyish brown, smooth or with thin fissures, becoming darker, rough, scaly or furrowed with age. **LEAF** Alternate, leathery, usually narrowly elliptic to lanceolate, often with wavy margins. **FLOWER** Greenish yellow, in terminal panicles.

glossy green above

FRUIT Fleshy, often fibrous drupe, sometimes with a turpentine flavour.

LEAF ROSETTE

slender stalks

RIPE FRUIT

yellowish green to reddish skin

yellow to orange flesh

dense crown

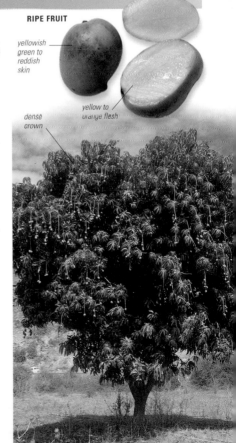

Pistacia lentiscus

Mastic

HEIGHT 2.4–3.6m (8–12ft)
TYPE Evergreen
OCCURRENCE Mediterranean region

Also known as Chios Mastic, this low, spreading tree usually has a crooked trunk. Only one variety (*Pistacia lentiscus* var. *chia*), grown on the Greek island of Chios, yields mastic resin, the original chewing resin used as a breath freshener. The resin is also used in water pipes, coffee, Turkish delight, and for medicinal purposes. **BARK** Pale grey-brown, turns dark grey-brown and rough, with large

TREE IN BLOSSOM

scaly plates. **LEAF** Alternate, pinnate; 4–10 oblong-lanceolate leaflets. **FLOWER** Males and females on separate trees, yellowish white with red stamens and stigmas. **FRUIT** Spherical, bright red drupe, ripening to black.

LEAFLETS

flower to 3cm (1¼in) long

fruit in clusters

to 3cm (1¼in) long

LEAVES, FLOWERS, AND FRUIT

FLOWER CLUSTER

Pistacia vera

Pistachio

HEIGHT up to 10m (33ft)
TYPE Deciduous
OCCURRENCE C. Asia, Afghanistan, Iran, Turkey

leaflet 5–10cm (2–4in) long

LEAVES AND FRUIT

Probably the earliest known cultivated tree, possibly dating back to 6,000BCE, the Pistachio is a small tree, known for its edible nut-like fruit. It is said that the Queen of Sheba reserved the harvest of the best pistachio trees for herself, and carried pistachios as a gift for King Solomon in 950BCE. **BARK** Grey-brown to russet, smooth, becoming rough. **LEAF** Alternate, trifoliate or pinnate with a terminal leaflet; 1–3 pairs of large, hairy, ovate to broadly lanceolate leaflets. **FLOWER** Males and females borne on separate trees; small, petalless, greenish brown, in panicles. **FRUIT** Edible, one-seeded drupe.

PISTACHIO NUTS

Pleiogynium timoriense

Burdekin Plum

HEIGHT 20–36m (55–120ft)
TYPE Semi-evergreen
OCCURRENCE Pacific Islands, Papua New Guinea, Australia

A spreading rainforest tree, the Burdekin Plum tree is known for its fleshy fruit. Marketed as "bush tucker", the fruit tends to be exceedingly acid and needs to be stored for several days to become soft and mellow. It is usually stewed or made into jams and jellies. **BARK** Dark grey or grey-brown, fissured, flaky. **LEAF** Alternate, pinnate with a terminal leaflet, glossy dark green. **FLOWER** Greenish yellow, small, in many-flowered, axillary panicles; males and females on separate trees. **FRUIT** Egg-shaped, edible drupe, dark purple when ripe, with a large single seed.

Schinus molle

Pepper Tree

HEIGHT 5–15m (16–50ft)
TYPE Evergreen
OCCURRENCE South America

Widely cultivated in dry subtropical areas, this tree has slender, drooping branches. It is often invasive in open wasteland. Its fruit was once used to make pink peppercorns. **BARK** Grey and smooth when young, turning yellowish brown, rough, and scaly. **LEAF** Alternate, pinnate with a terminal leaflet; leaflets lanceolate to linear-lanceolate, smooth to slightly toothed. **FLOWER** Yellowish white, small; males and females on separate trees, in axillary clusters at the tips of branches. **FRUIT** Lavender to pink drupes.

19–41 leaflets

small, spherical fruit

LEAVES AND FRUIT

Spondias dulcis

Ambarella

HEIGHT 6–18m (20–60ft)
TYPE Deciduous/Evergreen
OCCURRENCE Pacific Islands, S.E. Asia, introduced in West Indies

NEW LEAVES

The sour fruit of this tree is stewed and used in preserves, pickles, and sambal. It tastes of apples and pineapples, and has a pungent, resinous aroma. **BARK** Greyish to reddish brown, becoming fissured. **LEAF** Alternate, pinnate with a terminal leaflet; leaflets elliptic to obovate-oblong, with smooth or scalloped margins. **FLOWER** Cream to white, small, in terminal panicles; males and females on same tree. **FRUIT** Oval, thick-skinned drupes in clusters, containing yellow pulp.

9–25 leaflets

UNRIPE FRUIT

Ailanthus altissima

Tree of Heaven

HEIGHT 15–20m (50–70ft)
TYPE Deciduous
OCCURRENCE N. China, widely cultivated

This fast-growing tree has a rounded crown. Philip Miller (1691–1771), a noted English gardener, was the first to raise it from seeds sent to London from China. **BARK** Grey, finely fissured, becoming darker and rougher with age. **LEAF** Alternate, pinnate with a terminal leaflet, dark green; leaflets 13–31, ovate, finely hairy, untoothed or with 1–3 teeth at the base, bearing glands. **FLOWER** Small, greenish, males and females usually on separate trees, borne in terminal panicles; males with a foetid scent. **FRUIT** Flattened winged seed up to 4cm (1 1/2in) long, green at first, turning yellow-brown tinged with red.

FOLIAGE AND FLOWERS

notch near base
of leaflets

winged
fruit   **LEAVES AND FRUIT**

AN ORNAMENTAL WEED

Following its discovery by the West, this tree was planted widely in Europe. It was noted that silkworms produced a high quality thread when fed on its leaves instead of the mulberry's. In 1784, it was introduced into the USAby William Hamilton. A century later, biologists realized that it had invaded and colonized large waste areas in southern USA.

Leitneria floridana

Corkwood

HEIGHT up to 6m (20ft)
TYPE Deciduous
OCCURRENCE S.E. USA

Considered an endangered tree, only one species of the Corkwood can be found in scattered coastal and riverine floodplains of Missouri, Arkansas – where it is locally common – Florida, Texas, and in Georgia along the Altamaha river. This tree has spreading branches and a loose, open crown. **BARK** Dark grey, tinged with brown, divided by shallow fissures. **LEAF** Alternate, elliptic to elliptic-lanceolate, bright green above, covered with soft hairs beneath, on reddish stems. **FLOWER** Inconspicuous catkins on separate plants; both male and female catkins cylindrical; females upright and shorter. **FRUIT** Oblong, compressed, one-seeded, dry drupe.

Azadirachta indica

Neem

HEIGHT up to 16m (52ft)
TYPE Evergreen/Semi-evergreen
OCCURRENCE N.W. India, Myanmar, cultivated in tropical Asia and Africa

The people of India have long been aware of the medical properties of the Neem. These are recorded in early Sanskrit writings and are embedded in Ayurvedic medicine. Neem research was part of the upsurge of nationalistic sentiment started by Mahatma Gandhi. Often referred to as "the

village pharmacy" tree, the Neem's parts are used to treat diseases caused by fungi, viruses, and bacteria. Traditionally, neem seeds were used as an insect repellent and neem cake was spread on the soil as a fertilizer. **BARK** Red-brown to greyish, becoming fissured and flaky with age. **LEAF** Alternate, pinnate with or without a terminal leaflet; 4–7 pairs of sickle-shaped to lanceolate leaflets, with sharply toothed margins; two pairs of glands at base of leaf stalk. **FLOWER** Borne in axillary inflorescences, white, petals softly hairy on both sides, sweetly scented. **FRUIT** Single-seeded drupe, turning yellow when ripe.

NATURAL INSECTICIDE

Extracted from the kernel of the neem fruit, neem oil has valuable pesticidal and medicinal properties. Research has identified a compound in neem oil that works as an antifeedant, suggesting that the oil could have a great future as a selective, non-toxic insecticide. Its use as an environmentally safe alternative to synthetic insecticides and pesticides now draws interest from industrialized countries. The oil is also used in medicinal products for an array of blood, digestive, skin, and immune system disorders.

NEEM OIL

fleshy covering

to 1cm (³⁄₈in) long

SEED

UNRIPE FRUIT

1.2–2cm (³⁄₈–³⁄₄in) long

Cedrela odorata

West Indian Cedar

HEIGHT 12–30m (40–100ft)
TYPE Deciduous
OCCURRENCE West Indies, South America

The West Indian Cedar is a fast-growing species, usually with a rounded crown. It is an important avenue and shade tree in its native region and in Africa, where it is cultivated. It is also used as a shade tree in coffee and cocoa plantations. The wood of the tree has a strong aromatic odour and is resistant to insects. It is an important timber for furniture-making, especially for the manufacture of chests, and wardrobes. **BARK** Grey to brown, thick, becoming rough and furrowed. **LEAF** Alternate, pinnate, without a terminal leaflet.

10–30 leaflets

LEAVES

FLOWER Numerous, borne in terminal panicles, small, with yellow-green staminal tube. **FRUIT** Woody capsule, with winged seeds.

CEDAR WOOD FOR CIGAR BOXES

Cigars were originally packed in chests containing about 10,000 cigars. The bankers, H. Upmann, started shipping cigars in cedar boxes for their directors in London. They continued to use this packaging when they changed to the cigar business and it became standard for all major brands, because cedar wood helps to prevent cigars from drying out. Today, the wood is specially grown for the purpose.

CEDAR-LINED CIGAR BOX

Khaya senegalensis
Bisselon

HEIGHT up to 30m (100ft)
TYPE Evergreen
OCCURRENCE Africa

This tree is also called the African Mahogany. It was one of the first African mahoganies to be exported to Europe but today, due to its relatively small size and low weight, is seldom exported. The bark contains compounds that are used for medicinal and veterinary purposes.
BARK Grey, scaly. **LEAF** Alternate, pinnate; pale green leaflets. **FLOWER** In drooping, axillary panicles, creamish petals and staminal tube, with red disc. **FRUIT** Four-valved, woody capsule with winged seeds.

bark exudes red sap | knobbly surface

TRUNK | **BARK**

Dysoxylum traserianum
Australian Rosewood

HEIGHT 12–25m (40–80ft)
TYPE Evergreen
OCCURRENCE Australia (New South Wales, Queensland)

A common rainforest tree, the Australian Rosewood is also planted as an ornamental in large parks, including the Sydney Botanical Gardens. It was named after Charles Fraser, who was the first Superintendent of the Gardens. Large and fast-growing, the tree has a dense, leafy, spreading crown and a large, buttressed trunk. It needs moist soil to thrive. The wood is reddish and has a delicate perfume that is similar to roses. It has been used for carving, furniture, and cabinet-making. **BARK** Pale brown to yellowish grey, scaly. **LEAF** Alternate, pinnate without a terminal leaflet; 4–12 elliptic to obovate leaflets.
FLOWER Cream to white, fragrant, in terminal and lateral panicles.
FRUIT Cream tinged with pink, four-celled capsule, containing one or two seeds with a reddish aril.

Chukrasia tabularis
Yinma

HEIGHT up to 40m (130ft)
TYPE Deciduous
OCCURRENCE S. and S.E. Asia.

The Yinma has a fluted and buttressed trunk and its timber is valued for making furniture. **BARK** Dark brown, fissured.
LEAF Alternate, pinnate, with ovate to oblong leaflets. **FLOWER** Fragrant, creamy green to yellowish white, in axillary clusters. **FRUIT** Woody capsule.

6–12 leaflets | **LEAVES**

Lansium domesticum
Langsat

HEIGHT up to 30m (100ft)
TYPE Evergreen
OCCURRENCE Thailand, Malaya, Sumatra, Java, Borneo

The Langsat is a complex and variable species with wild and cultivated forms. There are two major varieties: Langsat, slender trees bearing oval fruit and Duku, spreading trees bearing rounded fruit. **BARK** Pale reddish brown or with fawn blotches, slightly furrowed and scaly. **LEAF** Alternate, pinnate with a terminal leaflet; 2–4 pairs of ovate-elliptic to oblong leaflets, slightly hairy beneath. **FLOWER** Borne in racemes on the branches or trunk, with greenish yellow petals and staminal tube. **FRUIT** Oval or globose berry, pale yellow to brown, skin sometimes exuding latex.

FRUIT

2.5–5cm (1–2in) wide

Lovoa trichilioides
Nigerian Golden Walnut

HEIGHT up to 45m (150ft)
TYPE Evergreen
OCCURRENCE S. to S.W. Africa

This well-known timber tree is found in lowland rainforest, but is also grown in plantations. **BARK** Smooth, with large irregular flaking pieces. **LEAF** Pinnate, without terminal leaflet; leaflets elliptic in six pairs, rounded or shortly pointed at the base. **FLOWER** Greenish white, with four sepals and petals, borne in large panicles. **FRUIT** Black or purplish black pendulous capsule, containing winged seeds.

FLOWER PANICLES

Sandoricum koetjape

Santol

HEIGHT up to 45m (150ft)
TYPE Evergreen
OCCURRENCE Cambodia, Laos, Malaya, (naturalized in Malaysia, Indonesia, Molucca Islands, Mauritius, Philippines, India)

Besides being valued for its fruit, this low-branched species is prized for its timber. **BARK** Pale. **LEAF** Spirally arranged, with three elliptic to oval leaflets, 20–25cm (8–10in) long, blunt at the base. **FLOWER** Borne in stalked panicles, with five greenish, yellowish, or pinkish yellow petals. **FRUIT** Oval to round drupe, containing milky fluid, 3–5 brown seeds in white translucent pulp.

pointed tip

wrinkled base of fruit

seed 2cm (¾in) long

SEED   **LEAFLET**

Melia azedarach

Persian Lilac

HEIGHT up to 40m (130ft)
TYPE Deciduous
OCCURRENCE Sri Lanka, India, China, S.E. Asia, Australia

Widely cultivated in tropical areas, this tree has a fluted trunk when mature. Forms of the Persian Lilac have been in cultivation for some 2,500 years. There are two groups of cultivars: the Chinese group, which has larger fruit, and the Indian cultivars. **BARK** Grey-brown, smooth, with lenticels, becoming lightly fissured. **LEAF** Alternate, usually bipinnate, with a terminal leaflet; 7–11 ovate to elliptic leaflets, dark green above, pale green, often sparsely hairy beneath. **FLOWER** Borne in axillary clusters, with white to lilac petals and staminal tube, densely hairy inside and sweetly scented. **FRUIT** Ovoid, plum-shaped drupe, yellow-brown when ripe; poisonous.

FLOWERS

Swietenia macrophylla

Baywood

HEIGHT up to 45m (150ft)
TYPE Evergreen/Deciduous
OCCURRENCE S. Mexico, Central and South America

Baywood is the most valuable timber tree in tropical Central and South America. Also known as Honduras Mahogany, its wood is fairly lightweight and strong, with a medium and uniform texture. It takes an excellent polish and is resistant to decay. **BARK** Pale brown, rough, deeply fissured. **LEAF** Alternate, pinnate without a terminal leaflet, slender yellow-green axis ending in a narrow point; 3–6 pairs of unequal-sided leaflets, 6–15cm (2¼–6in) long. **FLOWER** Small, greenish yellow, short-stalked, in panicles, 10–15cm (4–6in) long, five petals, ten brown stamens, fragrant. **FRUIT** Seeded capsule, erect, oval, 11–18cm (4¼–7in) long, 7.5cm (3in) wide, on long, stout stalks.

over 1cm (⅜ in) thick

BARK

Swietenia mahagoni

Mahogany

HEIGHT 12–16m (40–52ft)
TYPE Deciduous
OCCURRENCE USA (S. Florida), Bahamas, Antilles, Haiti, Jamaica

With its buttressed trunk and spreading crown, this tree has been prized since the 16th century, when its timber was first shipped to Europe. Most natural stands of mahogany were felled long ago. Today,

FRUIT AND LEAVES

open capsule

oblong fruit

FRUIT

the largest living specimen is believed to be in Florida's Everglades National Park. **BARK** Grey to dark reddish brown, smooth to slightly fissured, becoming scaly. **LEAF** Alternate, pinnate without a terminal leaflet, untoothed. **FLOWER** Greenish yellow, in panicles. **FRUIT** Woody capsule, stalked, upright, with winged seeds.

FLOWERS

greenish yellow fused stamens

Toona ciliata

Toon

HEIGHT up to 55m (180ft)
TYPE Deciduous
OCCURRENCE India, S. China, S.E. Asia
Malaysia, E. Australia

FLOWERS

5 petals

creamy white
flowers

Also known as the Red Cedar, this tall tree
has a cylindrical, sometimes buttressed,
trunk. It grows in sub-tropical rainforest
and scrubby areas, often bordering rivers
and streams. Its wood is highly valued for
cabinet-making and it has been virtually
logged out in its range due to extensive
exploitation of its timber. In Australia, it
used to be felled before conversion of areas
to agricultural land, but the remaining
forests where it occurs are now in a World
Heritage site. In the past, its flowers were
used as a source of red and yellow dyes
for silk, cotton,
and wool. The
tree has been
used medicinally,
particularly as an
astringent and a
tonic. **BARK** Greyish
white to brown,
usually fissured and
flaking. **LEAF** Alternate,
pinnate, with up to 20 ovate-lanceolate to
lanceolate leaflets, smooth to sparsely hairy.
FLOWER In large terminal panicles, white
to creamy white staminal tube, fragrant.
FRUIT Brown capsule, divides into five
segments when dry.

open
capsule

FRUIT

LEAVES AND FLOWERS

Xylocarpus granatum

Cannonball Mahogany

HEIGHT up to 20m (65ft)
TYPE Semi-evergreen
OCCURRENCE E. Africa, S.E. Asia, Tonga

The wood of this tree was once used for boat-building. Its bark is used for making dyes and medicines and its roots also have medicinal properties. **BARK** Pale to yellow-brown, smooth, scaling in irregular flakes. **LEAF** Alternate, pinnate; leaflets in 1–3 pairs, with rounded tips. **FLOWER** In axillary, white to pink clusters. **FRUIT** Spherical, hanging capsule.

elliptic to obovate
LEAFLETS

thinly branched buttresses

Calodendrum capense

Cape Chestnut

HEIGHT up to 20m (65ft)
TYPE Deciduous, rarely evergreen
OCCURRENCE South Africa to Tanzania and Ethiopia

An ornamental with a dense, compact, and rounded crown, this shade tree is suitable for planting in parks and streets. **BARK** Grey, smooth, mottled, and streaky.

LEAF Opposite, smooth, with untoothed edges. **FLOWER** In open terminal panicles, with five narrow petals, five pale pink stamens. **FRUIT** Woody, five-lobed, rough capsule.

ovate-oblong to elliptic leaves

pale pink flowers
LEAVES AND FLOWERS

Chloroxylon swietenia

Satinwood

HEIGHT up to 32m (105ft)
TYPE Deciduous
OCCURRENCE Madagascar, Sri Lanka, S. India

Satinwood grows in the dry, interior forests of its native range. It has hard, heavy, yellowish wood that polishes well. Its timber was once an important

Sri Lankan export. **BARK** Yellowish grey, deeply fissured. **LEAF** Pinnate, equal on both sides, up to 24cm (9½ in) long, 10–20 pairs of oblong leaflets. **FLOWER** Tiny, white, about 7mm (³/₁₆in) wide, on pyramidal racemes up to 15cm (6in) long, often produced when the tree is leafless. **FRUIT** Capsule, up to 3cm (1¼ in) long, oblong-ovoid and three-celled, each cell containing about four flat, winged seeds.

Citrus x aurantium

Bitter Orange

HEIGHT up to 10m (33ft)
TYPE Evergreen
OCCURRENCE China, Vietnam

The Bitter or Seville Orange has a round crown and its seedlings are often covered with spines. It is believed to have originally grown in the area of the China–Vietnam border and its long history of cultivation brought it through Arabia and into southern Europe by the 11th–12th centuries. The Spanish introduced it and the more widely cultivated Sweet Orange (*Citrus sinensis*) into South America and Mexico in the mid-1500s. Its fragrant white flowers are the

thick-skinned unripe fruit

finely toothed edges

FRUIT AND LEAVES

VERSATILE CITRUS

The Bitter Orange is used as a rootstock for other citrus trees, in herbal remedies, and to make marmalade. It is also planted as an ornamental, especially in the Mediterranean region.

ORNAMENTAL PLANTING

source of neroli oil. **BARK** Green to greyish brown. **LEAF** Alternate, ovate to ovate-oblong, smooth, with narrowly winged stalks. **FLOWER** White, fragrant, solitary or in short axillary racemes. **FRUIT** Spherical, greenish yellow to bright orange.

Citrus x aurantiifolia

Lime

HEIGHT up to 5m (16ft)
TYPE Evergreen
OCCURRENCE Known only in cultivation

winged stalks

The Lime tree has irregular, drooping branches and spiny twigs. A native to India, it was brought by the Arabs to Africa and the Middle East. It spread to Europe during the Crusades

LEAVES AND FRUIT

and was later taken to the Caribbean and Mexico following the Spanish conquest. The juice from the fruit is used in cooking, soft drinks, pickles, and for medicinal purposes. Its extracts and essential oils are used in aromatherapy, and in perfumes and cleansing products. **BARK** Green to greyish brown. **LEAF** Alternate, elliptic to ovate-oblong, with finely toothed margins. **FLOWER** White, up to ten, on short axillary racemes. **FRUIT** Ovoid to globose, with a thin skin.

FRUIT

greenish yellow skin

greenish pulp

Citrus x limon

Lemon

HEIGHT 3–6m (10–20ft)
TYPE Evergreen
OCCURRENCE Known only in cultivation

Unpalatable as a fresh fruit due to its acidic taste, lemon is mostly consumed in cooking and in drinks. **BARK** Green to greyish brown. **LEAF** Alternate, elliptic-ovate to oblong, with toothed margins, on winged stalks. **FLOWER** Axillary; solitary or in clusters of 2–3. **FRUIT** Ovoid, greenish to golden yellow, with thick and rough skin.

white flowers
elliptic-oblong leaves

LEAVES AND FLOWERS

FRUIT

Citrus reticulata

Mandarin

HEIGHT 3–6m (10–20ft)
TYPE Evergreen
OCCURRENCE S.E. Asia, S. Europe, Brazil, S.E. USA

The Mandarin was probably brought into cultivation in tropical Southeast Asia. It is one of the major parent species that gave rise to the remaining hybrid *Citrus*. **BARK** Green to greyish brown. **LEAF** Alternate, elliptic to lanceolate, on winged stalks. **FLOWER** White, solitary or in clusters of 2–3. **FRUIT** Rounded, with thin skin, indented on top.

LEAVES AND FRUIT

toothed edges

bright orange skin

FLOWER

Flindersia australis

Crow's Ash

HEIGHT 15–40m (50–130ft)
TYPE Evergreen/Semi-evergreen
OCCURRENCE E. Australia

The Crow's Ash or Australian Teak has a dense, spreading crown. It is an excellent urban shade tree. Its timber is yellow-brown. **BARK** Grey to dark brown, smooth, becoming scaly with rounded flakes. **LEAF** Alternate, pinnate, with a terminal leaflet; 3–13 elliptic to narrowly ovate leaflets, aromatic when crushed. **FLOWER** White to cream, in terminal panicles. **FRUIT** Woody five-valved capsule, covered with short, blunt prickles.

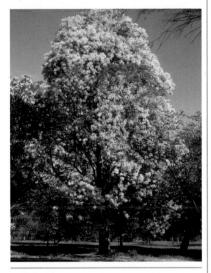

Limonia acidissima

Wood Apple

HEIGHT up to 7m (23ft)
TYPE Deciduous
OCCURRENCE S. Asia

The Wood Apple grows in the dry areas of its native habitat. Its fruit is a favourite of elephants. **BARK** Pale grey or whitish; branchlets with straight spines that are up to 4cm (1½in) long. **LEAF** Pinnate, with one terminal leaflet; 2–3 pairs of opposite, obovate, stalkless leaflets. **FLOWER** White, green, or reddish purple, with small petals and 7–12 stamens, numerous, on axillary clusters, often from leafless nodes. **FRUIT** Round, woody, many-seeded fruit, with sticky pulp.

Flindersia brayleyana

Queensland Maple

HEIGHT 25–35m (80–115ft)
TYPE Evergreen
OCCURRENCE Australia (Queensland)

boat-shaped valve

FRUIT POD

This tree is valued for its easily workable pinkish wood that is used for cabinet-making and indoor fittings. In Australia, it is planted as an ornamental.
BARK Grey, flaky. **LEAF** Opposite, pinnate with a terminal leaflet; 3–10 broadly elliptic leaflets. **FLOWER** White to cream, borne in terminal panicles. **FRUIT** Woody capsule, covered with short, blunt prickles, splitting into five valves.

Zanthoxylum simulans

Flatspine Prickly Ash

HEIGHT up to 6m (20ft)
TYPE Deciduous
OCCURRENCE China

This tree is found in mountain woods and thickets. Its leaves are aromatic when crushed. **BARK** Grey with conical knobs. **LEAF** Pinnate; up to 11 ovate, toothed leaflets. **FLOWER** Small, green, in clusters up to 5cm (2in) wide. **FRUIT** Round, warty, green, ripens to red.

glossy green leaflet

red-stalked fruit

LEAVES AND FRUIT

Sichuan Pepper
Zanthoxylum piperitum

HEIGHT up to 10m (33ft)
TYPE Deciduous
OCCURRENCE China, Japan, Korea

The fruit of this tree is used for flavouring and seasoning food. **BARK** Yellowish brown, smooth to shallowly fissured.

LEAF Alternate, pinnate with a terminal leaflet; usually 9–17, ovate to elliptic-lanceolate, toothed leaflets. **FLOWER** Greenish, in terminal clusters; males and females on separate trees. **FRUIT** Globose follicle, greenish, ripening to brown, with black seeds.

Chinese Dogwood
Cornus kousa

HEIGHT 3–15m (10–50ft)
TYPE Deciduous
OCCURRENCE China, Japan, Korea

This tree has a columnar habit. Its foliage turns red in autumn. **BARK** Greyish to red-brown. **LEAF** Opposite, dark green above, waxy and downy beneath. **FLOWER** Yellowish green, in dense heads on long stalks. **FRUIT** Red, fleshy drupe.

FRUIT AND LEAVES   strawberry-like fruit   ovate to ovate-elliptic leaves

Cornelian Cherry
Cornus mas

HEIGHT up to 8m (26ft)
TYPE Deciduous
OCCURRENCE C. and S. Europe, S.W. Asia

Cultivated in the past for its edible fruit, which has a plum-like flavour, this tree is now usually planted as a winter-flowering ornamental. It has numerous cultivars. **BARK** Dark brown, scaly. **LEAF** Opposite, ovate to elliptic, hairy on both sides. **FLOWER** Yellow, appearing before leaves. **FRUIT** Bright red, round drupe.

FLOWERS   short flower clusters

Canadian Dogwood
Cornus nuttalli

HEIGHT up to 20m (65ft)
TYPE Deciduous
OCCURRENCE W. North America

The flower of this tree is the floral emblem of British Columbia. **BARK** Grey, smooth, becoming scaly with age. **LEAF** Opposite, elliptic to obovate, dark green. **FLOWER** In clusters, with creamy white bracts. **FRUIT** Edible red drupe.

small and yellowish green   **FLOWERS**

Davidia involucrata

Handkerchief Tree

HEIGHT up to 20m (65ft)
TYPE Deciduous
OCCURRENCE China

Also called Dove Tree, the genus is named after Father Armand David, a French missionary, who was the first to report in 1869 that this tree had white flowers "fluttering like doves". During the decades that followed, French and British plant-hunters tried to introduce the tree into Europe. The form most grown today was raised in French nurseries at the end of the 19th century. **BARK** Orange-brown, peeling vertically in small flakes. **LEAF** Alternate, broadly ovate, heart-shaped base, smooth above, downy beneath. **FLOWER** Terminal, on short spur shoots, in small heads, surrounded by two asymmetrical white bracts. **FRUIT** Green with a purple bloom, solitary, usually pear-shaped.

FLOWER CLUSTERS

large white bracts

toothed leaf margin

FOLIAGE

Nyssa sylvatica

Black Gum

HEIGHT up to 25m (80ft)
TYPE Deciduous
OCCURRENCE E. North America

The Black Gum, also called Tupelo, has a pyramidal crown and drooping branches. It is planted as an ornamental and street tree due to its red autumn colour. It is also popular for environmental planting. **BARK** Dark grey, vertically ridged, breaking into irregular scales. **LEAF** Alternate, dark glossy green above, slightly hairy beneath. **FLOWER** Axillary, greenish, in stalked heads; males and females on same or separate trees. **FRUIT** Ovoid, blue drupe.

ovate to elliptic

LEAVES

Fouquieria columnaris

Boojum Tree

HEIGHT up to 18m (60ft)
TYPE Deciduous
OCCURRENCE Mexico (Baja California)

This strange-looking tree has a succulent main stem that has been often compared to an upside-down green carrot. It was given its unusual name by plant explorer Godfrey Sykes in 1923, after a fictitious character in a Lewis Carroll book. Its tall, gently tapering trunk has bristles with short branches, armed with spines. On older trees, the main trunk splits into two or more stems near the top. The tree grows on rocky hillsides, alluvial plains, and in deserts. **BARK** Pale yellow-green, tough, smooth but dimpled with twig scars. **LEAF** Alternate, obovate, fleshy, smooth. **FLOWER** Creamy yellow, tubular, borne on spike-like clusters. **FRUIT** Pale brown capsule, with three valves that curve backwards after opening.

thin secondary branches

FLOWERING BRANCHES

flowers in clusters

BOOJUM BOOSTERS

Trees of the Fouquieriacene family are pollinated by a variety of insects. One species, *E. splendens*, was thought to be pollinated by hummingbirds, but these are now known to feed on the nectar without carrying pollen between plants.

HUMMINGBIRD

Camellia sinensis

Tea

HEIGHT 10–15m (32–50ft)
TYPE Evergreen
OCCURRENCE China, N. India

The Tea plant is the source of the world's most popular beverage. Under cultivation, it is trimmed and kept as low bushes or hedges. The use of tea was originally restricted to China and Japan. The Dutch introduced it to Europe and dominated the trade for more than a century before yielding to the British. In 1823, the first wild tea plant was discovered in Assam, India. On 10 January 1839, the first samples of Assam tea were auctioned in London, a historic event that determined the future course of tea cultivation all over the world. Today, more tea is produced from Assam plants than from the Chinese type. It is fermented to give black tea as

FLOWER AND FRUIT

TEA HARVESTING

Tea leaves are harvested every 7–15 days, depending on the development of the tender shoots. Slow-developing leaves give a better flavour. They are dried to make green, black, or oolong teas. **PICKING TEA**

opposed to Chinese unfermented green tea. **BARK** Grey, rough. **LEAF** Alternate, leathery, lanceolate to elliptic, slightly hairy when young, becoming smooth. **FLOWER** White, large, axillary, solitary, with 5–7 petals and numerous yellow stamens. **FRUIT** Capsule that splits open when seeds ripen.

glossy surface

LEAVES

Franklinia alatamaha

Franklin Tree

HEIGHT up to 5–7m (16–23ft)
TYPE Deciduous
OCCURRENCE North America

Discovered in Georgia in 1765, this tree was named after Benjamin Franklin. It was last seen in the wild in 1803 and is now known only in cultivation. The tree has a dense, rounded crown. **BARK** Dark brown, smooth. **LEAF** Alternate, obovate, finely toothed, dark green above, paler with fine hairs beneath. **FLOWER** Axillary, solitary, large, with five white petals. **FRUIT** Spherical, dry, woody capsule.

LEAVES AND FLOWER | *numerous yellow stamens*

Diospyros ebenum

Ebony

HEIGHT up to 30m (100ft)
TYPE Evergreen
OCCURRENCE S. India, Sri Lanka

This tree has nearly uniform black wood, the densest and darkest of the Indian-Asian ebony timbers. It is slow-growing and has a buttressed, sometimes fluted trunk. **BARK** Black to grey-black, flaking in small rectangular pieces. **LEAF** Alternate, elliptic to ovate-oblong. **FLOWER** Males and females on separate trees; males: yellowish, with white corolla, borne in clusters of 3–5; females: yellowish white, solitary. **FRUIT** Large, spherical to ovoid berry.

Diospyros quaesita

Calamander

HEIGHT up to 35m (115ft)
TYPE Evergreen
OCCURRENCE Sri Lanka

Calamander timber is black, with brown bands. It is valued for its durability and ornamental value, but the tree is now rare because of its slow growth and irregular flowering period. **BARK** Black, very rough, peeling to reveal a brown layer. **LEAF** Alternate, 8–18cm (3¼–7in) long, leathery, elliptic-oblong to lanceolate. **FLOWER** Males: yellow, in small clusters; females: yellowish white to white, solitary. **FRUIT** Spherical berry.

Diospyros kaki

Kaki

HEIGHT up to 27m (88ft)
TYPE Deciduous
OCCURRENCE China, cultivated in Japan

Also called Sharon Fruit, the Kaki has a short, crooked trunk and a dense crown. It has over 1,000 cultivars. Its fruit are of two types. The astringent type, with high levels of soluble tannins, cannot be eaten until fully ripe and is best grown in cooler regions. The non-astringent type needs hot summers. **BARK** Greyish brown, scaly, and divided into square plates.

FRUIT yellow to orange coloration

LEAF Alternate, leathery, ovate to elliptic or rounded, dark green above, pale green and hairy beneath, at least on the veins.

untoothed margins **LEAVES**

FLOWER Males and females on separate trees; males: yellowish or red, with white corollas, borne in clusters of 3–5; females: yellowish white, solitary.
FRUIT Large, spherical to ovoid berry, with a large, persistent calyx.

Diospyros virginiana

Persimmon

HEIGHT up to 15–20m (50–65ft)
TYPE Deciduous
OCCURRENCE E. USA

Often planted as an ornamental, this tree has a broadly spreading crown. Its ripe fruit is pulpy and can be fermented to make persimmon beer. **BARK** Dark brown-grey to black, with square, scaly, thick plates. **LEAF** Alternate, leathery, ovate-oblong to elliptic. **FLOWER** Males and females on separate trees, both yellowish white and bell-shaped; males in clusters of 3–5; females solitary. **FRUIT** Large, spherical to ovoid, yellow to orange berry.

persistent calyx

FRUIT smooth surface **LEAF**

Halesia carolina

Snowdrop Tree

HEIGHT up to 12m (40ft)
TYPE Deciduous
OCCURRENCE S.E. USA

The Snowdrop Tree is a small ornamental that provides a spectacular display of flowers in spring. Its trunk is short or multi-stemmed and its crown is rounded. **BARK** Reddish brown, scaly. **LEAF** Alternate, elliptic to ovate-oblong, thinly hairy on both sides, with finely toothed margins and a long-pointed tip. **FLOWER** White, with bell-shaped corolla, borne in clusters of 3–5 at the nodes on old wood. **FRUIT** Pear-shaped, four-winged, green drupe.

bell-shaped flowers

FLOWERING SHOOT

Styrax officinalis

Styrax

HEIGHT up to 7m (23ft)
TYPE Deciduous
OCCURRENCE Mediterranean region

Resin from the bark of this tree was once used by the Sumerians in ointments. **BARK** Grey-brown, becoming vertically fissured. **LEAF** Alternate, with whitish, star-shaped hairs. **FLOWER** White, with yellow anthers, in axillary, drooping clusters. **FRUIT** Greenish yellow, ovoid drupe.

LEAVES AND FLOWERS

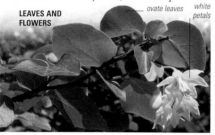

ovate leaves

white petals

Couroupita guianensis

Cannonball Tree

HEIGHT up to 30m (100ft)
TYPE Evergreen/Deciduous
OCCURRENCE Tropical South America

The flowers of this narrow-crowned tree have an unusual sweet scent and are pollinated by bats. **BARK** Brown, smooth, becoming slightly fissured. **LEAF** Alternate, elliptic to oblong or obovate, smooth, except for veins below. **FLOWER** Six reddish-tinged sepals, six pinkish to orange-red petals; only one flower opens at a time. **FRUIT** Large, brown capsule.

curved disc at centre

FLOWER

spherical capsule   **RIPE FRUIT**

Bertholletia excelsa

Brazil Nut

HEIGHT up to 50m (165ft)
TYPE Deciduous
OCCURRENCE Tropical South America

This tall tree has large woody fruit. **BARK** Grey-brown, fissured. **LEAF** Alternate, leathery, smooth, with smooth or wavy margins. **FLOWER** Pale yellow to white, in axillary spikes or terminal panicles. **FRUIT** Capsule with 10–25 seeds (nuts).

FRUIT

hard, woody shell

longitudinally fissured bark

Chrysophyllum cainito

Star Apple

HEIGHT up to 30m (100ft)
TYPE Evergreen
OCCURRENCE West Indies, cultivated in tropical America, S.E. Asia, Africa

This tall tree has a broad and dense crown. **BARK** Brown, rough, and fissured. **LEAF** Alternate, oblong to obovate, dark green above, brown beneath. **FLOWER** Yellowish to purple-white, borne in axillary clusters. **FRUIT** Egg-shaped to spherical berry, with thick rind.

LEAVES, FRUIT, AND FLOWERS

fruit 5–10cm (2–4in) wide   densely hairy undersides   small flowers

Argania spinosa

Argan

HEIGHT up to 10m (33ft)
TYPE Evergreen
OCCURRENCE Morocco

This tree has a dense, wide crown. It is valued for the oil that is extracted from its nuts. **BARK** Grey to yellow-brown, cracked, and divided in small plates. **LEAF** Alternate, usually in clusters, lanceolate-oblong. **FLOWER** Greenish white, in axillary clusters. **FRUIT** Green to brown, ovoid berry with 1–3 seeds.

yellow stamens

FLOWERS

Manilkara bidentata

Balata

HEIGHT up to 33m (110ft)
TYPE Evergreen
OCCURRENCE N. South America, West Indies

The timber of the Balata tree is hard, heavy, and durable. It is used for cabinet-making and to make violin bows. The tree was also tapped or felled for its latex, which was the source of balata gum. **BARK** Brown, thick, fissured and scaly; pink inner bark. **LEAF** Alternate, dark green, elliptic, up to 23cm (9in) long, often covered in a black mould. **FLOWER** Small, fragrant, whitish, bell-shaped, in clusters of 3–10. **FRUIT** Smooth berry, with sticky pulp and one shiny, blackish seed.

Palaquium gutta

Gutta Percha

HEIGHT up to 45m (150ft)
TYPE Evergreen
OCCURRENCE Malay Peninsula, Sumatra, Borneo

This tree has a columnar trunk, usually with small buttresses. Its flowers smell of burnt sugar. Its latex was once used for wire insulation but has been replaced by synthetics. It is now used for dental filling. **BARK** Greyish brown, fissured. **LEAF** Alternate, obovate-ovate to elliptic, dark green above, golden brown with fine silky hairs beneath. **FLOWER** Pale green, in axillary clusters. **FRUIT** Green, globose to egg-shaped, finely hairy nut.

Manilkara zapota

Sapodilla

HEIGHT 5–20m (16–65ft)
TYPE Evergreen
OCCURRENCE Mexico, West Indies, tropical Central America

Sapodilla is grown for its edible fruit. The tree's latex, called "chicle", was used in the past as the first chewing gum.
yellow-brown flesh **BARK** Dark brown, rough. **LEAF** Alternate, ovate-elliptic to oblong-lanceolate, parallel veins. **FLOWER** Solitary, in leaf axils. **FRUIT** Reddish to yellow-brown berry.

shiny black seeds

FRUIT

Pouteria caimito

Abiu

HEIGHT 10–35m (33–115ft)
TYPE Evergreen
OCCURRENCE Tropical South America

This tree has a pyramidal or rounded crown. It is mostly grown in home gardens. **BARK** Grey-brown, with white latex. **LEAF** Alternate, variable shape, usually smooth. **FLOWER** White to pale yellow, solitary or in clusters of 2–5, fragrant. **FRUIT** Round to ovoid yellow berry.

LEAVES

Pouteria sapota

Sapote

HEIGHT 7–20m (23–65ft)
TYPE Evergreen/Semi-evergreen
OCCURRENCE Mexico, Central America, South America, S.E. Asia

This tree has a narrow or spreading crown with thick branches. **BARK** Reddish brown. **LEAF** Alternate, obovate, dark green above, pale green to pale brown beneath. **FLOWER** White to pale yellow, in clusters of 6–15 in axils of fallen leaves. **FRUIT** Dark brown, globose berry with soft, pink to red flesh, sweetish taste.

FRUIT AND FOLIAGE

Pouteria campechiana

Canistel

HEIGHT 8–20m (26–65ft)
TYPE Evergreen
OCCURRENCE Mexico

Grown for its fruit, this tree has been introduced into tropical South America, the Philippines, and the Seychelles. **BARK** Dark grey-brown, furrowed. **LEAF** Alternate, obovate-elliptic, smooth. **FLOWER** White to pale yellow, solitary or in clusters. **FRUIT** Yellow berry.

LEAVES AND FRUIT — smooth skin

Synsepalum dulcificum

Miraculous Berry

HEIGHT up to 3m (10ft)
TYPE Evergreen
OCCURRENCE W. Africa

An unusual trait of this tree's fruit is that it can make bitter or sour food taste sweet. **BARK** Fibrous. **LEAF** Alternate, obovate to oblanceolate, smooth, in clusters. **FLOWER** White, small, in axillary clusters. **FRUIT** Small, single-seeded, bright red berry. — elongated leaves

LEAVES AND FRUIT — oval berry

Arbutus menziesii

Madrono

HEIGHT up to 40m (130ft)
TYPE Evergreen
OCCURRENCE Canada (British Columbia), USA (California, Oregon, Washington)

A highly ornamental horticultural species, this tree is prized for its peeling bark, showy flowers, and brightly coloured fruit. It is named after Archibald Menzies, a Scottish botanist and surgeon, who was the first to discover it in 1792. **BARK** Red-brown, smooth, peeling, becoming fissured with age; green when freshly exposed. **LEAF** Alternate, smooth or slightly downy when young, dark green above, dull or waxy beneath. **FLOWER** White or tinged pink, borne in large, broad, upright, terminal panicles. **FRUIT** Orange-red, rough and warty, berry-like drupe, with mealy flesh.

small, urn-shaped flowers

BARK

elliptic to obovate leaves

FLOWERS AND LEAVES

Arbutus unedo

FLOWERS AND LEAVES

Strawberry-tree

HEIGHT up to 12m (40ft)
TYPE Evergreen
OCCURRENCE S.W. Ireland, Mediterranean region

The Strawberry-tree grows mostly in thickets and woodland in rocky places. The fruit is edible but not tasty. It has a very high sugar content and sometimes ferments on the tree. In several Mediterranean countries, it is used to make wines and liqueurs. The Strawberry-tree is incorporated in the heraldic emblem of the Spanish city of Madrid, with a bear stretching out to eat the fruit of the tree. **BARK** Red-brown, not peeling but shredding into strips. **LEAF** Alternate, elliptic to oblong or obovate, smooth, dark glossy green above, paler beneath. **FLOWER** Small, white or tinged pink, borne in drooping terminal clusters. **FRUIT** Orange-red, spherical drupe, with mealy flesh.

leaf to 10cm (4in) long

rough, warty skin

urn-shaped flowers

rough, fissured surface

FRUIT   **BARK**

Rhododendron arboreum

Rhododendron

HEIGHT up to 15m (50ft)
TYPE Evergreen
OCCURRENCE S.W. China, Himalayas, Sri Lanka

This species was the first rhododendron to be introduced to Europe from the Himalayas. It is broadly columnar in shape. **BARK** Red-brown, rough, and shredding. **LEAF** Alternate, oblong to lanceolate, glossy dark green above, silvery to rusty brown beneath; poisonous. **FLOWER** Red, pink, or white, bell-shaped, in dense terminal clusters of up to 20. **FRUIT** Brown woody capsule; tiny seeds.

pointed tip

LEAVES

Cordia myxa

Sebesten Plum

HEIGHT 3–15m (10–50ft)
TYPE Deciduous/Semi-evergreen
OCCURRENCE N. Africa, India, S.E. Asia, Australia

Widely cultivated, this tree often has a crooked trunk. **BARK** Grey-brown to blackish, shallowly fissured. **LEAF** Alternate, smooth to hairy below. **FLOWER** White, in cymes. **FRUIT** Brownish yellow, oval drupe.

FOLIAGE

Cordia alliodora

Cypre

HEIGHT up to 20m (65ft)
TYPE Evergreen/Semi-deciduous
OCCURRENCE Tropical South America, West Indies

Cypre wood is in great demand for making boat decks, fine cabinetry, veneers, flooring, and panelling. Its flowers, fruit, and leaves are used medicinally. **BARK** Grey to brown, becoming rough and fissured. **LEAF** Alternate, elliptic-oblong, smooth or with scattered hairs. **FLOWER** Small, white, in terminal panicles. **FRUIT** Oblong nutlet.

branches in horizontal layers

Wigandia caracasana

Wigandia

HEIGHT up to 3.6m (12ft)
TYPE Evergreen
OCCURRENCE South America

Wigandia is a coarse shrub and is sometimes grown as an ornamental because of its large, showy leaves and violet flowers. However, its leaves and stem have stinging hairs, which can cause severe allergic reactions. It is considered a noxious weed in Australia. **BARK** Green-brown. **LEAF** Alternate, ovate, toothed, long-stalked, with glandular stinging hairs. **FLOWER** Purple-blue petals, bell-shaped, in large terminal cymes. **FRUIT** Capsule that splits open on ripening.

Eucommia ulmoides

Hardy Rubber Tree

HEIGHT up to 20m (65ft)
TYPE Deciduous
OCCURRENCE C. China

rounded to spreading habit

Very rare in the wild, this tree is widely cultivated in China for medicinal use and as a street tree. It produces latex, but is not exploited for rubber. **BARK** Greybrown, rough. **LEAF** Alternate, usually elliptic, smooth. **FLOWER** Greenish brown, axillary; males in clusters; females solitary; on separate trees. **FRUIT** Elliptic to oblong, winged nut.

densely toothed margins

LEAVES

MALE FLOWERS

Cinchona calisaya

Quinine

HEIGHT up to 25m (80ft)
TYPE Evergreen
OCCURRENCE South America

This tropical tree is the primary source of the antimalarial drug quinine, which is found in its bark. **BARK** Greybrown, vertically and horizontally fissured. **LEAF** Opposite, elliptic to oblong or ovate or obovate, smooth above, smooth to downy beneath. **FLOWER** White to pink, fragrant; in terminal panicles, short- and long-styled on separate trees. **FRUIT** Ovate-oblong capsule.

large glossy leaves

smooth margins

FOLIAGE

FLOWERS AND BUDS

Coffea arabica

Arabica Coffee

HEIGHT 4–5m (13–16ft)
TYPE Evergreen
OCCURRENCE Ethiopia, cultivated in tropical regions

FLOWERS

5-lobed flowers

There are probably at least 25 species of coffee growing wild, all indigenous to tropical Africa, especially Ethiopia. All species of Arabica Coffee are woody, ranging from small shrubs to large trees, and have horizontal branches in opposite pairs. This species accounts for 74 per cent of world production of coffee.
BARK Brown, with fine vertical fissures.
LEAF Opposite, glossy dark green, ovate to elliptic, smooth. **FLOWER** Borne in clusters of 5–20 in leaf axils, with five white petals, fragrant. **FRUIT** Ovoid berry, about 1.25cm (½in) long; green ripening to yellow and then red, black when dried, with two seeds.

berry ripens to red

COFFEE ON THE GO

Coffee was transported to the Arabian Peninsula around 600CE and the custom of coffee-drinking then spread throughout the Ottoman Empire. Coffee houses opened in Vienna in 1555 and in England in 1650. It was not until the 1690s that the Dutch introduced coffee into Java. A plant from Java was sent to Amsterdam where it set fruit. Coffee plants were then sent to Paris and Surinam.

COFFEE BEANS

Coffea canephora

Robusta Coffee

HEIGHT up to 10m (33ft)
TYPE Evergreen
OCCURRENCE W. Africa

An important species planted in Africa and Asia, this tree has long, drooping branches. Once chewed as a stimulant, the coffee beans are now used exclusively for the production of instant coffee, or sometimes blended with Arabica coffee. **BARK** Brown, with fine vertical fissures. **LEAF** Opposite, glossy dark green, often toothed or wavy margins, oblong-elliptic. **FLOWER** Borne in clusters of 5–20 in leaf axils, with 6–8 white petals. **FRUIT** Red, ovoid berry.

berry 1.8–2.5cm (¾–1in) long

FRUIT

Neolamarckia cadamba

Kadam

HEIGHT 25–45m (80–150ft)
TYPE Deciduous
OCCURRENCE India, China, S.E. Asia

The Kadam tree occurs in many of the Hindu writings about Lord Krishna. **BARK** Pale brown, smooth, becoming grey-brown, fissured, ridged, and flaky. **LEAF** Opposite, elliptic, smooth, with narrowly triangular terminal stipules. **FLOWER** Numerous, in round heads, at ends of short side twigs. **FRUIT** Greenish capsule, turning brown, in spherical heads.

FLOWERHEAD

yellowish white flowers

Alstonia scholaris

Dita

HEIGHT up to 40m (130ft)
TYPE Evergreen
OCCURRENCE India, S. China, S.E. Asia, tropical Australia

Often seen in parks and along streets, this tree has a distinctive pagoda-like crown. Its wood was once used to make writing tablets. **BARK** Grey; exudes white sap. **LEAF** In whorls of 4–10, with many lateral veins. **FLOWER** White, with overlapping lobes, in terminal or axillary inflorescences. **FRUIT** Long, paired follicles.

elliptic to obovate

LEAVES

Dyera costulata

Jelutong

HEIGHT up to 80m (260ft)
TYPE Deciduous
OCCURRENCE S. Thailand, Malay Peninsula, Sumatra, Borneo, Sulawesi

The wood of this tree is commonly used to make pencils, picture frames, and cabinets. **BARK** Grey to brown, mottled. **LEAF** Arranged in whorls of 5–8, usually at the ends of the twigs, elliptic to obovate. **FLOWER** Axillary inflorescences, with small, white corollas. **FRUIT** Long, paired follicles, containing ellipsoidal seeds.

FOLIAGE

Plumeria rubra

Frangipani

HEIGHT up to 10m (33ft)
TYPE Deciduous
OCCURRENCE Mexico, South America

This tree with fragrant flowers is central to Mayan creation myths. **BARK** Pale green to pale brown, smooth; exudes white latex. **LEAF** Alternate, elliptic, with pointed tips. **FLOWER** Large, in terminal clusters. **FRUIT** Grey-green, oblong follicles.

FLOWERS IN BLOOM   *pink-yellow lobes*

Rauvolfia serpentina

Serpentine Root

HEIGHT up to 3m (10ft)
TYPE Evergreen
OCCURRENCE Sri Lanka, India, China, Malay Peninsula

This medicinal tree is usually unbranched. It contains the alkaloid reserpine, which is used in some medicinal drugs. **BARK** Thin, yellowish green. **LEAF** Elliptic to obovate, in whorls of up to three, near tips of stems. **FLOWER** White or tinged with purple, with overlapping lobes, in terminal and lateral cymes. **FRUIT** Oval, orange ripening to purple-black, paired drupes.

untoothed edges

LEAVES AND FLOWERS   *red stalks*

Tabernaemontana divaricata

Crepe Jasmine

HEIGHT up to 5m (16ft)
TYPE Evergreen
OCCURRENCE Myanmar, Thailand, India

Widely cultivated in the tropics as an ornamental, this tree contains alkaloids that also make it a useful medicinal plant. Its flowers exude an intense, penetrating perfume. All parts of this tree are poisonous. **BARK** Green to pale brown. **LEAF** Opposite, elliptic. **FLOWER** White, in terminal inflorescences of 1–8; ovoid buds. **FRUIT** Oval follicles in pairs.

pointed leaf tip   *5 petals*

FLOWER AND LEAVES

Tabernanthe iboga

Iboga

HEIGHT up to 2m (6ft)
TYPE Evergreen
OCCURRENCE W. Africa, Gabon, Cameroon

The Iboga has an upright and branching trunk. Its leaves, seeds, and root bark contain alkaloids, including a psychoactive compound "Ibogaine", which is illegal in some countries, such as the USA. Known as the "Tree of Life", the Iboga tree has been used for hundreds of years as a source of stimulant and aphrodisiac preparations by people living in its native habitat. Extracts from the tree have been used experimentally to treat impotence and to break drug addiction. **BARK** Green to pale brown; exudes white latex. **LEAF** Opposite, dark green, elliptic to ovate or oblanceolate, smooth and untoothed. **FLOWER** White corollas, spotted with pink; in axillary clusters of up to 12. **FRUIT** Oval, orange-red.

Brugmansia x candida

Angel's Trumpets

HEIGHT 1.5–5m (5–16ft)
TYPE Evergreen
OCCURRENCE Peru

Often planted in gardens, this species is a hybrid of *B. aurea* and *B. versicolor*. It includes numerous cultivars, some with double flowers. All parts of the plant are highly toxic. It has spectacular flowers which are sweetly scented, particularly in the evenings. Angel's Trumpets can be grown in frost-free Mediterranean or sub-tropical climates. **BARK** Greyish, thin. **LEAF** Alternate, up to 40cm (16in) long, with soft hairs.

FLOWER Solitary, white, pink, to yellow, up to 60cm (24in) long, with recurved petals. **FRUIT** Green, ovoid to spindle-shaped, pendulous capsule.

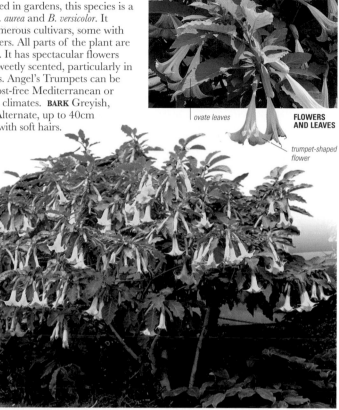

ovate leaves

FLOWERS AND LEAVES

trumpet-shaped flower

Solanum betaceum

Tree-tomato

HEIGHT 2–8m (6–26ft)
TYPE Evergreen
OCCURRENCE South America, Africa, S.E. Asia, New Zealand

The commercial production of this tree's fruit is restricted to New Zealand, where it began in 1920. Internationally, the trade remains on a small scale. **BARK** Greenish brown, thin. **LEAF** Alternate, ovate, heart-shaped base, with soft hairs. **FLOWER** Bell-shaped, fragrant, pink to pale blue, in axillary clusters. **FRUIT** Ovoid, smooth, purplish red to orange-red or yellow berry.

UNRIPE FRUIT

Fraxinus excelsior

Ash

HEIGHT up to 45m (150ft)
TYPE Deciduous
OCCURRENCE Europe, W. Asia

A broadly columnar, tall tree, the Ash has a spherical to round crown and is commonly found on limestone in moist woods and on riverbanks. **BARK** Grey-brown and smooth, becoming ridged and furrowed. **LEAF** Opposite, pinnate with a terminal leaflet; 7–15 ovate-oblong to lanceolate leaflets, dark green above, hairy beneath on the midrib, toothed margins. **FLOWER** Small, purplish, with sepals and petals absent, in short, axillary clusters, opening from black buds before the leaves appear. **FRUIT** Winged key, glossy green turning pale brown, in hanging clusters.

tapered tip

LEAVES AND FRUIT

winged fruit in drooping clusters

flowers in dense clusters

FLOWERS

ELASTIC ASH WOOD

The wood of the Ash is known for its strength and flexibility; it is easily bent when steamed or seasoned. Once used to make shafts and wheel rims for carriages and wagons, it is now used to make sturdy baskets, oars, and agricultural implements.

BASKET

Fraxinus ornus

Manna Ash

HEIGHT up to 20m (65ft)
TYPE Deciduous
OCCURRENCE S. Europe, S.W. Asia

Also called Flowering Ash for its showy flower clusters, this tree has a round crown and a broadly spreading habit. In Sicily, the tree is tapped to form "manna" from the solidified sap. This contains high concentrations of mannitol, a sugar that can be used as a sweetener for people with diabetes. **BARK** Grey, smooth. **LEAF** Opposite, pinnate with a terminal leaflet; 5–9 ovate to lanceolate leaflets, dark green above, hairy beneath on the midrib, sharply toothed margins, and distinctly stalked lateral leaflets. **FLOWER** White, small, with four slender petals, borne before the leaves, in short, fluffy axillary clusters. **FRUIT** Green lanceolate key, ripening to pale brown, with a flattened wing, hanging in clusters.

pointed leaflets

flowers in conical clusters

FLOWERING BRANCHES

Fraxinus pennsylvanica

White Ash

HEIGHT up to 25m (80ft)
TYPE Deciduous
OCCURRENCE N. and C. USA

Often planted as an ornamental, this fast-growing tree has a broadly columnar shape. **BARK** Grey-brown, with interlacing ridges. **LEAF** Opposite, pinnate with a terminal leaflet; 5–9 ovate to lanceolate leaflets, green above, hairy beneath on the midrib. **FLOWER** Greenish purple, petalless, small; males and females borne on separate trees, in short clusters. **FRUIT** Green winged key, ripening to pale brown.

tapered tips

slightly furrowed

LEAVES

BARK

Olea europaea

Olive

HEIGHT up to 15m (50ft)
TYPE Evergreen
OCCURRENCE Middle East, Mediterranean region, N. Africa

white flowers in clusters

grey-green leaves

fruit to 4cm (1½in) long

FRUIT

LEAVES AND FLOWERS

OLIVES AND THEIR OIL

Olive trees are grown throughout the Mediterranean region for their edible fruit. Harvested in late summer, olives are pickled in brine to remove bitter chemicals or they are pressed to extract their oil.

OLIVE OIL

PICKING OLIVES

The wild Olive is a small, bushy plant, but cultivated trees have a typical gnarled trunk. It grows best in a warm climate and tolerates periods of drought. It is a long-lived species; individual trees can survive for up to 500 years. Probably domesticated by the Minoans around 2500BCE, the Olive was spread throughout the Mediterranean region by the Greeks and Romans. Franciscan missionaries brought Olive trees to California from Mexico in the 1700s.
BARK Grey, furrowed, sometimes peeling.
LEAF Opposite, lanceolate, or ovate (wild trees), grey-green above, paler beneath due to small silvery scales. **FLOWER** White, fragrant, small, four-toothed, borne in dense axillary clusters in summer.
FRUIT Ovoid drupe, green turning brownish green to black.

Myoporum acuminatum

Boobialla

HEIGHT 2–8m (6–26ft)
TYPE Evergreen
OCCURRENCE Australia (New South Wales, Queensland)

A species that grows on sandy soil and rocky sites, this broad-crowned tree can be used for hedging and street planting, particularly in coastal areas, as it is resistant to saline spray. **BARK** Grey-brown, deeply fissured. **LEAF** Alternate, toothed near tip. **FLOWER** White, with purple spots, in axillary inflorescences of 3–8. **FRUIT** Ovoid, purple or purple-black drupe.

pointed tip *elliptic leaves*

FOLIAGE

Catalpa bignonioides

Indian Bean

HEIGHT up to 18m (60ft)
TYPE Deciduous
OCCURRENCE S.E. USA, naturalized elsewhere

This bean tree is much branched, with a spreading habit and a round crown. It is frequently used as an ornamental. **BARK** Pale brown tinged with red, with irregular scales. **LEAF** Opposite or in threes, unlobed or shallowly lobed. **FLOWER** Large; white corollas with two lobes, frilled at the margin, with rows of yellow spots and many purple spots. **FRUIT** Bean-like, pendulous pod.

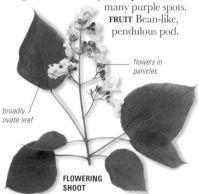

flowers in panicles

broadly ovate leaf

FLOWERING SHOOT

Crescentia cujete

Calabash Tree

HEIGHT up to 12m (40ft)
TYPE Evergreen
OCCURRENCE West Indies, tropical South America

The Calabash Tree has dense, tiered, spreading branches with a broad crown and a relatively short trunk. Its fruit are dried and polished to make utensils and musical instruments. **BARK** Whitish to silver grey, rough. **LEAF** Alternately arranged in clusters on short shoots, oblanceolate to obovate, tapering at the base. **FLOWER** Yellow-green, with purple markings, large, cup-shaped, solitary or in clusters, usually borne on the trunk; night-flowering. **FRUIT** Large, round gourd; hard shell.

12–30 cm (5–12in) wide

FRUIT

Jacaranda

HEIGHT 5–15m (16–50ft)
TYPE Deciduous
OCCURRENCE Argentina, Bolivia

Its striking display of flowers makes this tree a popular ornamental for streets and parks. **BARK** Pale brown, rough and fissured with age. **LEAF** Opposite, bipinnate; 13–41 small, smooth or downy leaflets. **FLOWER** Purplish blue, in terminal panicles. **FRUIT** Oval pod; winged seeds.

FLOWERS

tubular corolla

Sausage-tree

HEIGHT 10–15m (33–50ft)
TYPE Deciduous
OCCURRENCE Tropical Africa

The flowers of this tree are pollinated by nectar-eating bats; it rarely fruits in their absence. **BARK** Pale brown, rough, often cracked. **LEAF** Opposite, pinnate, with

drooping panicle   *grey-green capsule*   **FRUIT**

3–6 pairs of elliptic to lanceolate leaflets. **FLOWER** Red to purplish, bell-shaped. **FRUIT** Pendulous, sausage-shaped capsule.

Midnight Horror

HEIGHT 5–20m (16–65ft)
TYPE Evergreen/Semi-deciduous
OCCURRENCE India, E. Asia

The night-blooming flowers of this tree have a harsh, musty smell that attracts pollinating bats. **BARK** Pale grey-brown, smooth or finely cracked. **LEAF** Opposite, pinnate, with 3–4 ovate to oblong leaflets, clustered at ends of branches. **FLOWER** Large, trumpet-shaped, reddish purple outside, yellow to cream inside, in terminal clusters. **FRUIT** Long, pendent woody capsule.

slender crown   **WINGED SEED**

Spathodea nilotica

Flame-tree

HEIGHT up to 18m (60ft)
TYPE Evergreen
OCCURRENCE Tropical Africa

upright pods The Flame-tree is grown for its shade and colour. It is used for fire resistant landscaping, as its wood is difficult to burn. **BARK** Pale grey and warty. **LEAF** Opposite, pinnate; 11–15 pairs of oval to ovate leaflets, hairy beneath. **FLOWER** Large, bell-shaped, red-orange, with yellow edges, in racemes. **FRUIT** Greenish brown pods; numerous *terminal leaflet* papery seeds.

LEAVES AND FLOWERS

Tabebuia chrysantha

Yellow Trumpet Tree

HEIGHT up to 25m (80ft)
TYPE Deciduous
OCCURRENCE Mexico, Central America, Venezuela

This is the national tree of Venezuela. **BARK** Pale to dark grey and scaly. **LEAF** Palmate, with 5–7 stalked, oval to oblong leaflets. **FLOWER** Golden yellow, trumpet-shaped, in terminal panicles. **FRUIT** Hairy capsule.

Tabebuia impetiginosa

Pink Trumpet Tree

HEIGHT up to 20m (65ft)
TYPE Deciduous
OCCURRENCE South America

This tree is cultivated as an ornamental. **BARK** Grey, fissured. **LEAF** Opposite, ovate-elliptic leaflets. **FLOWER** Pinkish purple, tubular, in panicles. **FRUIT** Capsule.

Tabebuia serratifolia

Washiba

HEIGHT up to 45m (150ft)
TYPE Deciduous
OCCURRENCE Tropical Central and South America

The showy flowers of the Washiba bloom when the tree has no leaves. Its hard, durable timber has been used for marine and naval construction, bridges, flooring, and furniture. It is also planted as an ornamental and street tree in South America, but is now rare in the wild due to over-exploitation. **BARK** Pale brown to grey, fissured, scaly. **LEAF** Opposite, pinnate with one terminal leaflet; five ovate-oblong to elliptic, toothed leaflets. **FLOWER** Yellow, tubular, in terminal and lateral clusters. **FRUIT** Long capsule, with winged seeds.

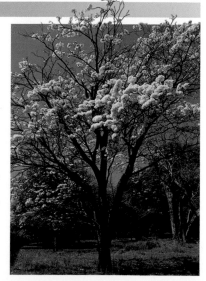

Citharexylum spinosum

Fiddlewood

HEIGHT up to 15m (50ft)
TYPE Deciduous/Evergreen
OCCURRENCE Caribbean, N. South America

A popular ornamental and street tree in tropical and sub-tropical areas, Fiddlewood has hard and durable wood that was historically used for tools. It was called "bois fidèle" or faithful tree by the French, which was bastardized to "fiddlewood" in English. Despite the name *spinosum*, the tree bears no spines. Where the tree is deciduous, the leaves turn orange before falling. **BARK** Pale brown, becoming scaly, with longitudinal thin strips. **LEAF** Opposite or in whorls of three, ovate to oblong or elliptic. **FLOWER** White, small, tubular, borne in axillary and terminal, spike-like inflorescences. **FRUIT** Oblong drupe, borne on pendulous stalks, red, turning black, containing four seeds.

irregular crown

Gmelina arborea

Yamar

HEIGHT up to 20m (65ft)
TYPE Deciduous
OCCURRENCE India to S. China, Malay Peninsula, Indonesia

This broad-crowned, fast-growing tree is grown in plantations for its wood. **BARK** Pale ashy grey to greyish yellow, smooth. **LEAF** Opposite, broadly ovate, with brownish hairs beneath. **FLOWER** In axillary clusters, with five unequal lobes: upper two curved backwards, next two forward-pointing and orange-red, bottom lobe lemon yellow. **FRUIT** Oblong to obovoid, yellowish green, fleshy drupe.

Premna serratifolia

Headache Tree

HEIGHT up to 5m (16ft)
TYPE Evergreen
OCCURRENCE S. and S.E. Asia, Australia, Pacific Islands

Used occasionally for living fence poles and garden stakes, this tree is valued for its tolerance to salt spray and saline soil.

BARK Yellowish brown with vertical furrows, soft, thin, flaky. **LEAF** Opposite, oblong to broadly ovate, sometimes hairy along veins. **FLOWER** Greenish white petals, forming a short, hairy tube, with two unequal lobes, scented, in terminal compound corymbs. **FRUIT** Round, bluish black, fleshy drupe, 3–6mm (1 1/4–2 1/4in) wide.

Tectona grandis

Teak

HEIGHT up to 50m (165ft)
TYPE Deciduous
OCCURRENCE Asia: India to Thailand, Cambodia, Vietnam, Laos, Java

One of the best-known tropical hardwood species, Teak has been exploited for its durable and versatile wood for hundreds of years. British colonists in India and Burma (now Myanmar), and Dutch colonists in Indonesia, established Teak plantations to provide a ready supply of timber for ship-building, general construction, and fine furniture. The tree can take up to 60 years to mature and can be exceptionally long-lived. There are two contenders for the oldest Teak tree, both about 47m (154ft) tall; one in Palghat district, Kerala, India with a girth of 6.42m (21ft) and the other in Uttaradit province, Thailand, with a girth of 9.57m (32 ft), estimated to be more than 1,000 years old. The trunk of the Teak tree is fluted. **BARK** Pale brown, thin, flaky in narrow, vertical strips.

FRUIT

papery calyx

LEAF Opposite, large, ovate to broadly obovate, rough above, soft hairs beneath. **FLOWER** White, with a small, funnel-shaped corolla, the calyx densely covered with brown hairs, numerous, borne in terminal and lateral, wide pyramidal inflorescences, at the ends of shoots. **FRUIT** Thin, inflated calyx surrounding a stone containing four cavities, each with one seed.

LEAVES

30–50cm (12–20in) long

TEAK WOOD FURNITURE

The dark brown wood of the Teak tree has a distinct grain, dries with little degradation, and is easily worked with hand or power tools. The untreated wood weathers well, resists rot, and is not attacked by termites. These properties make it one of the most valuable woods for furniture-making.

TEAK WOOD CHAIR

Paulownia tomentosa

Foxglove-tree

HEIGHT up to 20m (65ft)
TYPE Deciduous
OCCURRENCE China, cultivated in Korea, Japan, North America, Europe

Also known as the Empress Tree, after Anna Paulovna, queen of William II of the Netherlands, this tree was first planted in Jardin des Plantes, Paris, in 1834. It was introduced into North America a few years later and naturalized. Centuries ago, the tree was cultivated in Japan where it was traditionally valued, particularly for making the stringed

to 30cm (12in) long

tubular flowers

FLOWERS

LEAVES

heart-shaped base

instrument "Koto".
BARK Brown-grey, smooth, visible lenticels when young, splitting lengthwise with age.
LEAF Opposite, ovate, 3–5 lobes, hairy, untoothed or lobed margins. **FLOWER** Bell-shaped, large, pale purple with darker spots, yellow stripes inside, in terminal panicles. **FRUIT** Woody, ovoid capsule, up to 5cm (2in) long, hairy, ripening from green to brown.

RIPE FRUIT

ovoid capsule

Paulownia x taiwaniana

Princess Tree

HEIGHT up to 20m (65ft)
TYPE Deciduous
OCCURRENCE Island of Taiwan

This tree is a natural hybrid between *P. fortunei* and *P. kawakami*. It grows quickly and is cultivated mainly for its fine, light timber. It can also be pruned to supply leaves and flowers as fodder for livestock.

It is highly ornamental with masses of sweetly scented, trumpet-shaped flowers in spring. **BARK** Greyish, rough.
LEAF Opposite, ovate, thin, 10–30cm (4–12in) long, with 3–5 lobes, pointed tip.
FLOWER Petals 5–6cm (2–2¼in) long, pale purple with deep violet spots on yellow "throat"; in terminal, pyramidal panicles.
FRUIT Woody capsule, oblong-ovoid, 3.5–4.5cm (1½–1¾in) long.

Ilex aquifolium

Holly

HEIGHT up to 20m (65ft)
TYPE Evergreen
OCCURRENCE Europe, W. Asia

The Holly has been cultivated since ancient times. There are numerous cultivars with variations in the density of prickles, in patterns of variegation, and the colour of berries. Its glossy leaves also vary in shape. Its wood is heavy and fine-grained and has been used for inlay work in furniture, chess pieces, and printing blocks. **BARK** Pale grey, smooth.
LEAF Alternate, ovate to elliptic, wavy margins with spines.
FLOWER Small, white, sometimes purple-tinged, fragrant; males and females on separate trees, borne in axillary clusters.
FRUIT Berry, usually shiny bright red, but yellow in some cultivars; poisonous.

FESTIVE WREATH

In ancient Rome, the festival of Saturnalia took place during the winter solstice. It was a time of high spirits and gift-giving, which included sending sprigs of Holly to friends. Some pagan peoples brought Holly indoors to ward off evil spirits. Gradually, these traditions were absorbed into Christianity, and the Holly became associated with Christmas.

green ovary

white flowers

dense clusters of berries

MALE FLOWERS

FEMALE FLOWERS

leaf to 10cm (4in) long

FRUIT-BEARING SHOOT

pyramidal to columnar crown

Ilex paraguariensis
Maté

HEIGHT up to 20m (65ft)
TYPE Evergreen
OCCURRENCE South America

The first Maté plantations were founded by the Jesuits in 1650CE. Today, Argentina accounts for about 45 per cent of the total crop. A tall, multi-stemmed bush in the wild, Maté is pruned to 3–6m (10–20ft) in cultivation to stimulate growth and to make the leaves easier to pick. The leaves are used to make a tea-like drink. **BARK** Grey-brown, smooth. **LEAF** Alternate, obovate, leathery. **FLOWER** Axillary; males in clusters of 3–11; females 1–3, on separate trees. **FRUIT** Reddish to black, spherical drupe.

LEAVES
white flowers
toothed margins
unripe fruit

FLOWERS AND FRUIT

MATÉ TEA

Maté is traditionally drunk from a gourd with a metal straw which has a filter to strain out leaf fragments. The bottom of the gourd is filled with burned or toasted leaves and hot water. Burnt sugar, lemon juice, and/or milk is used to flavour the tea.

TEA

GOURD AND STRAW

Pseudopanax crassifolius
Lancewood

HEIGHT 6–18m (20–60ft)
TYPE Evergreen
OCCURRENCE New Zealand

The crown of this tree is rounded at maturity and its juvenile foliage differs from adult leaves. **BARK** Greyish, smooth. **LEAF** Juveniles: very long, linear, toothed; adults: oblanceolate, smooth, toothed. **FLOWER** Greenish, in terminal umbels; males with five petals; females petalless. **FRUIT** Globose, black, fleshy drupe.

Schefflera actinophylla
Umbrella-tree

HEIGHT 5–12m (16–40ft)
TYPE Evergreen
OCCURRENCE Papua New Guinea, tropical Australia

This tree is so named because of its compound leaves that form an umbrella-shaped rosette. **BARK** Grey, smooth. **LEAF** Alternate, digitate, with 5–16 elliptic to obovate, smooth leaflets. **FLOWER** Bright red, stalkless, clustered on straight branches. **FRUIT** Purple-black, drupe.

Steganotaenia araliacea
Carrot Tree

HEIGHT 3–5m (10–16ft)
TYPE Deciduous
OCCURRENCE S.W. and C. Africa

All parts of this tree smell strongly of carrots, hence its common name. **BARK** Pale greenish grey, papery and peeling. **LEAF** Alternate, drooping, crowded at the ends of branches; pinnate with ovate, deeply toothed leaflets and a terminal leaflet. **FLOWER** Tiny, white to yellow, in compound umbels. **FRUIT** Small, flat, ovate to pear-shaped, with three prominent ribs.

TREE IN LEAFLESS PHASE

Pittosporum undulatum
Cheesewood

HEIGHT up to 15m (50ft)
TYPE Evergreen
OCCURRENCE Australia

This tree was introduced into horticulture in 1789, and is now well established in cultivation. It is commonly used for hedges and windbreaks. However, it can be very invasive in scrubland. **BARK** Dark grey, smooth. **LEAF** Alternate, ovate to elliptic or lanceolate, clustered at ends of branches, aromatic when crushed. **FLOWER** White, turning yellow, borne in short terminal panicles. **FRUIT** Globose capsule, with red-brown seeds.

LEAF AND FLOWER — *wavy margins* — *flowers in short clusters*

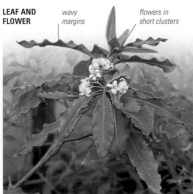

Pittosporum tobira
Tobira

HEIGHT 5–6m (16–20ft)
TYPE Evergreen
OCCURRENCE China, Japan

Widely cultivated in areas with a Mediterranean climate, this species is sometimes used as a low hedge or as a small ornamental tree. It has a rounded crown. **BARK** Dark grey, smooth. **LEAF** Alternate, oblanceolate to obovate, leathery, sometimes curved back, aromatic when crushed. **FLOWER** White, turning yellow, in short terminal panicles, fragrant. **FRUIT** Globose capsule with red-brown seeds.

white petals
glossy leaves

FLOWERS AND LEAVES

Sambucus canadensis
American Elder

HEIGHT up to 5m (16ft)
TYPE Deciduous
OCCURRENCE North America

The fruit of this tree have more Vitamin C per unit weight than oranges or tomatoes. **BARK** Pale yellowish brown, soft, spongy, fissured. **LEAF** Opposite, pinnate with a terminal leaflet; 5–7 lanceolate to elliptic, toothed leaflets, smooth or slightly hairy beneath. **FLOWER** Creamy white, numerous, in flat, terminal panicles. **FRUIT** Small, berry-like drupe, 3–5 nutlets.

FRUIT *dark purple drupes*

Sambucus nigra

Elder

HEIGHT up to 10m (32ft)
TYPE Deciduous
OCCURRENCE Europe

BRANCHLET

pointed leaflets

flowers with broad flattened heads

CORDIALS AND WINES

Both the flowers and fruit of the Elder tree are used to make wine. Elder fruit is also used to make jellies and the flowers to make a non-alcoholic cordial. The use of elder flowers for this purpose has greatly increased in the last 25 years. An estimated 100 tonnes of wild flowers are harvested annually in Britain for cordial-making. Elder is also used to make medicinal herbal remedies.

DRIED FLOWERS AND INFUSION

The Elder tree is common in damp woods and wasteland. It often springs up around farm buildings and along walls, where its seeds are scattered in bird droppings. Elder grows rapidly, and its branches form a dense, shrubby growth with age. Many cultivated forms have been bred, with different leaf colours and forms, as well as ones with coloured flowers or larger fruit. **BARK** Pale yellowish brown, soft, spongy, fissured.

LEAF Opposite, pinnate with a terminal leaflet; 5–7 ovate to elliptic leaflets, slightly hairy beneath, sharply toothed; exuding a foul odour when crushed. **FLOWER** Creamy white, strongly fragrant, numerous, borne in terminal flat panicles. **FRUIT** Berry-like, purple-black drupe, with 3–5 one-seeded nutlets.

broadly columnar to rounded head

FRUIT

drupe to 6mm (¼in) wide

Lobelia giberroa

Giant Lobelia

HEIGHT up to 10m (32ft)
TYPE Evergreen
OCCURRENCE Kenya

One of the strange herbaceous plants of African mountains that have developed a tree-like habit, this species has a hollow stem. There are also related species that are stemless. **BARK** Brownish, not highly developed. **LEAF** In rosettes, alternate, oblanceolate, hairy, with toothed margins. **FLOWER** Green with mauve stamens, borne in a long terminal inflorescence. **FRUIT** Capsule.

LEAFY ROSETTE

sparsely branched stems

Montanoa quadrangularis

Arboloco

HEIGHT up to 20m (65ft)
TYPE Evergreen
OCCURRENCE Colombia, Venezuela

A fast-growing tree, Arboloco is found in open habitats. This species has been used for construction of houses and buildings, animal enclosures, and fences. Its white pith is used in handicrafts. **BARK** Brown-grey. **LEAF** Opposite, ovate to triangular to almost palmate, toothed to indented margins or lobed in older leaves. **FLOWER** Borne in terminal cymes, numerous, daisy-like with white ray florets and yellow central disc. **FRUIT** Head of brown-black seeds.

Dendrosenecio johnstonii

Giant Groundsel

HEIGHT 5–10m (16–32ft)
TYPE Evergreen
OCCURRENCE E. African mountains

The Giant Groundsel grows around Mount Kilimanjaro in northern Tanzania, in a belt of alpine grassland, shrubs, and bogs. This gigantic, odd-looking plant has tree-like characteristics. Its sparsely branched stems terminate in large rosettes of leaves. These are densely furred as protection against the intense light and harsh climatic conditions in its mountainous habitat. The old dead leaves act as a screen around its trunk. **BARK** Brownish, not highly developed. **LEAF** In rosettes, broadly ovate to elliptic, hairy, with toothed margins. **FLOWER** Borne in terminal inflorescences, numerous, to 1m (3ft) long, daisy-like with white ray florets and yellow central disc. **FRUIT** Head of brown-black achenes.

leaf-clad stems

ELDER
The structure of the flowerheads of the Elder tree (*Sambucus nigra*) is clearly seen here. The buds eventually open as fragrant greenish white and pink blossom. The Elder is a common inhabitant of damp woodlands throughout Europe.

Glossary

A number of specialist botanical and scientific terms have been used in this book. Use this glossary to obtain a concise definition of these terms. Terms in italic type are defined elsewhere in the glossary.

ACHENE A small, dry and hard, one-seeded fruit that does not split open for seed distribution.

ALTERNATE Describes leaves that are borne singly at each node, in two vertical rows, on either side of an axis. (See Leaf Arrangements, p.347.)

ANTHER Part of the *stamen* that releases pollen; usually borne on a filament.

ARIL Coat that covers some seeds; often fleshy and brightly coloured.

AXIL Upper angle between a part of a plant and the stem that bears it.

AXILLARY Borne in an *axil*, usually referring to flowers.

BIPINNATE A compound leaf arrangement (see p.347) in which the *leaflets* are themselves *pinnate*.

BRACT Modified leaf at the base of a flower or flowerhead. A bract may be small and scale-like, or large and petal-like, or it may resemble normal foliage.

BRACTEOLE Secondary *bract* sheathing a flower in an *inflorescence*.

BURR *1.* Prickly, spiny, or hooked fruit, seed head, or flowerhead. *2.* Woody outgrowth on the trunk of some trees.

BUTTRESS Trunk base that is fluted or swollen, giving stability to a tree in shallow soil conditions.

CALYX (*pl.* calyces) Collective name for *sepals*, joined or separate, which form the outer whorl of the *perianth*.

CAPSULE A type of dry fruit that splits open to disperse ripe seed.

CARPEL Female flower part consisting of a *style*, a *stigma*, and an *ovary*.

CATKIN A type of *inflorescence*, usually pendulous, in which scale-like *bracts* and tiny, often petalless flowers are arranged in a *spike*.

CLONE A genetically identical group of plants derived from one individual by vegetative reproduction.

LEAF SHAPES

Leaves occur in a great variety of shapes, and a selection of the most common types is shown below. Some leaves do not match one of these shapes exactly and may be a combination of two.

These shapes apply to both simple leaves, which are undivided, and compound leaves, which are divided into two or more component parts, each of which is known as a leaflet.

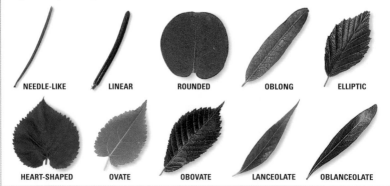

NEEDLE-LIKE　　LINEAR　　ROUNDED　　OBLONG　　ELLIPTIC

HEART-SHAPED　　OVATE　　OBOVATE　　LANCEOLATE　　OBLANCEOLATE

COLUMNAR A tree shape that is taller than broad, with parallel sides. (see Tree Habit, p.348.)

CONE The seed-bearing structure of conifer trees.

COROLLA *1.* Collective name for petals. *2.* Inner whorl of *perianth* segments in some monocotyledons.

CORYMB Broad, flat-topped or domed *inflorescence* of stalked flowers or flower-heads arising at different levels on alternate sides of an axis. (See Flower Arrangements, p.346.)

CULTIVAR Contraction of "cultivated variety". A cultivated plant that retains distinct characteristics when propagated.

CYME Branched *inflorescence* with each axis ending in a flower. (See Flower Arrangements, p.346.)

DECIDUOUS A tree that loses its leaves and remains leafless for some months of the year, usually in winter (temperate zones) or the dry season (tropical zones).

DIGITATE A *palmate* compound leaf divided into five *leaflets* arising from a single basal point. (See Compound Leaf Arrangements, p.347.)

DRUPE A type of fruit consisting of one or several hard seeds (stones) surrounded by a fleshy outer covering.

ELLIPTIC A flat leaf shape that is broadest at the centre, tapering towards each end. (See Leaf Shapes, facing page.)

ENDOCARP The hard outer covering of the seed of a succulent fruit.

ENDOSPERM Specialized food store within the fertilized seed of angiosperms (flowering plants) that nourishes the embryo during germination.

EVERGREEN A tree that bears leaves throughout the year.

FOLLICLE Dry fruit, formed from a single *carpel*, that splits along one side to release one or more seeds.

HABIT The overall shape of a tree. (See Tree Habit, p.348.)

FLOWER PARTS

Most flowers are made up of petals, sepals, and the male and/or female flower parts (some flowers are exclusively male or female). The main distinction is between those that have distinct sepals and petals (advanced) and those that do not (primitive).

showy petal

style borne on a stigma

anther borne on a thin filament

sepals distinct from petals

ADVANCED FLOWER

stigmas arranged spirally

tepals (petals and sepals that are indistinguishable)

anthers

PRIMITIVE FLOWER

HERITAGE TREE A tree of considerable age that has some important cultural or historical significance.

HYBRID Naturally or artificially produced offspring of genetically distinct parents of different species. Hybrids show new characteristics.

INFLORESCENCE Arrangement of flowers around a single axis.

LANCEOLATE Leaf that is broadest below the centre, tapering to a narrow tip. (See Leaf Shapes, p.344.)

FLOWER ARRANGEMENTS

Flowers are arranged on a single stem either singly or in groups called inflorescences. Groups of flowers are displayed in a characteristic pattern around the stem – a descriptive feature and a means of identification. The most common types of inflorescence are shown here.

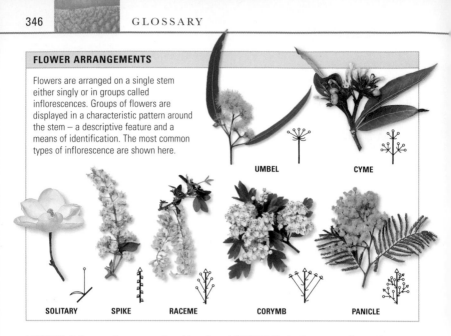

UMBEL   **CYME**

SOLITARY   **SPIKE**   **RACEME**   **CORYMB**   **PANICLE**

LATERAL *1*. Located on or to the side of an axis. *2*. Side shoot arising from the stem of a plant.

LEAFLET Single division of a compound leaf. Also known as a pinna.

BARK TYPES

As the trunk of a tree grows, the bark has to crack or peel to accommodate its increasing girth. Every species has a distinctive bark texture, some examples are shown here.

SMOOTH IN EARLY YEARS

IRREGULAR PLATES

RIDGED AND FISSURED

VERTICAL PEELING

HORIZONTAL PEELING

ROUGH FLAKING

LENTICEL Raised pore on the surface of bark or some fruits that provides access for air to the inner tissues.

MESOCARP The soft, fleshy, middle portion of the wall of a succulent fruit between the skin and the hard layer.

MIDRIB Primary (usually central) vein running from the stalk to the tip of a leaf or leaflet. Also called midvein.

NATIVE A species that occurs naturally in a particular region, as opposed to one that has been introduced.

NATURALIZED A non-native species that has become established in the wild in a region where it was introduced.

NODE Point on a stem, sometimes swollen, at which leaves, leaf buds, and shoots arise.

OBLANCEOLATE Leaf shape that is broadest above the centre, tapering to a narrow basal point. Also called inversely lance-shaped. (See Leaf Shapes, p.344.)

OBLONG Describes a leaf shape with two sides of roughly equal length. (See Leaf Shapes, p.344.)

OBLONG-ELLIPTIC Describes a leaf shape that is oblong with ends that are round.

OBOVATE A leaf shape that is egg-shaped in outline and broadest above the middle. (See Leaf Shapes, p.344.)

OIL DOTS The tiny reservoirs that occur on the surfaces of leaves of some trees, known for their aromatic oils; sometimes visible as black spots.

OPPOSITE A leaf arrangement in which the leaves are borne in pairs at each *node*, in the same place but on opposite sides of an axis. (See Simple Leaf Arrangements, right.)

OVARY Female flower part that contains the ovules, which develop into seeds (see also *carpel*).

OVATE Describes a leaf shape that is broadest below the middle. (See Leaf Shapes, p.344.)

OVOID Describes a solid form that is broadest below the middle; usually refers to a fruit.

PALMATE A compound leaf that is fully divided into *leaflets* arising from a single basal point. (See Compound Leaf Arrangements, right.)

PANICLE A branched *raceme*. (See Flower Arrangements, facing page.)

PEA-LIKE Describes a flower with an erect standard petal, two lateral wing petals, and two lower, keeled petals enclosing the stamens and *pistil*.

SIMPLE LEAF ARRANGEMENTS

Simple leaves are not divided into secondary units. They are arranged in one of two patterns: opposite (paired on either side of the stem) or alternate (in a staggered arrangement).

OPPOSITE   ALTERNATE

COMPOUND LEAF ARRANGEMENTS

Leaves that are divided into individual leaflets are known as compound leaves. Leaflets may be arranged symmetrically around the tip of the stem or along its length.

PINNATE   PALMATE

LEAF MARGINS

The lamina, or leaf blade, of both simple and compound leaves may have a smooth edge (entire) or it may be shaped with indentations. The individual pattern is particular to each species of tree and can serve as an identification feature. As shown below, the indentations may be toothed, lobed, or wavy but in addition there are also other less common variations.

ENTIRE   TOOTHED   LOBED   WAVY

PEDICEL The stalk supporting a flower, flowerhead, or fruit.

PERIANTH Collective term for the petals and *calyx*.

PERICARP The part of the fruit that encloses the seed.

PINNATE A compound leaf arrangement in which the *leaflets* (pinnae) are arranged either alternately or in opposite pairs on a central axis. (See Compound Leaf Arrangements, p.347.)

PIONEER SPECIES Species that are usually the first to colonize inhospitable sites and cleared ground, leading the way for other vegetation. They improve soil quality and protect land from erosion.

PISTIL Female reproductive organ of a flower, composed of one or several fused or separate *carpels*.

RACEME *Inflorescence* of stalked flowers radiating from a single, unbranched axis, with the youngest flowers near the tip. (See Flower Arrangements, p.346.)

SEMI-DECIDUOUS OR SEMI-EVERGREEN A tree that loses its leaves for only a short period during the year or that sheds a proportion of its leaves periodically but is never entirely leafless.

SEPAL One of the usually green parts of an advanced flower outside the petals. (See Flower Parts, p.345.)

SPIKE An *inflorescence* in which stalkless flowers are arranged on an unbranched axis. (See Flower Arrangements, p.346.)

STAMEN Male part of a flower, usually composed of an *anther* borne on a filament.

STAMINAL TUBE A structure formed from joined *stamens*.

STIGMA Female part of a flower found at the tip of the *pistil* that receives pollen. (See Flower Parts, p.345.)

STIPULE Leaf-like or bract-like structure borne, usually in pairs, at the point where a leaf-stalk arises from a stem.

STYLE Female part of flower connecting the *ovary* and the *stigma*. (See Flower Parts, p.345.)

SUCKER *1*. Shoot that arises below the soil level, usually from the roots rather than from the stem or crown of the plant. *2*. Shoot that arises from the stock of a grafted or budded plant.

SYNCARP An aggregate or multiple fruit that is produced from fused *pistils*; the individual fruits join together in a mass and grow together to form a single fruit.

TEPAL The term that is given to the *sepals* and petals when they are indistinguishable from one another as in the case of primitive angiosperms. (See Flower Parts, p.345.)

TERMINAL A term that describes the position at the end of a stem or shoot.

UMBEL Flat- or round-topped *inflorescence* in which numerous stalked flowers are borne in a terminal position from a single point. (See also Flower Arrangements, p.346.)

TREE HABIT

A tree's shape is species specific and can help in identification. However, habit can vary depending on age and habitat and other external features such as climate. For example, a tree growing in the open will differ greatly in shape compared to one of the same species growing in dense forest.

CONICAL   SHRUB-LIKE   SPREADING   COLUMNAR

Tree Families

Refer to this alphabetical list to find out which tree families and genera are represented in this book and on which page(s) their species can be found.

Adoxaceae *Sambucus* (pp.339–40). **Amaranthaceae** *Charpentiera; Haloxylon* (p.148). **Anacardiaceae** *Anacardium; Gluta; Harpephyllum; Mangifera; Pistacia; Pleiogynium; Schinus; Spondias* (pp.296–9). **Annonaceae** *Annona; Asimina; Cananga; Polyalthia* (pp.116–8). **Apocynaceae** *Alstonia; Dyera; Plumeria; Rauvolfia; Tabernaemontana; Tabernanthe* (pp.325–6). **Aquifoliaceae** *Ilex* (pp.337–8). **Araucariaceae** *Agathis; Araucaria* (pp.92–3). **Araliaceae** *Pseudopanax; Schefflera* (p.338). **Asparagaceae** *Cordyline; Dracaena; Yucca* (pp.126–7). **Asphodelaceae** *Aloe* (pp.125–6). **Betulaceae** *Alnus, Betula; Carpinus; Corylus; Ostrya* (pp.257–62). **Bignoniaceae** *Catalpa; Crescentia; Jacaranda; Kigelia; Oroxylum; Spathodea; Tabebuia* (pp.331–3). **Bixaceae** *Bixa; Cochlospermum* (p.269). **Boraginaceae** *Cordia; Wigandia* (p.322). **Burseraceae** *Boswellia; Bursera; Commiphora* (pp.294–5). **Buxaceae** *Buxus* (p.145). **Cactaceae** *Carnegiea* (p.149). **Campanulaceae** *Lobelia* (p.341). **Canellaceae** *Canella* (p.113). **Cannabaceae** *Celtis* (p.229). **Caricaceae** *Carica; Vasconcellea* (pp.267–8). **Caryocaraceae** *Caryocar* (p.179). **Casuarinaceae** *Casuarina* (p.263). **Cercidiphyllaceae** *Cercidiphyllum* (p.153). **Chrysobalanaceae** *Chrysobalanus; Parinari* (pp.167–8). **Combretaceae** *Terminalia* (p.153). **Compositae** *Dendrosenecio; Montanoa* (p.341). **Cornaceae** *Cornus; Davidia; Nyssa* (pp.310–11). **Cucurbitaceae** *Dendrosicyos* (p.242). **Cunoniaceae** *Davidsonia* (p.184). **Cupressaceae** *Calocedrus; Chamaecyparis; Cryptomeria; Cunninghamia;* × *Cupressocyparis; Cupressus; Juniperus; Metasequoia; Platycladus; Sequoia; Sequoiadendron; Taxodium; Tetraclinis; Thuja; Thujopsis; Xanthocyparis* (pp.99–104). **Cycadaceae** *Cycas* (p.69). **Dicksoniaceae** *Dicksonia* (p.65). **Dipterocarpaceae** *Dryobalanops; Hopea; Neobalanocarpus; Shorea* (pp.282–4). **Ebenaceae** *Diospyros* (pp.316–7). **Ericaceae** *Arbutus; Rhododendron* (pp.321–2). **Erythroxylaceae** *Erythroxylum* (p.181). **Eucommiaceae** *Eucommia* (p.323). **Euphorbiaceae** *Aleurites; Baccaurea; Euphorbia; Hevea; Mallotus; Vernicia* (pp.177–9). **Fagaceae** *Castanea; Chrysolepis; Fagus; Quercus* (pp.243–55). **Fouquieriaceae** *Fouquieria* (p.314). **Ginkgoaceae** *Ginkgo* (p.71). **Guttiferae** *Calophyllum; Garcinia* (p.180). **Hamamelidaceae** *Liquidambar; Parrotia* (p.154). **Juglandaceae** *Carya ; Juglans; Pterocarya* (pp.264–6). **Labiatae** *Gmelina; Premna; Tectona* (pp.334–5). **Lauraceae** *Chlorocardium; Cinnamomum; Endiandra; Eusideroxylon; Laurus; Persea; Sassafras; Umbellularia* (pp.118–22). **Lecythidaceae** *Bertholletia; Couroupita* (p.318). **Leguminosae** *Acacia; Albizia; Amherstia; Bauhinia; Butea; Cassia; Castanospermum; Ceratonia ; Cercis; Colophospermum; Colvillea; Cynometra; Dalbergia; Delonix; Dipteryx; Erythrina; Falcataria; Gleditsia; Gymnocladus; Inocarpus; Koompassia; Laburnum; Leucaena; Parkia; Peltogyne; Peltophorum; Pericopsis; Prosopis; Pterocarpus;*

Robinia; Samanea; Sophora; Tamarindus (pp.185–209). **Loranthaceae** *Nuytsia* (p.152). **Lythraceae** *Lawsonia* (p.153). **Magnoliaceae** *Liriodendron; Magnolia* (p.114). **Malvaceae** *Adansonia; Bombax; Brachychiton; Ceiba; Durio; Guazuma; Lagunaria; Ochroma; Pachira; Theobroma; Tilia; Triplochiton* (pp.269–81). **Melastomataceae** *Tibouchina* (p.167). **Meliaceae** *Azadirachta; Cedrela; Chukrasia; Dysoxylum; Khaya; Lansium; Lovoa; Melia; Sandoricum; Swietenia; Toona; Xylocarpus* (pp.301–8). **Moraceae** *Antiaris; Artocarpus; Broussonetia; Ficus; Maclura; Milicia; Morus* (pp.230–41). **Moringaceae** *Moringa* (p.268). **Muntingiaceae** *Muntingia* (p.282). **Musaceae** *Ravenala* (p.140). **Myricaceae** *Morella* (p.256). **Myristicaceae** *Myristica* (p.114). **Myrtaceae** *Corymbia; Eucalyptus; Eugenia; Melaleuca; Metrosideros; Psidium; Syzygium* (pp.153–67). **Nothofagaceae** *Nothofagus* (p.243). **Oleaceae** *Fraxinus; Olea* (pp.328–30). **Oxalidaceae** *Averrhoa* (p.184). **Palmae** *Areca; Arenga; Borassus; Caryota; Ceroxylon; Cocos; Copernicia; Corypha; Elaeis; Hyphaene; Jubaea; Lodoicea; Metroxylon; Phoenix; Raphia; Roystonea; Trachycarpus; Washingtonia* (pp.127–40). **Pandanaceae** *Pandanus* (p.124). **Paulowniaceae** *Paulownia* (p.336). **Phytolaccaceae** *Phytolacca* (p.152). **Pinaceae** *Abies, Cedrus; Larix; Phyllocladus; Picea; Pinus; Pseudotsuga; Tsuga* (pp.76–91). **Pittosporaceae** *Pittosporum* (p.339). **Platanaceae** *Platanus* (pp.144–5). **Podocarpaceae** *Podocarpus* (pp.96–7). **Polygonaceae** *Triplaris* (p.148). **Proteaceae** *Grevillea; Macadamia* (pp.142–3). **Quillajaceae** *Quillaja* (p.184). **Rhamnaceae** *Hovenia; Ziziphus* (pp.225–6). **Rhizophoraceae** *Rhizophora* (p.181). **Rosaceae** *Crataegus; Cydonia; Eriobotrya; Malus; Prunus; Pyrus; Sorbus* (pp.210–25). **Rubiaceae** *Cinchona; Coffea; Neolamarckia* (pp.323–5). **Rutaceae** *Calodendrum; Chloroxylon; Citrus; Flindersia; Limonia, Zanthoxylum* (pp.308–1?). **Salicaceae** *Pangium; Populus; Salix* (pp.291-2). **Santalaceae** *Santalum* (pp.152–3). **Sapindaceae** *Acer; Aesculus; Blighia; Dimocarpus; Koelreuteria; Litchi; Nephelium* (pp.285–93). **Sapotaceae** *Argania; Chrysophyllum; Manilkara; Palaquium; Pouteria; Synsepalum* (pp.318–20). **Schisandraceae** *Illicium* (p.112). **Sciadopityaceae** *Sciadopitys* (p.97). **Scrophulariaceae** *Myoporum* (p.331). **Simaroubaceae** *Ailanthus; Leitneria* (p.300). **Solanaceae** *Brugmansia; Solanum* (p.327). **Staphyleaceae** *Staphylea* (p.154). **Styracaceae** *Halesia; Styrax* (pp.317–318). **Taxaceae** *Cephalotaxus; Taxus; Torreya* (pp.97–9). **Theaceae** *Camellia; Franklinia* (pp.315–6). **Thymelaeaceae** *Aquilaria; Gonystylus* (p.285). **Ulmaceae** *Trema; Ulmus; Zelkova* (pp.226–9). **Umbelliferae** *Steganotaenia* (p.339). **Urticaceae** *Cecropia; Dendrocnide; Musanga* (p.242). **Verbenaceae** *Citharexylum* (p.334). **Winteraceae** *Drimys* (p.113). **Xanthorrhoeaceae** *Kingia; Xanthorrhoea* (pp.124–5).

Index

A

Abiu 320
Abies
  alba 76
  grandis 76
  koreana 76
  nordmanniana 76
  procera 77
Acacia
  False 207
  Prickly 187
Acacia
  aneura 185
  dealbata 185
  farnesiana 185
  longifolia 186
  mangium 186
  mearnsii 186
  melanoxylon 186
  nilotica 187
  pycnantha 188
  seyal 188
  xanthophloea 188, 190–191
Acer
  campestre 285
  negundo 285
  palmatum 286
    palmatum dissectum 290–291
  pseudoplatanus 287
  rubrum 287
  saccharum 288
acid rain 27
Adansonia
  digitata 270
  gregorii 270
Aesculus hippocastanum 289
African Baobab 42
African Blackwood 196
African Mahogany 303
African Teak 240
Afromosia 205
Agarwood 285
Agathis
  australis 92
  robusta 92
Akee 289
Alan 284
Albizia julibrissin 189
Alder 257
  Green 56
  Grey 258
Alerce 106
Aleurites moluccana 177
Alexandrian Laurel 180
Algarroba 205
Allanthus altissima 300
Almond 141, 217
  Indian 155
almond nuts 45
Alnus
  crispa 256
  glutinosa 257
  incana 258

Aloe
  bainesii 126
  dichotoma 125
Aloe Tree 126
Alpine Ash 156
Alstonia scholaris 325
Ambarella 299
American Beech 245
American Black Birch 258
American Chestnut 243
American Elder 339
American Hornbeam 260
Amherstia nobilis 189
Anacardium occidentale 296
Anatto 269
angiosperms 110
  primitive 112
Angel's Trumpets 327
Angsana 207
Annona
  cherimola 116
  glabra 116
  muricata 116
Antarctic Beech 243
Antiaris toxicaria 231
Apple
  Flowering 211
  Pond 116
  Star 318
  Turkish Crab 211
  Wild 211
  Wood 311
Apricot 212, 214–215
Aquilaria malaccensis 285
Arabica Coffee 324
Araucaria
  araucana 93, 94–95
  bidwillii 92
  columnaris 92
  cunninghamii 96
  heterophylla 96
  hunsteinii 96
Arboloco 341
Arbutus
  menziesii 331
  unedo 331
Areca catechu 127
Arenga pinnata 127
Argan 319
Argania spinosa 319
Arolla Pine 86
aromatherapy 50
Artocarpus
  altilis 230
  heterophyllus 231
Ash 328
  Alpine 156
  Crow's 311
  Flowering 329
  Manna 329
  Mountain 164
  White 329
Ashoka, King 238
Asimina triloba 117

Aspen 172, 174–175
  Canadian 172
  Big-tooth 168
aspirin 50, 51
  and White Willow 173
Atlas Cedar 77
Australian Rosewood 303
Averrhoa
  bilimbi 184
  carambola 184
Avocado 121
Ayurvedic medicine 301
Azadirachta indica 301

B

Babaco 268
Babul 187
bacteria, nitrifying 21
Baccaurea ramiflora 177
Balata 319
Balsa 275
Balsam Poplar 169
Banyan 233
Baobab 42, 270, 272–273
bark 18, 37
Bark
  Cassia 119
  Winter's 113
barren lands 34
Basket Willow 173
Bastard Cedar 275
Bauhinia variegata 189
Bay, Bull 115
Bay Tree 121
Baywood 306
Beach Pine 86
Bean
  Black 192
  Indian 331
  Kentucky Coffee 201
  Tonka 199
Beaverwood 229
Beech
  American 245
  Antarctic 243
  Black 243
  Common 246
  Japanese 245
  Myrtle 243
Beefwood 263
Bella Umbra 152
Bertholletia excelsa 318
Betel 127
Betula
  alleghaniensis 258
  lenta 258
  pendula 259
  utilis 258
Betulus papyrifera 259
Big-tooth Aspen 168
Bilimbing 184
biodiversity 61
biomass 48

Birch
  American Black 258
  Himalayan 258
  Paper 259
  Silver 259
  Yellow 258
Bird Cherry 218
Bisselon 303
Bitter Orange 309
Bixa orellana 269
Black Bean 192
Black Beech 243
Black Cottonwood 172
Black Gin 124
Black Gum 313
Black Locust 207
Black Mulberry 241
Black Oak 254
Black Poplar 172
Black Walnut 265
Black Wattle 186
Blackbutt 161
Blackthorn 218
Blackwood 186
  African 196
Bladdernut 154
Bligh, Captain 289
Blighia sapida 289
Blue Gum 157
Blue Pine 91
Boab 270
boat, wood-framed 47
Bodhi Tree 238
Bombax ceiba 269
bonsai trees 53
Boobialla 331
Boojum Tree 314
Borassus flabellifer 130
Boswellia sacra 94, 294
Bo-tree 238
  special reverence for 43
Box 145
Box Elder 285
Brachychiton acerifolius 270
branches 19
Brazil Nut 318
Brazilian Rosewood 197
Brazilian Tulipwood 196
Breadfruit 230
Bristlecone Pine 86, 88–89
broadleaf forests
  temperate 28
  tropical 30
Broad-leaved Paperbark 164
Broussonetia papyrifera 232
Brugmansia x *candida* 327
Buddha 43, 238, 283
Bull Bay 115
Bunya-bunya 92
Burdekin Plum 299
Burr Oak 254
Bursera simaruba 295
Butea monosperma 192
Butternut 265
Buttonwood 145
Buxus sempervirens 145

C
Calabash Tree 331
Calamander 316
Californian Nutmeg 99
Californian Redwood 103
Californian Yew 97
Calophyllum inophyllum 180
Calocedrus decurrens 99
Calodendrum capense 308
cambium 21
Camellia sinensis 315
Camphor Laurel 120
Canada Poplar 169
Canadian Aspen 172
Canadian Dogwood 312
Cananga odorata 117
Canary Palm 139
Candelabra Tree 177
Candlenut 177
Canella winterana 113
Canella 113
Canistel 320
Cannonball Tree 318
Cannonball Mahogany 308
canoes 40
Cape Chestnut 308
Cape York Red Gum 156
carbon cycle 58, 59
cardboard boxes 49
Caribbean Pitch Pine 86
Carica papaya 267
caring, for trees 54–55
Carl von Linné 14, 69
Carnauba Wax Palm 133
Carnegiea gigantea 149, 150–151
Carob 193
Carpinus
  betulus 260
  caroliniana 260
Carolus Linnaeus (Carl von
  Linné) 14, 69
Carrot Tree 339
Carya illinoinensis 264
Caryocar nuciferum 179
Caryota urens 131
Cashew 296
Cassia Bark 119
Cassia
  fistula 192
  javanica 192
Castanea
  dentata 243
  pumila 245
  sativa 244
Castanospermum australe 192
Casuarina equisetifolia 263
Catalpa bignonioides 331
Caucasian Fir 76
cave paintings 41
Cecropia peltata 242
Cedar of Lebanon 78, 80–81
Cedar
  Atlas 77
  Bastard 275
  Deodar 77
  Hiba 107
  Incense 99

Cedar cont.
  Japanese 100
  of Lebanon 78
  Red 102
  West Indian 302
  Western Red 107
  White 107
  Yellow 107
Cedrela odorata 302
Cedrus
  atlantica 77
  deodara 77
  libani 78, 80–81
Ceiba
  pentandra 274, 276–277
  speciosa 271
Celtis
  australis 229
  occidentalis 229
Cephalotaxus harringtonia 97
Ceratonia siliqua 193
Cercidiphyllum japonicum 153
Cercis
  canadensis 194
  siliquastrum 194
Ceroxylon alpinum 131
Chamaecyparis
  lawsoniana 99
  pisifera 99
Champak 115
Chanel No. 5 117
Charpentiera densiflora 148
Cheesewood 339
Chengal 282
Cherimoya 116
Cherry Laurel 216
Cherry
  Bird 218
  Cornelian 312
  Flowering 218
  Jamaican 282
  Morello 216
  Surinam 164
  Wild Sweet 213
  Winter-flowering 218
  Yoshino 222
Chestnut 244
  American 243
  Cape 308
  Golden 245
  Horse 289
  Sweet 244
Chilean Wine Palm 137
Chinese Arbor-vitae 106
Chinese Date 225
Chinese Dogwood 312
Chinese Weeping Willow 173
Chinquapin 245
Chios Mastic 298
Chir 87
Chlorocardium rodiei 118
chlorophyll 19
Chloroxylon swietenia 308
chocolate 45, 281
Christmas-tree 164
Chrysobalanus icaco 167
Chrysolepis chrysophylla 245

Chrysophyllum cainito 318
Chukrasia tabularis 303
Chusan Palm 139
cicada 208
Cider Gum 157
cigar boxes 302
Cinchona calisaya 323
Cinnamomum
   aromaticum 119
   camphora 120
   verum 119
Cinnamon 119
Citharexylum spinosum 334
Citrus
   x *aurantiifolia* 310
   x *aurantium* 309
   x *limon* 310
   reticulata 310
   sinensis 309
clarinet 196
classification
   artificial 14
   botanical 14
Clove 166
Coast Coral Tree 199
coal 17
Coca 181
cocaine 181
Cochlospermum religiosum 269
Cocoa 281
cocoa beans 44, 281
Coconut
  Double 137
  Palm 132, 134–135
Cocoplum 167
Cocos nucifera 132
Coffea
   arabica 324
   canephora 325
Coffee
  Arabica 324
  Robusta 325
coffee beans 45
coir 132
Colophospermum mopane 195
Colvillea racemosa 195
Colville's Glory Tree 195
Commiphora myrrha 295
Common Beech 141, 246,
  248–249
Common Fig 234
Common Lime 279
coniferous forests 26
Conifers, description 74
conservation, of trees 60–61
Cook Pine 92
Coolibah 161
Copernicia prunifera 133
coppices, hazel 261
coppicing 56, 57
Coral Tree 199
Cordia
   alliodora 322
   myxa 322
Cordials 340
Cordyline
   australis 126

Cordyline cont.
   fruticosa 126
cork 51
corks, bottle 255
Cork Oak 255
Corkwood 300
Cornelian Cherry 312
Cornus
   kousa 312
   mas 312
   nutalli 312
Corsican Pine 87
Corylus
   avellana 261
   colurna 262
   maxima 262
Corymbia ficifolia 155
Corypha umbraculifera 133
Cottonwood 169
  Black 172
Couroupita guianensis 318
Crab Apple 211
  Turkish 211
Crack Willow 22
Crataegus monogyna 210
Crepe Jasmine 326
Crescentia cujete 331
crops, processed 45
Crow's Ash 311
Cryptomeria japonica 100
Cucumber Tree 184, 242
Cupressus
   macrocarpa 100
   empervirens 100
   lusitanica 100
  x *Cupressocyparis leylandii* 101
cycads
  and tree evolution 17
  description of 68
Cycas circinalis 69
Cydonia oblonga 210
Cynometra cauliflora 195
Cypre 322
Cypress
  Italian 100
  Lawson's 99
  Leyland 101
  Mexican 100
  Monterey 100
  Sawara 99
  Swamp 106

D

Dalbergia
   decipularis 196
   melaxylon 196
   nigra 197
Damar 284
Date, Chinese 225
Date Palm 138
David, Armand 313
Davidia involucrata 313
Davidsonia pruriens 184
Davidson's Plum 184
Dawn Redwood 102
deforestation, rainforest 58
Delonix regia 198

Dendocnide excelsa 242
Dendosenecio johnstonii 341
Dendrosicyos socotranus 242
Deodar 77
deserts 34
Dicksonia antarctica 65
dicotyledons
  comparison with
   monocotyledons 123,
  description of 141
Dimocarpus longan 292
Diospyros
   ebenum 141, 316
   kaki 317
   quaesita 316
   virginiana 317
Dipteryx odorata 199
Dita 325
Dogwood
  Canadian 312
  Chinese 312
Doronoki 169
Double Coconut 137
Douglas Fir 91
Doum Palm 137
Dove Tree 313
Downy Oak 250
Dracaena cinnabari 126, 128–129
Dragon Tree 126, 128–129
Drake, Sir Francis 113
Drimys winteri 113
Dryobalanops aromatica 284
Durian 271
Durio zibethinus 271
Durmast Oak 250
Dyera costulata 325
Dysoxylum fraserianum 303

E

early people 40
Ebony 141, 316
Elaeis guineensis 136
Elder 340, 342–343
  American 339
  Box 285
Elm
  English 228
  Siberian 229
  White 227
  Wych 227
elm bark beetle 228
endangered tree species 61
Endiandra palmerstonii 120
English Elm 228
English Oak 251
environmental problems 58
Eriobotrya japonica 210
erosion control 59
Erythroxylum coca 181
Erythrina
   caffra 199
   crista-galli 199
ethanol 48
Eucalyptus
   brassiana 156
   camaldulensis 156,
    158–159

Eucalyptus cont.
  deglupta 156
  delegatensis 156
  diversicolor 157
  globulus 157
  gunnii 157
  marginata 160
  microcorys 161
  microtheca 161
  pauciflora 161, 162–163
  pilularis 161
  regnans 164
Eucommia ulmoides 323
Eugenia uniflora 164
Euphorbia
  candelabrum 177
  ingens 177
evolution, of trees 16

F

Fagus
  crenata 245
  grandifolia 245
  sylvatica 246, 248–249
Falcataria moluccana 200
False Acacia 207
False Sago 69
Faya 256
felling 57
Fever Tree 188, 190–191
fibre 51
fibreboard 48
Ficus
  benghalensis 233
  benjamina 234
  carica 234
  elastica 235
  macrophylla 235,
    236–237
  religiosa 238
  sumatrana 239
  sycomorus 239
Fiddlewood 334
Field Maple 285
field notes 36
field work 36
Fig 234
  Moreton Bay 235
  Strangler 239
  Sycamore 239
  Weeping 234
Filbert 262
Fir
  Caucasian 76
  Douglas 91
  Grand 76
  Korean 76
  Noble 77
  Nordmann 76
  Silver 76
  White 76
Fire Tree 152
Flamboyant 198
  Yellow 204
Flame of the Forest 192
Flame-tree 270, 333
Flatspine Prickly Ash 311

Flindersia
  australis 311
  brayleyana 311
Floss Silk Tree 271
Flowering Apple 211
Flowering Ash 329
Flowering Cherry 218, 220–221
flowering trees, description 110
flowers 19
  and tree reproduction 22
  and tree identification 37
food 40
forest
  Beech 29
  Birch–Alder 29
  commercial 56
  coniferous 24, 26–27
  maintenance 57
  management 56–57, 60
  Oak 29
  prehistoric 16
  Southern Beech 29
  Sparse African 30
  temperate broadleaf 24, 28
  tropical broadleaf 24, 30
  tropical rainforest 24
  wildlife in *Eucalyptus* 31
  zones 24–25
fossil cycad frond 68
Fouquieria columnaris 314
Foxglove-tree 336
Frangipani 326
Frankincense 35, 294
Frankincense Tree 154
Franklin, Benjamin 316
Franklin Tree 316
Franklinia alatamaha 316
Fraxinus
  excelsior 328
  ornus 329
  pennsylvanica 329
fruit 19, 37
  and nuts from trees 44
  growing commercially 44
fuel, modern wood 48

G

Garcinia mangostana 180
gardens, trees in 53
Gean 213
Giant Groundsel 341
Giant Lobelia 341
Gin, Black 124
Ginkgo 68
ginkgos 17, 70
Ginkgo biloba 71
Gleditsia triacanthos 201
global warming 58
Gluta renghas 296
Gmelina arborea 334
Golden Chestnut 245
Golden Rain 202, 292
Golden Shower 192
Golden Wattle 188
Golden Weeping Willow 176
Gonystylus bancanus 285
Grand Fir 76

Grass-tree 125
Green Alder 256
Greenheart 118
Grevillea robusta 142
Grey Alder 258
Groundsel, Giant 341
Guacimilla 226
Guava 165
Guazuma ulmifolia 275
Gum
  Alpine Ash 156
  Black 313
  Blackbutt 161
  Blue 157
  Cape York Red 156
  Coolibah 161
  Cider 157
  Kamarere 156
  Karri 157
  Jarrah 160
  Mountain Ash 164
  Red-flowering 155
  River Red 156
  Sandarac 106
  Snow 161
  Sweet 154
  Tallowwood 161
gum 51
gum arabic 187
Gumbo Limbo 295
Gutta Percha 319
Gymnocladus dioica 201
Gympie Stinger 242

H

Halesia carolina 317
Haloxylon persicum 148
habitat conservation 61
hamadryads 42–43
Handkerchief Tree 313
hardwood 46
Hardy Rubber Tree 323
Harpephyllum caffrum 297
Hawthorn 210
Hazel 261
  Turkish 262
Headache Tree 334
heartwood 21
Hemlock
  Western 91
  White 91
Henna 155
Hevea brasiliensis 33, 178
Hiba 107
Hibiscus, Norfolk Island 275
Himalayan Birch 258
Holly 337
Holm Oak 247
Homo erectus 40–41
Homo sapiens 41
honey, from Jarrah trees 160
Honey-locust 201
Hoop Pine 96
Hop Hornbeam 262
Hopea odorata 282
Hornbeam 260
  American 260

Hornbeam cont.
  Hop 262
Horse Chestnut 289
Horse-radish Tree 268
Hovenia dulcis 225
Hyphaene thebaica 137

I

Iboga 326
Ibogaine 326
identification, of trees 36
Ilex
  aquifolium 337
  paraguariensis 338
Illicium verum 112
Incense Cedar 99
Incense Tree 295
incense
  frankinscence 294
  myrrh 295
Indian Almond 155
Indian Bean 331
Indian Rubber Tree 326
Indian Willow 118
insecticide, natural 301
International Union for the
  Conservation of Nature
  (IUCN) 15
Iroko 240
Ironwood 154
Italian Cypress 100

J

Jacaranda 332
Jacaranda mimosifolia 332
Jack Pine 83
Jak 231
Jamaican Cherry 282
Jambolan 167
Jam-tree 282
Japanese Beech 245
Japanese Cedar 100
Japanese Larch 79
Japanese Maple 286, 290–291
Japanese White Pine 83
Jarrah 160
Jelutong 325
Joshua Tree 127
Jubaea chilensis 137
Judas Iscariot 194
Judas Tree 194
Juglans
  cinerea 265
  nigra 265
  regia 266
Juniper 101
Juniperus
  communis 101
  virginiana 102

K

Kadam 325
Kaffir Plum 297
Kaki 317
Kamala 179
Kamarere 156

Kapok 274, 276–277
Kapur 284
Karri 157
Katsura 153
Kauri 92
  Queensland 92
Keaki 229
Kempas 202
Kentucky Coffee Bean 201
Kepayang 168
Khaya senegalensis 303
Kigelia africana 332
Kingia australis 124
Kitul Palm 131
Klinki Pine 96
Koelreuteria paniculata 292
Koompassia
  excelsa 202
  malaccensis 202
Korean Fir 76
Koto, instrument 336
Kusamaki 97

L

Laburnam 202
Laburnum anagyroides 202
Lagunaria patersonia 275
Lancewood 338
Langsat 304
Lansium domesticum 304
Lapacho 333
Larch 79
  Japanese 79
Larix
  decidua 79
  kaempferi 79
  laricina 79
Lasiandra 167
latex 51
Laurel
  Alexandrian 180
  Camphor 120
  Cherry 216
Laurus nobilis 121
Lawsonia inermis 155
Lawson's Cypress 99
layering 23
Lead Tree 203
Leitneria floridana 300
Lemon 310
Leucaena leucocephala 203
Levant Storax 154
Leyland, C.J. 101
Leyland Cypress 101
Lilac, Persian 305
Lime 310
  Common 279
  Silver 280
  Small-leaved 279
Limonia acidissima 311
Linnaeus, Carolus (Carl von
  Linné) 14, 69
Liquidambar
  orientalis 154
  styraciflua 154
Liriodendron tulipifera 115
Litchi chinensis 293

Lobelia giberroa 341
Locust 204
Lodoicea maldivica 137
London Plane 144
Longan 292
Longbow 98
Long Jack 148
Loquat 210
Lotus 226
Lovoa trichilioides 304
Lychee 293

M

Macadamia 143
Macadamia integrifolia 143
Maclura pomifera 240
Madrono 321
Magnolia
  champaca 115
  grandiflora 115
Mahatma Gandhi 301
Mahogany 33, 306
  African 303
  Cannonball 308
Mayas 274, 281
Maidenhair Tree 71
Malay Tree 167
Mallotus philippensis 179
Malus
  sylvestris 211
  trilobata 211
Mandarin 310
Mangifera indica 297
Mangium 186
Mango 297
Mangosteen 180
Mangrove, Red 181, 182–83
Manilkara
  bidentata 319
  zapota 319
Manna 329
Manna Ash 329
Maple
  Field 285
  Japanese 286, 290–291
  Queensland 311
  Red 287
  Sugar 288
Maritime Pine 83
Mastic 298
Maté 338
medium density fibreboard
  (MDF) 49
Melaleuca quinquenervia 164
Melia azedarach 305
Menzies, Archibald 321
Mesquite 206
Metasequoia glyptostroboides 102
Metrosideros excelsa 164
Metroxylon sagu 137
Mexican Cypress 100
Mexican Pine 87
Midnight Horror 332
Millennium Seed Bank 61
Milicia excelsa 240
Miller, Philip 300
Miraculous Berry 320

Mobola 168
Money Pine 79
Monkey Puzzle 93, 94–95
monocotyledons 122
monsoon woodland 30
Montanoa quadrangularis 341
Monterey Cypress 100
Mopane 195
Morella
  cerifera 256
  faya 256
Morello Cherry 216
Moreton Bay Fig 235
Moringa oleifera 268
Morus
  alba 241
  nigra 241
Mountain Ash 164
Mountain Papaya 268
Mulberry 241
  Black 241
  Paper 232
  White 241
Mulga 185
Mume 216
Muntingia calabura 282
Musanga cecropioides 242
Myoporum acuminatum 331
Myristica fragans 114
Myrobalan 213
Myrrh 295
Myrtle, Wax 256
Myrtle Beech 243
myths 42

N
Nam-nam 195
Nashi 224
Neanderthal 41
Neem 301
Nelson, Lord 251
Neobalanocarpus heimii 282
Neolamarckia cadamba 325
Nephelium lappaceum 293
Nettle Tree 229
Nigerian Golden Walnut 304
nitrogen cycle 21
Noble Fir 77
Nordmann Fir 76
Norfolk Island Hibiscus 275
Norfolk Island Pine 96
Norway Spruce 82
Nothofagus
  antarctica 243
  cunninghamii 243
  solanderi 243
nuts, as food 44–45
Nutmeg 114
  Californian 99
Nuytsia floribunda 152
Nyssa sylvatica 313

O
Oak
  Burr 254
  Cork 255
  Downy 250

Oak cont.
  Durmast 250
  English 251
  Holm 247
  Pedunculate 251
  Red 254
  Scarlet 247
  Sessile 250
  Shingle 250
  Silky 142
  Turkey 247
  Valonia 250
  White 247
Obeche 280
Ochroma pyramidale 275
oil
  aromatic 51
  clove
  olive 330
  palm 136
Oil Palm 136
Olea europaea 330
Olive 330
Ombu 152
Ooray 184
Opopanax 185
Orange
  Bitter 309
  Osage 240
  Sweet 309
Orchids 33
Orchid Tree 189
Oroxylum indicum 332
Osage Orange 240
Ostrya carpinifolia 262

P
Pachira aquatica 278
Pagoda Tree 209
Palaquium gutta 319
Palm Lily 126
Palm
  Canary 139
  Carnauba Wax 133
  Chilean Wine 137
  Chusan 139
  Coconut 132
  Date 138
  Double Coconut 137
  Doum 137
  Kitul 131
  Oil 136
  Palmyra 130
  Raphia 139
  Royal 139
  Sago 137
  Sugar 127
  Talipot 133
  Traveller's 140
  Washingtonia 140
  Wax 131
Palmyra Palm 130
Pandanus tectorius 124
Pangium edule 168
Papala 148
Papaya 267
  Mountain 268

paper
  recycling 49
  handmade 48
Paperbark 164
  Broad-leaved 164
Paper Birch 259
papermaking 48
Paper Mulberry 232
Para Rubber 33, 178
Parasol Pine 97
Parinari curatellifolia 168
Parkia
  biglobosa 204
  speciosa 204
Parrotia persica 154
Paulovna, Anna 336
Paulownia
  x *taiwaniana* 336
  tomentosa 336
Pawpaw 117
Peach 219
Pear 223
  Nashi 224
  Whitty 225
  Willow 224
Pecan 264
Pedunculate Oak 251
Pehuenche, The 93
Peltophorum pterocarpum 204
Pepper Tree 299
Pepperwood 122
Pericopsis elata 205
Persea americana 121
Persian Lilac 305
Persimmon 317
pest and disease control 55
Petai 204
phloem 21
Phoenix
  canariensis 139
  dactylifera 138
photosynthesis 20
Phytolacca dioica 152
Picea
  abies 82
  sitchensis 82
Pine
  Arolla 86
  Beach 86
  Blue 91
  Bristlecone 86, 88–89
  Caribbean Pitch 86
  Chir 87
  Cook 92
  Corsican 87
  Hoop 96
  Jack 83
  Japanese White 83
  Klinki 96
  Maritime 83
  Mexican 87
  Norfolk Island 96
  Parasol 97
  Scots 90
  Screw- 124
  Stone 83
  Weymouth 87
  White 87

Pink Shower 192
Pink Trumpet Tree 333
Pinus
    banksiana 83
    caribaea 86
    cembra 86
    contorta 86
    longaeva 86, 88–89
    nigra 87
    parviflora 83
    patula 87
    pinaster 83
    pinea 83, 84–85
    roxburghii 87
    strobus 87
    sylvestris 90
    wallichiana 91
Pipal Tree 238
Pistachio 298
Pistacia
    lentiscus 298
    vera 298
Pittosporum
    tobira 339
    undulatum 339
planting, of trees 54
  commercial 56
plants, climbing 32
Platanus
    x *hispanica* 144
    occidentalis 145
Platycladus orientalis 106
Pleiogynium timoriense 299
Pliny the Elder 14
Plum Yew 97
Plum 216
Podocarpus macrophyllus 97
pollination 22
pollution
    and climatic change 58
    gene 61
    protection from air 55
Polyalthia longifolia 118
Pond Apple 116
Poplar
    Balsam 169
    Black 172
    Canada 169
    White 168
Populus
    alba 168, 170–171
    balsamifera 169
    x *canadensis* 169
    deltoides 169
    grandidentata 168
    maximowiczi 169
    nigra 172
    tremula 172, 174–175
    tremuloides 172
    trichocarpa 172
Pouteria
    caimito 320

Pouteria cont.
    campechiana 320
    sapota 320
prehistoric trees 16, 17
Premna serratifolia 334
preserves, apricot 212
Prickly Acacia 187
Prickly Ash, Flatspine 311
Pride of Burma 189
primitive angiosperms 112
Princess Tree 336
problems, of trees 55
Prosopis
    chilensis 205
    glandulosa 206
pruning 55
Prunus
    africana 212
    armeniaca 212, 214–215
    avium 213
    cerasifera 213
    cerasus 216
    x *domestica* 216
    dulcis 141, 217
    laurocerasus 216
    mume 216
    padus 218
    persica 219
    serrulata 218, 220–221
    spinosa 218
    subhirtella 218
    x *yedoensis* 222
Pseudopanax crassifolius 338
Pseudotsuga menziesii 91
Psidium guajava 165
Pterocarpus
    indicus 207
    santalinus 207
Pterocarya fraxinifolia 266
Pyrus
    communis 223
    pyrifolia 224
    salicifolia 224
pulp 48–49

Q

Quillaja saponaria 184
Queen of Sheba 298
Queensland Kauri 92
Queensland Maple 311
Queensland Walnut 120
Quercitron 254
Quercus
    alba 247
    cerris 247
    coccinea 247
    ilex 247
    imbricaria 250
    macrocarpa 254
    macrolepis 250
    petraea 250, 252–253
    pubescens 250
    robur 251
    rubra 254
    suber 255
    velutina 254
Quillai 184

Quince 210
Quinine 323
quinine 50, 323
Quiver Tree 125

R

Rain Tree 208
rainforest
    South American 32
    sub-tropical 30
    tropical 24, 32
Rainbow Shower 192
Raisin Tree 225
Rambai 177
Rambutan 293
Ramin 285
Raphia farinifera 139
Raphia Palm 139
Rauvolfia serpentina 326
Ravenala madagascariensis 140
Red Cedar 102
Red Mangrove 181, 182–183
Red Maple 287
Red Oak 254
Red Sandalwood 207
Red Stinkwood 212
Redbud 194
Red-flowering Gum 155
Redwood
    Californian 103
    Dawn 102
    Wellingtonia 103
Rengas 296
reproduction, in trees 22
resin 51
Rhizophora mangle 181, 182–183
Rhododendron 322
Rhododendron arboreum 322
River Red Gum 156, 158–159
Robin Hood 251
Robinia pseudoacacia 207
Robusta Coffee 325
roots 18
Rosewood
    Australian 303
    Brazilian 197
Rowan 224
Royal Palm 139
Roystonea regia 139
rubber 33, 178
Rubber, Para 33, 178
Rubber Plant 235
Rubber Tree
    Hardy 323
    Indian 326

S

Sago Palm 137
Saguaro 149, 150–151
Sal 283
Salix
    alba 173
    babylonica 173
    fragilis 23
    purpurea 173
    x *sepulcralis* 176
Samanea saman 208

Sambucus
  canadensis 339
  nigra 340, 342–343
Sandalwood 153
  Red 207
Sandarac Gum 106
Sandoricum koetjape 304
Santalum album 153
Santol 304
Sapodilla 319
Sapote 320
Sassafras albidum 122
Sassafras 122
Satinwood 308
Sau 200
Sausage-tree 332
Sawara Cypress 99
Saxaul 148
Scarlet Oak 247
Sequo-yah 103
Sessile Oak 250,
  251–252
Schefflera actinophylla 338
Schinus molle 299
Sciadopitys verticillata 97
Scottish Crossbill 90
Scots Pine 90
Screw-pine 124
Sebesten Plum 322
seed banks 61
seed dispersal 23
Seed trees 66
Sequoiadendron giganteum 103
Sequoia sempervirens 103
Serpentine Root 326
shaman's drum 43
Shaving-brush Tree 278
shelter 40
shelterbelts 59
Shingle Oak 250
Shittim 188
Shorea
  albida 284
  javanica 284
  robusta 283
Shower
  Pink 192
  Rainbow 192
  Golden 192
Siberian Elm 229
Sichuan Pepper 312
Silk Tree 189
  Floss 271
Silk-cotton Tree 269
Silky Oak 142
Silver Birch 259
Silver Fir 76
Silver Lime 280
Silver Wattle 185
Simul 269
Sitka Spruce 82
Sloe 218
Snow Gum 161, 162–163
Snowdrop Tree 317
Soapbark Tree 184
Soft Tree Fern 65
Softwood 46

soil
  salinity 35
  stabilization 58
Solanum betaceum 327
Solomon, King 298
Sophora japonica 209
Sorbus
  aria 224
  aucuparia 224
  domestica 225
  torminalis 225
Soumbala 204
Soursop 116
Spathodea nilotica 333
Species Plantarum 14
spices 114, 166
spirits 42
Spondias dulcis 299
spore trees 64
Spruce
  Norway 82
  Sitka 82
Staphylea pinnata 154
Star Anise 112
Star Apple 318
Starfruit 184
Steganotaenia araliacea 339
Stinkwood, Red 212
Stone Pine 83, 84–85
Storax, Levant 154
Strangler Fig 239
Strawberry-tree 321
structure, of trees 18
Styrax officinalis 318
Styrax 318
suckering 23
Sugar Maple 288
Sugar Palm 127
Surinam Cherry 164
Swamp Cypress 106, 108–109
Swarri Nut 179
Sweet Chestnut 244
Sweet Gum 154
Swietenia
  macrophylla 306
  mahagoni 306
Sycamore 287
Sycomore Fig 239
Sydney Golden Wattle 186
Sykes, Godfrey 314
Synsepalum dulcificum 320
syrup
  maple 288
  palm 130
Syzygium
  aromaticum 166
  cumini 167
  malaccense 167

T

Tabebuia
  chrysantha 333
  impetiginosa 333
  serratifolia 333
Tabernaemontana divaricata 326
Tabernanthe iboga 326
Talipot Palm 133

Tallowwood 161
Tamarack 79
Tamarind 209
Tamarindus indica 209
tannin 51
tapa cloth 232
Taxodium distichum 106
Taxus
  baccata 98
  brevifolia 97
Tea 315
  Maté 338
Teak 33, 335
  African 240
temperate broadleaf forest 28
thinning 57
Tectona grandis 335
Terminalia catappa 155
Tetraclinis articulata 106
Theobroma cacao 281
Theophrastus 14
Thingwa 282
Thuja
  occidentalis 107
  plicata 107
Thujopsis dolobrata 107
Ti 126
Tibouchina urvilleana 167
Tilia
  americana 278
  cordata 279
  x *europaea* 279
  tomentosa 280
Tobira 339
Tonka Bean 199
Toon 307
Toona ciliata 307
Torreya californica 99
Tourist Tree 295
Trachycarpus fortunei 139
transpiration 21
Tradescant, John 144
Traveller's Palm 140
Tree Aloe 126
Tree Euphorbia 177
tree ferns 17
Tree Fern, Soft 65
tree migration 17
Tree of Heaven 300
Tree-tomato 327
Trema micrantha 226
Triplaris weigeltiana 148
Triplochiton scleroxylon 280
tropical
  broadleaf forest 30
  rainforest 32
Trumpet Tree 242
  Pink 333
  Yellow 333
trunk 18
Tsuga
  canadensis 91
  heterophylla 91
Tualang 202
Tulip-Tree 115
Tulipwood, Brazilian 196
Tung 179

Turkey Oak 247
Turkish Crab Apple 211
Turkish Hazel 262
turpentine 51

U

Ulmus
    americana 227
    glabra 227
    procera 228
    pumila 229
Umbellularia californica 122
Umbrella Tree 242
Umbrella-tree 338
Upas Tree 231
urban environment, trees in 53

V

Valonia Oak 250
varnish 51
Vasconcellea x *heilbornii* 268
Vernicia fordii 179

W

Wallich, Nathaniel 189
Walnut 266
    Black 265
    Nigerian Golden 304
    Queensland 120
Washiba 333
washi paper-making 232
Washingtonia 140
Washingtonia filifera 140
Wattle
    Black 186
    Golden 188
    Silver 185
    Sydney Golden 186
wax 133
Wax Myrtle 256
Wax Palm 131
weapons 41
Weeping Fig 234
Weeping Willow 176
Wellingtonia 103, 104–105
West Indian Cedar 302
Western Hemlock 91
Western Red Cedar 107
White Ash 329
White Cedar 107
White Elm 227
White Fir 76
White Hemlock 91
White Mulberry 241
White Oak 247
White Pine 87
White Poplar 168, 170–171
White Willow 173
Whitebeam 224
Whitewood 278
Whitty Pear 225
Wigandia caracasana 322
Wigandia 322
Wild Apple 211
Wild Service Tree 225
Willow Pear 224

Willow
    Basket 173
    Chinese Weeping 173
    Golden Weeping 176
    Indian 118
    Purple Osier 173
    Weeping 176
    White 173
wind, protection from 59
Wine, elder 340
Wingnut 266
Winter, William 113
Winter-flowering Cherry 218
Winter's Bark 113
wood
    for fire 40
    products 48
    pulp 48–49
    types 46
    uses 46–47
Wood Apple 311
wood-framed
    boat 47
    house 47
woodland, monsoon 30
Wych Elm 227

X

Xanthocyparis
    nootkatensis 107
    xanthophloea 188
Xanthorrhoea australis 125
xylem 21
Xylocarpus granatum 308

Y

Yamar 334
Yellow Birch 258
Yellow Cedar 107
Yellow Flamboyant 204
Yellow Trumpet Tree 333
Yew 98
    in churchyards 42
    Californian 97
    Plum 97
Yinma 303
Ylang-ylang 117
Yoshimune Tokugawa 222
Yoshino Cherry 222
Yucca brevifolia 127
Yggdrasil 42

Z

Zanthoxylum
    piperitum 312
    simulans 311
Zelkova serrata 229
Ziziphus
    jujuba 225
    lotus 226

Acknowledgments

DORLING KINDERSLEY would like to thank the following: David Burnie and Sabina Knees for reviewing the text; Steve Parker and Phil Wilkinson for supplying additional text; Miezan Van Zyl for administrative and proof-reading assistance; Corrine Manches for administrative help.

PICTURE CREDITS

Picture librarians: Richard Dabb; Lucy Claxton.
Picture researchers: Neil Fletcher, Will Jones, David Penrose, Jo Walton.

Abbreviations key: a = above, b = bottom, c = centre, f = far, l = left, t = top, r = right.

Dorling Kindersley would like to thank the following for permission to reproduce copyright material:

Akg-images: 42tr.
Alamy: AGStockUSA, Inc: 44–45. Apex News and Pictures Agency: 60b. Archivberlin Fotoagentur GmbH: 50b. Peter Arnold Inc: 182–183. Bildagentur-online.com/th-foto: 36tl. Brand X Pictures: 78tr. CuboImages srl: 36c. Sue Cunningham Photographic: 32c. Andrew Fox: 286tl. ImageState: 12. Inmagine: 45tl. Mike Lane: 144tr. Luis C. Marigo: 182–183. Jamie Marshall: 181bl. Renee Morris: 25tr. The National Trust Photolibrary: 342–343. Ron Niebrugge: 123l. Donald Pye: 21bl. Jeremy Samson: 270tr. Nick Servian: 309b. Frantisek Staud: 53tr.
Dr M. Balick: 226br.
Belpress.com: Photofruit: 304bl.
Paul Bolsted: 187tc, clb; 333cra.
Kenneth L. Bowles: 314clb.
Dr Gerald D. Carr: 86br; 92cra; 107br; 122cb; 137br; 148cra, cla, clb, bl; 152tr; 155cra; 164cra; 167cla; 180cra, cla; 181cla; 189cfr; 192bl; 195cra; 198clb; 203cfr; 207cla, cra; 208cla; 209bl, br; 230tr, cfr; 263cla; 269tr; 274tc; 275bl, br, cra, cla; 289br, bl; 306cfr, bl, crb, br; 307cfl, tr; 315cla; 318clb, bl; 320bl; 326crb; 327c; 332cfl; 333cla, cfl; 335crb; 338br.
Geoffrey Carr: 173bl.
William M. Ciesla: 187cfr.
Bruce Coleman Collection: Tore Hagman: 4–5.
Clemson University: 264tcr.
Constructionphotography.com/Mediacolors. com: 47br.
Charles W. Cook: 245cla.
Corbis: 25tl; 45tr; 104–105; 176tr. Archivo Iconografico SA: 41t. Yann Arthus-Bertrand:

272–273. Craig Aurness: 19c; 123r. David Ball: 52br. Tom Bean: 2; 3. Gary Braasch: 57b. Richard A. Cooke: 64bl. Terry W. Eggers: 28–29. Michael Freeman: 38–39. Darrell Gulin: 74cr; 97; 111. Lindsay Hebberd: 43b. Robert Holmes: 236–237. Karen Huntt: 52tl. George H.H. Huey: 41br. Peter Johnson: 31cra. Wolfgang Kaehler: 70c; 70t. Layne Kennedy: 7. Frank Lane Picture Agency: 67b. 149t. Wayne Lawler/Ecoscene: 158–159. George D. Lepp: 150–151. Joe Macdonald: 190–191. John McAnulty: 290–291. Gunter Marx Photography: 27tr; David Muench: 10, 88–89, 132b, 264b. Charles O'Rear: 84–85. Douglas Peebles: 33tr, 134–135; 198b. Clay Perry: 65br. Reuters: 45crb. Reuters/Sukree Sukplang: 136cr. David Samuel Robbins: 40b. Hans Georg Roth: 47cfr. M.L. Sinibaldi: 174–175, 220–221. Paul A. Souders: 27tl. Alan Towse/Ecoscene: 49cfr. Vanni Archive: 309tr. Ron Watts: 49br. Nevada Wier: 130bl. Roger Wilmshurst/Frank Lane Picture Agency: 337b. Doug Wilson: 141b. Michael S. Yamashita: 46–47. Ed Young: 219b.
Jean Delacre: 226tr, c.
M. Fagg, Australian National Botanic Gardens: 311cfl.
Olivier Filippi: 106bcr; 298br; 319tl.
Flora Fauna International: Evan Bowen Jones: 205tr.
FLPA: Tim Fitzharris: 108–109. Frans Lanting: 32b, 49t. Minden Pictures/Michael & Patricia Fogden: 15bc; 16cl, tl, tr, cl; 17tl, tr. Minden Pictures/Martin Withers: 67br. Tui de Roy: 94–95. Roger Wilmhurst: 19tc.
Forestry Department, Food and Agriculture Organisation of the United Nations: Susan Braatz: 58ca. Roberto Faidutti: 303cla, cal. Christel Palmberg Lerche: 303tr.
J.B. Friday: 153tl; 200tc, cr, cfr, bl; 293cla.
Garden Picture Library: Pernilla Bergdhal: 2. Jacqui Hurst: 80–81.
Getty Images: Jens Schlueter: 26bc.
Chris Gibson: 173br; 310clb; 318cla; 327cra.
Paul Gullan: 161cfl; 188cla, tr.
Nigel Hicks: 178cb, tr; 274clb; 315bc; 324cb.
Josh Hillman/Florida Nature: 179clb, crb.
Holt Studios: Nick Spurling: 56b.
Dr. A. Jagel, Ruhr-Universität Bochum: 106br.
Henriette Kress: 107bl; 112bl; 212cra; 212bl; 338tl, cla.
Rolf Kyburz/Kplams.com: 130cfl, clb.
Paul Latham: 116cla; 180br; 204cla; 231cla; 240bl; 242bl; 268cbr, cra; 293crb; 304cfr; 310bl; 325cla; 341cfl.
Amanda Mason: 331br.
Archie Miles: 250b.
National Geographic: Lynn Abercrombie:

295bl. Walter Meayers Edwards: 75. Darlyne A. Murawski: 66.

National Parks Board, Singapore: 86cra; 114cra, bl; 118crb; 166cfl, tr; 180bl; 192cla; 195br; 202bl, tr; 242cla; 268bl; 269bl; 278cla; cra; 282cfl, tr, cra, crb; 303br; 306cra, cal; 318br; 320br; 325bl; 335cfl.

Natural History Museum: Dr G.S. Robinson: 284tc.

Natural Visions: Heather Angel: 22bl; 113bl; 137bl; 202br; 204cra; 219cr. 232cra; 278cfr; 283bl, br; 302tc; 316tr, c; 318car, cra.

Nature Picture Library: Juan Manuel Borrero: 217tl. Hanne & Jens Eriksen: 294cfr, bl. Martha Holmes: 23crb. Jose B. Ruiz: 319cra.

Neil Fletcher: 185clb; 257bl.

NHPA: George Bernard: 57t. Simon Booth: 28cfr. Simon Colmer: 15br. Nigel J. Dennis: 125bl. Khalid Ghani: 33cla. Martin Harvey: 42b. Daniel Heuclin: 136b. Ernie Janes: 228b; 248–249; 255b. Matt Johnston: 138cl. Mike Lane: 294tr. Harold Palo Jr: 281b. Tim Scoones: 35br. John Shaw: 1; 20cr; 288br.

Dave Osbourne: www.walkgps.com: 160b.

Alan Outen: 122bl; 126cfl; 177br; 224cla; 281cfl; 308clb; 317br; 332cfr; 339bl.

Oxford Scientific: Peter Adams: 62–63. Kathie Atkinson: 231br. Deni Bown: 199tr; 284bl; 299br. Prof. Jack Dermid: 206crb. Michael Fogden: 295tr. Mike Powels: 40c.

Jerry A. Paine: 264cal.

Photolibrary.com/Oxford Scientific: 116bl; 148br.

Christian Puff: 325cra.

Gordon Ridgewell: 146–147.

Rik Schuiling: 292cla, cra.

Royal Botanic Gardens Kew/Photo: Andrew McRobb: 61br.

Royal Saskatchewan Museum: 23bcl.

José Manuel Sánchez de Lorenzo Cáceres: 205bl; 297tr.

A.D. Schilling: 96tl; 164br; 233cra; 283car; 310br; 322cla.

Science Photo Library: Diccon Alexander: 126br, 128–129, 276–277. David Aubrey: 252–253. Pallava Bagla: 253b; 301b. Andrea Balogh: 68l. Alex Bartel: 193b. Darryl T. Branch: 70b. Robert Brook: 56t. Dr Jeremy Burgess: 15bl.

Peter Etchells: 132tc. Eye of Science: 20bl. Vaughan Fleming: 64br. Simon Fraser: 43cra; 67tr; 170–171; 206t. Bob Gibbons: 136tr. Adam Hart-Davis: 330b. David Henderson: 217b. K. Jayaram: 198t. Matt Johnston: 138cfl. Andrew Lambert Photography: 48cfl. Martin Land: 68r. Michael Marten: 246b. Susumu Nishinaga: 214–215. Claude Nuridsany & Marie Perennou: 21cr. Bjorn Svensson: 61t. Steve Taylor: 72.

Thomas Schoepke: 119bc; 296cla, car.

Shu Suehiro: 314cfl.

Soraya Sierra: 179tr.

J. Dan Skean Jr: 113cra; 116clb, br; 293tr.

Forest & Kim Starr (USGS): 92br; 142cla, cb; 155ca; 164bl, bcl; 167cra, bl, br; 185br; 186cra; 198crb; 200bl; 203tr, cla, cb; 204bc; 208cb; 230cla, bl; 232bl; 233cl, bl; 234cla, cfr; 235br; 256tl, car, bl, bcl; 263cfr, cb; 299cfr; 302tcl; 304bcr, br; 307clb, cbr; 319br; 323clb, br; 334clb; 335tr.

Geoff Stein: 97cfl; 118cla; 120cra, cfl; 131bl; 133cra, cla, bl, bcr; 138br; 139cra; 140bl; 149bl; 177bl; 184cfl; 189bl; 199clb, bl; 206br; 235cla, cra; 238cb; 239car; 269br; 270br; 299cfl; 308crb; 314cr.

Still Pictures: Mark Edwards: 58br; 59br. Peter Frischmuth: 44cl.

Mike Thiv: 61cfr, 242br.

Top Tropicals/www.toptropicals.com: Tatiana Anderson: 271tr, c. Marina Rybka: 69bc.

Alan Watson: 65tc; 96bl; 124cla, bl; 127tr; 130cr; 140cal, cfl, cra; 152bl, br; 155br; 156bl; 157br, cla, cal; 160car; 164cla; 178cfl; 181ca; 185cra; 188bl; 195cla; 227bc; 239cla, br; 243cla; 270bl; 274br; 275crb; 295cl; 296bl, bc; 308cla, tr; 338bl; 339cla.

Alan Watson/Forest Light: 90bc; 120br.

Paul Wray: 168cbr; 172bl; 201cfr; 240cra; 243br; 254cal; 260bl; 265cra; 278br; 288tc, tcr.

Kazuo Yamasaki: 245bl.

DK Images: Peter Anderson: Courtesy of the Roskilde Viking Ships Museum, Denmark: 251br. Judith Miller/Lyon and Turnbull Ltd: 142cr. Hamptons: 197tr. Freeman's: 328br. Windsor and Newton: 186bl.

Other photographs provided by: Chris Gibson, Neil Fletcher, A.D. Schilling, Heinz Schneider, Jens Schou, Justyn Willsmore.